SAGE was founded in 1965 by Sara Miller McCune to support the dissemination of usable knowledge by publishing innovative and high-quality research and teaching content. Today, we publish over 900 journals, including those of more than 400 learned societies, more than 800 new books per year, and a growing range of library products including archives, data, case studies, reports, and video. SAGE remains majority-owned by our founder, and after Sara's lifetime will become owned by a charitable trust that secures our continued independence.

Los Angeles | London | New Delhi | Singapore | Washington DC | Melbourne

INDIRECT TAX REFORM
in India

Thank you for choosing a SAGE product!
If you have any comment, observation or feedback,
I would like to personally hear from you.

Please write to me at **contactceo@sagepub.in**

Vivek Mehra, Managing Director and CEO, SAGE India.

INDIRECT
TAX
REFORM
in India
1947 to GST and Beyond

YASHWANT SINHA
VINAY K. SRIVASTAVA

Los Angeles | London | New Delhi
Singapore | Washington DC | Melbourne

First published in 2020 by

SAGE Publications India Pvt Ltd
B1/I-1 Mohan Cooperative Industrial Area
Mathura Road, New Delhi 110 044, India
www.sagepub.in

SAGE Publications Inc
2455 Teller Road
Thousand Oaks, California 91320, USA

SAGE Publications Ltd
1 Oliver's Yard, 55 City Road
London EC1Y 1SP, United Kingdom

SAGE Publications Asia-Pacific Pte Ltd
18 Cross Street #10-10/11/12
China Square Central
Singapore 048423

Published by Vivek Mehra for SAGE Publications India Pvt Ltd. Typeset in 10.5/13pt Berkeley by Fidus Design Pvt Ltd, Chandigarh.

Library of Congress Control Number: 2019953820

ISBN: 978-93-5328-971-3 (HB)

SAGE Team: Rajesh Dey, Sandhya Gola and Anupama Krishnan

Contents

Section A. Indirect Tax Reforms after Independence

Section B. The New Regime of Goods and Services Tax

List of Illustrations

Figures

Tables

List of Abbreviations

ABC	Accounts-based control
AITUC	All India Trade Union Congress
ARA	Advance Ruling Authority
AT	Appellate Tribunal
AVT	Ad valorem taxes
CAB	Constitution (Amendment) Bill
CAG	Comptroller and Auditor General
CBC	Clearance-based control
CBDT	Central Board of Direct Taxes
CBEC	Central Board of Excise and Customs
CBIC	Central Board of Indirect Taxes and Customs
CEA	Central Excise Act, 1944
CED	Central Excise Duty
CENVAT	Central Value Added Tax
CETA	Central Excise Tariff Act, 1985
CGST	Central GST
CST	Central Sales Tax
EC	Empowered Committee
FRBMA	Fiscal Responsibility and Budget Management Act
GDP	Gross domestic product
GoI	Government of India
GSPs	GST Suvidha Providers
GST	Goods and Services Tax
GSTN	Goods and Services Tax Network
GSTR	Goods and Services Tax Return

HSN	Harmonized System Nomenclature
HST	Harmonized Sales Tax
IGST	Integrated GST
IMF	International Monetary Fund
IRAS	Internal Revenue and Tax Authority of Singapore
IT	Information technology
ITC	Input tax credit
ITEC	Indirect Taxation Enquiry Committee
MANVAT	VAT at manufacturing stage
MODVAT	Modified value added tax
NDA	National Democratic Alliance
NIPFP	National Institute of Public Finance and Policy
OECD	Organisation for Economic Co-operation and Development
PAC	Public Accounts Committee
PBC	Production-based control
PST	Provincial Sales Tax
QST	Quebec Sales Tax
RNR	Revenue Neutral Rate
SED	Special Excise Duty
SGST	State GST
SSI	Small-scale industry
SST	Sales and Service Tax
TDS	Tax deducted at source
TIN	Tax Identification Number
ToR	Terms of reference
TRC	Tax Reform Committee
TVA	Tax on value added
UPA	United Progressive Alliance
UTGST	Union Territory GST
VAIT	Confederation of All India Trader
VAT	Value Added Tax
VRR	VAT revenue ratio

Preface

Indirect tax was first introduced in India in 1944 in the form of excise duty on Indian products as a measure of protection for goods imported from the UK. In course of time, it became a well-established tax to shore up government finances. The need for reform in indirect taxes was felt soon after Independence and one committee after another was appointed for this purpose. The most important of these was the L. K. Jha Indirect Tax Enquiry Committee of 1974. The committee submitted its report in 1978 and recommended the introduction of the value added tax (VAT). The French economist Maurice Laure had first introduced the concept of VAT in 1954. Since VAT is applicable to both goods and services, it is also called goods and services tax (GST). Over the last four decades, VAT has emerged as an important instrument of indirect taxation and a main source of revenue in 160 countries of the world, accounting for approximately 20 per cent of the tax revenue of the entire world.

In India, it took eight years of preparation before modified VAT or MODVAT was introduced by Finance Minister V. P. Singh on selected products in 1986. The Raja Chelliah Committee recommended the introduction of VAT in 1991. The preparation for the introduction of VAT went on over the years. Ultimately, Finance Minister Yashwant Sinha announced his intention to introduce VAT in India in his budget speech of 1999 and finally CENVAT or central VAT was introduced on all commodities in 2002.

Simultaneously, Yashwant Sinha had also started the process of introduction of VAT at the state level by calling a meeting of chief ministers on 16 November 1999. Subsequently, an empowered committee of state finance ministers was formed to take the process forward. This empowered group proved to be a highly successful experiment in cooperative federalism and was the predecessor of the GST Council of today.

The process of introduction of VAT went through its share of ups and downs and, though all the details were carefully worked out, the actual introduction could not take place on account of political and traders' opposition. It was finally introduced by the UPA government in 2005.

The concept of GST was first mooted by Vijay Kelkar in a report he submitted to the then Finance Minister Jaswant Singh in 2003. The matter could not be taken forward as the Vajpayee government in which he was minister lost the 2004 general elections and had to demit office. The finance minister in the next government, P. Chidambaram, mentioned the idea of implementing GST in his budget speech of 2007–2008. Later, the Thirteenth Finance Commission headed by Kelkar also conducted an in-depth study and submitted a detailed report on GST to the government in 2009. The rest is history.

The book covers all these developments in detail but apart from dealing with the political economy of GST, it also covers the current problems, the conceptual infirmities and the reforms needed urgently to undo the disruption it has caused so far. The book should be of interest to parliamentarians, politicians, policy practitioners, economists, journalists, students of economics, commerce and management, and to civil services aspirants.

Acknowledgements

This book, *Indirect Tax Reform in India: 1947 to GST and Beyond*, would not have come into existence without the encouragement and support of many of our associates and well-wishers.

While preparing this book, we have tried to collect the latest information available from government publications, published and unpublished sources, journals and articles by eminent economists.

We express our sincere thanks to all those individuals and institutions that have helped us in completing this book.

We must acknowledge the cooperation of Mr Rajesh Dey (Managing Editor) and all the members of SAGE for bringing out this book nicely and timely.

Last but not least, we would like to acknowledge the support of our families whose faith and love for us was a constant source of inspiration.

Introduction

Historical Background of Indirect Taxes in India

The word 'tax' is derived from the Latin word *taxare*. The meaning of 'taxare' is 'to estimate' or 'to value'. *Black's Law Dictionary* gives the following definition of tax: 'A tax is any contribution imposed by government upon individuals, for the use and service of the state, whether under the name of toll, tribute, tallage, gabel, impost, duty, custom, excise, subsidy, aid, supply, or other name'.[1] Taxes are levied and collected by the state on the sale or purchase of merchandise. Taxes provide revenue to the state, which is the basis of state functioning. Tax structure is one of the most significant aspects of any system of administration by a government. In India, the government has followed a progressive and proportional taxation system since Independence. The slab-wise taxation is applicable to income tax, while proportional tax is applicable to indirect taxes such as customs duty, excise duty, service tax, VAT and wealth tax. All governments have paid attention to reforming the taxation system and closing the loopholes to discourage the evaders in order to enlarge revenue and improve compliance.

---

[1] *Black's Law Dictionary,* https://thelawdictionary.org/tax/

What Is Tax?

Tax is a legal and compulsory payment levied by the state on an income, a product or an activity. Generally, the tax which is levied directly on the income of an individual or company is a direct tax and the tax which is levied on goods or services is an indirect tax. The union, states and local bodies can levy taxes in India. They should be in accordance with the laws passed by the state legislature and the Parliament under authority granted to them by the Constitution.

Progressive Tax

Progressive tax is a tax in which the tax rate increases as the taxable amount increases. Income tax is an example of this tax. It is based on the concept of 'ability to pay'. It is a redistribution of income from the rich to the poor Lower income persons are generally exempted or pay less tax, whereas higher income persons usually pay a comparatively higher tax.

Regressive Tax

The regressive tax is a tax in which the tax rate decreases as the amount subject to taxation increases. There is an inverse relationship between the tax rate and taxable income. Under this, the rate of tax decreases as the income of taxpayers increases.

Proportional Tax

Proportional tax is a method where the authority charges a flat tax from all taxpayers regardless of income. It applies the same tax rate across lower-, middle- and higher-income taxpayers. A proportional tax is also frequently called a flat tax. It is based on the principle that since everybody is equal, taxes should also be charged the same way.

Why Tax?

The motive to levy tax is to finance government expenditure that is incurred on conferring common services and benefits to the people. Governments need funds to carry out public expenditure or government activities. The most important use of taxes is to finance public goods and services. The government performs numerous functions in the discharge of its responsibilities such as maintenance of law and order, health care, education, development of infrastructure and defence of the country. A huge amount of money is required to perform these functions. The question arises: Where will this money come from? How would the government get revenue to perform all these activities for the country's development? Governments, therefore, levy taxes in the form of tax, fees, fines and surcharges and get money from the public.

'Just like a leech, calf and bee draw only small-but-very-small quantities from their respective feeds (i.e., blood, milk and honey), similarly a King should, by his orders, take from his subjects, very small amounts of taxes.'

—Manu[2]

'A king who enriches his treasury by oppressive methods would, before long, be deprived of his prosperity and meet with destruction. The fire generated by the heat of oppression does not quench without consuming the prosperity and family of the king.'

—Rishi Yajnavalkya[3]

'Just as the sun extracts water from the reservoirs and gives it back in the form of showers, so does the ruler extract tax from his subjects and give it back to them in the form of prosperity.'

—Kalidas[4]

[2] *Manusmriti* (7.129).

[3] Speech by Hon'ble Justice Mr Arun Mishra, Chief Justice, Rajasthan High Court, in National Tax Conference at Jodhpur on 23 April 2011.

[4] Sury, *Taxation in India*, 3.

'The king should take wealth from his subjects at the proper time. Like an intelligent man milking his cow every day, the king should milk his kingdom every day. As the bee collects honey from flowers gradually, without causing harm to the tree: The king should draw wealth gradually from his kingdom for storing it.'

—Bhishma to Yudhishthira[5]

'Note, besides, that it is no more immoral to directly rob citizens than to slip indirect taxes into the price of goods that they cannot do without.'

—Albert Camus[6]

Genesis

The procedure of taxation is very old. It is said that the taxation system started from the time around 3100–2686 BC in Ancient Egypt. At that time the main occupation of the people was agriculture and they used to pay one-fifth or 20% of their total crop to Pharaoh (ancient Egyptian rulers) as tax.[7]

Taxation is also mentioned in the Bible which says, 'When the crop comes in, give a fifth of it to Pharaoh'.

The concept of taxation has been in existence from ancient times. Political thinking has always considered the issue of public finance to be of prime importance. The history of tax in India can be found in *Manusmriti* and *Arthashastra*. These provide detailed description of the ways and means of creating an abundant treasury. These treatises discuss the methods of revenue collection and modes of taxation.

---

[5] Mahabharata, Book 12: Santi Parva: Rajadharmanusasanaparva.

[6] https://www.brainyquote.com/quotes/albert_camus_394950

[7] Shyam, *History of Tax.*

Manusmriti

We get an idea of taxation in *Manusmriti*, although the period of *Manusmriti* is not firmly established and is a matter of debate. William Jones and Karl Wilhelm Friedrich Schlegel assigned *Manusmriti* to the period of around 1250 BCE and 1000 BCE, respectively.[8] A lead is available in *Manusmriti*[9]:

> [the] king should arrange the collection of taxes in such a manner that the tax payers do not feel the pinch of paying taxes. It lays down that traders and artisans should pay 1/5th of their profits in silver and gold, while the agriculturists pay 1/6th, 1/8th and 1/10th of their produce depending upon their circumstances.[10]

Arthashastra

We can get some indication of the presence of commodity taxation such as tolls and duties on liquor and salt, almost like the excises of today, even during the Mauryan times during 322–187 BCE. Kautilya (also known as Chanakya) wrote a very famous book *Arthashastra*. The book describes how duties on cotton, oils, salt, liquor, metal, etc., have to be levied. Kautilya has described in detail the system of tax management during the Mauryan times. At that time, the main source of tax was agricultural crop. The taxes also included service tax, sales tax and tax on the import of goods. All taxes were specific and there was no room for arbitrariness. The tax collectors predetermined the schedule of all the payment, its time, manner and quantity. The land revenue was fixed at 17 per cent of the total production. The export–import tax was fixed on ad valorem basis. The import duty on foreign goods was 20 per cent. Likewise, ferry charges, tolls, road charges and other levies were also fixed taxes for

---

[8] https://en.wikipedia.org/wiki/Manusmriti

[9] The Manusmriti or 'law of Manusmriti', also known as Mānava-Dharmaśāstra, is the most important and earliest work of the Dharmaśāstra textual tradition of Hinduism.

[10] Lawbaba, 'Concept and History of Indirect Taxation'.

internal–external emergencies like wars; taxes for floods, famines, etc., were also raised separately. It was also known as *lagaan*. Kautilya lays down that the king could raise war loans during war or emergencies. He says in *Arthashastra* that the king can raise the land revenue from one-sixth to one-fourth during emergencies. He further says that the people who do business must pay donations. Kautilya emphasized equity and justice in taxation. The affluent had to pay higher taxes as compared to the poor.

The taxes of the above-said period must be considered as the beginning of indirect taxes in India. The present taxation system is almost similar to that of about 2,300 years ago.

What Is Indirect Tax?

The tax levied on goods and services is called indirect tax. The examples of indirect taxes are sales tax, excise tax, service tax, custom duty, VAT, etc. The structure of indirect tax of the country is very complex. There are a number of taxes levied by the central government, state governments and local bodies. The business concerns are facing the problem of complex tax structure.

Pre-Independence Taxes

Mughal Period

During the Mughal period, the main source of revenue was tax on farm produce, and peasants paid taxes to headmen or local chieftains. Todar Mal—the revenue minister of Akbar—did a survey of crop yields, prices and areas cultivated for a 10-year period. On the basis of that, he fixed taxes on each crop. A province was divided into revenue circles. Every circle had its own rates of revenue for each crop. The revenue system was known as *zabt*. The Mughals also imposed *jizya*, primarily on non-Muslim communities, which was later ended by Emperor Akbar, though the last Mughal Emperor Aurangzeb levied *jizya* on Hindus again in 1679. The people were also paying tax in kind in the form of agricultural produce to the king.

British Rule

The country witnessed numerous sensational changes in the whole taxation system during the British Rule. Though the taxation system was mainly in favour of the British government and its exchequer, but it was also based on modern and scientific principles of taxation. Excise duty was first levied on salt in 1870, followed by cotton yarn in 1894, motor spirit in 1917 and kerosene in 1922. An enquiry into the taxation system was conducted by the Indian Taxation Enquiry Committee in 1925.

At that time, the economic scenario was naturally very different from today. The country was a dependency of the United Kingdom. British India included Burma, the whole of Bengal and the Punjab, Baluchistan and Sind. The geography of India included the entire area which now forms four countries—India, Pakistan, Bangladesh and Burma.

The maritime States imposed their own customs duties, while many of the others levied import and export duties on their trade with British India. There was no plan of economic development, nor was there any attempt at building up a welfare State. Organized industry except in cotton and jute was in an initial stage of development and the bulk of the country's requirements by way of manufactures was met by imports from abroad. In the field of public finance customs dominated central revenues, while land revenue dominated the revenues of British Indian provinces. The salt tax was an important source of revenue for the Central Government, while excise duties on liquor constituted the second major source of revenue for the British Indian provinces. There was no prohibition and no sales tax. Income tax was an important source of revenue for the Central Government, but the maximum rate of income tax and super tax was only 47% on incomes above ₹5.5 lakhs. The situation remained substantially the same in the field of public finance till the beginning of the War. During the War and post-war years, changes took place in quick succession.[11]

Tax on sale of goods was made a provincial subject by the Government of India Act, 1935. Sales tax was first time introduced in India in the Province of Bombay under the Bombay Tobacco (Amendment) Act,

---

[11] GoI, *Report of the Taxation Enquiry,* Vol. 1, 4.

1938. The act came into effect on 24 March 1938. This sales tax was levied on the sale of tobacco within certain very limited urban and suburban areas. Madras was the second state which levied a general sales tax in 1939, which was later followed by other states as well. Subsequently, various indirect taxes were included into the taxation system. There were about 20 types of indirect taxes in India.

During the British Rule, the country was exporting only raw materials which used to come back as finished products. The major export was to Great Britain. The British used to discourage Indian producers to produce finished products. The Indian market overflowed with British-made products.

The period in the 18th and 19th centuries in Europe witnessed the advent of the Industrial Revolution which meant the use of machines for producing goods, and emergence of many new industries. The European market was soon flooded with machine-made goods, clothing fabric being the most prominent. The European market was soon saturated and the sale of more manufactured products there was not possible anymore. Then the British chose India as their new market. The British introduced machine-made cloth in the Indian market, but India was already self-sufficient in textiles. The British product was also costlier than the Indian products. Thus, price became a major problem. To solve the problem, they levied a new tax on goods manufactured in India. This tax was called 'excise duty'. Due to this, the price of imported goods came at par with goods manufactured in India. The Indian Khadi and handloom industry suffered greatly and incurred heavy losses because of the imposition of excise duty.

Post-Independence Taxes

The real history of modern indirect taxes begins from around the middle of the 20th century. The Central Excises and Salt Act came into existence in 1944. Indirect taxes included central taxes, state taxes and local body taxes. Central taxes were levied on manufacturing activities, import–export and sale of services. State taxes were levied on sale of goods within the state, and local body taxes were municipal taxes, entertainment tax, etc.

Constitutional Provisions

Under the Constitution of India adopted in 1950, there are three lists—Union List (List 1), State List (List 2) and Concurrent List (List 3)—in the Seventh Schedule. It has given power to the union and states to make any changes in their lists. As per Article 246 of the Constitution, the Parliament has the absolute power to make legislation in respect of the items which are given in Union List. States have power to make laws with respect to any of the matters contained in the State List. In reference to matters contained in Concurrent List, that is, List 3 of the Seventh Schedule, both central government and state governments have the power to make laws.

Central Indirect Taxes

Prior to the introduction of GST, the main sources of revenue via indirect taxes were custom duty,[12] central excise duty (CED)[13] and service tax.[14] (See Table I.1.) The union also levied central sales tax (CST)[15] on all inter-state consignment of goods and all inter-state sale and purchase of goods. CST, however, was assigned to the state of origin.

Central Excise Duty

Excise duty is levied as per the provisions of Central Excise Act (CEA), 1944, and Central Excise Rules, 1944.

---

[12] Entry 83 of Union List provides for the 'duties of customs including export duties'.

[13] Entry 84 of Union List empowers the central government to levy 'duties of excise on tobacco and other goods manufactured or produced in India except (a) alcoholic liquors for human consumption; (b) opium, Indian hemp and other narcotic drugs and narcotics, but including medicinal and toilet preparations containing alcohol or any substance included in the subparagraph (b) of this entry'.

[14] Entry 97 of Union List, Entry 92C included in List 1 by Constitution (88th Amendment) Act, 2003 to levy service tax. But service tax was being levied under Entry 97 because amendment was not notified.

[15] Entries 92A and 92B.

CED was a tax imposed by the government on all the goods manufactured or produced in the country. Earlier, it was the main source of revenue for the central government and was the backbone of the economy. It was regulated by two acts: (a) the CEA, 1944, and (b) the Central Excise Tariff Act (CETA), 1985. The CEA, 1944, covered the provisions on tax, valuations and administrations, whereas CETA, 1985, carried complete list of excisable goods and applicable tax rates in each case. As it was collected by the manufacturers from the buyers of the goods, hence it was called an indirect tax.

The CEA came into force in the year 1944. After that, it was gradually changed from year to year. But, as already noted, excise duty was levied on salt for the first time in 1870.

> This was followed by levies on cotton textiles in 1894, petroleum (motor spirit) in 1920s, kerosene in 1922, silver in 1930s (unimportant after the formation of Burma in 1933), sugar and steel ingots in 1934, tyres in 1941, manufactured tobacco and vegetable products in 1943 and coffee and tea in 1944.[16]

Excise duty was abolished immediately after India's independence in 1947. Excise duty on mill cloth however was introduced in 1949 to meet the shortfall in the revenue and to help the handloom industry.[17] But it was not enough to meet the government's needs. Generation of funds became a major problem for the post-Independence government. The Taxation Enquiry Commission, 1953–1954 had observed as follows: 'For any substantial receipts from commodity taxation and appreciable restraint on consumption in the economy as a whole, it will be necessary to extend excise and sales taxation to the consumption of lower income groups and of goods which are commonly classed as necessaries.'[18]

Within the first decade of Independence, the number of items under excise duty doubled to 33, adding items such as cigarettes, soap,

[16] Krishnan, 'Milestones in Central Excise'.

[17] *Budget Speech, 1949–50* of Dr John Mathai.

[18] Taxation Enquiry Commission, 1953–1954.

sewing machine and electric bulb. In the next decade, the number reached up to 80 and further reached to 130 in 1975. In 1975, the central excise tariff witnessed inclusion of a residuary entry referred to as 'Tariff Item 68' which covered all items other than those covered under the first 67. Although initially these goods were subjected to a small 1 per cent duty, Item 68 proved to be a tax-mopping device for successive finance ministers as the rate was increased to 12 per cent by 1985. In the latter part of the same year, the CETA, 1985, was introduced which provided for levy of excise duty on almost all items of manufacture, barring a few exceptions.

Customs Duty

Custom duty is also an indirect tax. The central government levied it on import and export of goods in 1962 to prevent illegal imports and exports. It soon became the second major source of central revenue in India. The government levied and collected duty on imports–exports, laid down the import–export procedures and imposed prohibitions on importation and exportation of goods, etc. The main purpose behind levying customs duty was to encourage growth of domestic industries by providing them with enough protection. However, while achieving this main goal, it also contributed substantially to the exchequer. Excessive protectionism however led to the imposition of inordinately high customs duties in India and, in several cases, it was more than 300 per cent prior to the reforms introduced in 1991. A phased reduction in the peak rate was undertaken in each of the 28 budgets since 1991, and accordingly the peak rate of customs duty was reduced to 10 per cent.

Central Sales Tax

The CST prior to GST was levied by the central government on inter-state consignment of goods and inter-state sale and purchase of goods. CST however is not retained by the centre but assigned to the state of origin, as per Central Sales Tax Act, 1956, made under Article 269 of the Constitution. The CST rate was 2 per cent where specified concessional form was available and where the specified form was not available—the CST rate was made equal to the VAT rate in the respective states where the goods were located at the time of sale.

Service Tax

There was a debate on taking services under tax bracket in the 1990s. At that time, it was contributing 40 per cent of GDP.[19] The then Finance Minister Manmohan Singh took the initiative to tax the services. He introduced service tax in his budget speech of 1994–1995 on selected services at a rate of 5 per cent. Over the years, service tax came to be levied on 120 types of specified services at a rate of 12 per cent plus 2 per cent education cess and 1 per cent secondary and higher secondary education cess on taxable services. Service tax has now been subsumed into GST.

Value Added Tax

The VAT was a consumption tax added to a product's sales price. It was levied on the domestic consumption of goods and services. In 1976, L. K. Jha had suggested levying VAT in the form of MANVAT.[20] The reforms in indirect taxes were started in 1986 by the then Finance Minister V. P. Singh. He introduced a new concept of tax: MODVAT. Initially, it was applied to a few selected commodities under the union excise duties. Few years later, government extended MODVAT to almost all commodities and reduced excise duty rates. In the budget speech of 2000–2001, Yashwant Sinha converted MODVAT scheme into CENVAT scheme which was further converted into GST later.

States Indirect Taxes

The main source of revenue for states has been tax on sale and purchase,[21] excise duty on alcoholic beverages, opium and narcotics,[22] octroi and entry tax,[23] electricity tax,[24] and taxes on luxuries,

---

[19] Mehra, 'Birth of Service Tax'.

[20] VAT at the manufacturing level.

[21] Entry 54 of the State List.

[22] Entry 51 of the State List.

[23] Entry 52 of the State List.

[24] Entry 53 of the State List.

Table I.1 Revenue Realization from Indirect Taxes (in Rupees Crore)

Year	Revenue Realization from					Share in Total Indirect Taxes (%)			
	Customs Duties	Excise Duties	Service Tax	GST[a]	Total	Customs Duties	Excise Duties	Service Tax	GST
1989–1990	18,036	22,406	NA		40,442	44.6	55.4	NA	
1990–1991	20,644	24,514	NA		45,158	45.7	54.3	NA	
1991–1992	22,257	28,110	NA		50,367	44.2	55.8	NA	
1992–1993	23,776	30,832	NA		54,608	43.5	56.5	NA	
1993–1994	22,193	31,697	NA		53,890	41.2	58.8	NA	
1994–1995	26,789	37,347	407		64,543	41.5	57.9	0.6	
1995–1996	35,757	40,187	862		76,806	46.6	52.3	1.1	
1996–1997	42,851	45,008	1,059		88,918	48.2	50.6	1.2	
1997–1998	40,193	47,962	1,586		89,741	44.8	53.4	1.8	
1998–1999	40,668	53,246	1,957		95,871	42.4	55.5	2.0	
1999–2000	48,419	61,902	2,128		112,449	43.1	55.0	1.9	
2000–2001	47,542	68,526	2,613		118,681	40.1	57.7	2.2	
2001–2002	40,268	72,555	3,302		116,125	34.7	62.5	2.8	
2002–2003	44,852	82,310	4,122		131,284	34.2	62.7	3.1	
2003–2004	48,629	90,774	7,891		147,294	33.0	61.6	5.4	
2004–2005	57,611	99,125	14,200		170,936	33.7	58.0	8.3	
2005–2006	65,067	111,226	23,055		199,348	32.6	55.8	11.6	
2006–2007	86,327	117,613	37,598		241,538	35.7	48.7	15.6	

(continued)

(continued)

Year	Revenue Realization from					Share in Total Indirect Taxes (%)			
	Customs Duties	Excise Duties	Service Tax	GST[a]	Total	Customs Duties	Excise Duties	Service Tax	GST
2007–2008	104,119	123,611	51,301		279,031	37.3	44.3	18.4	
2008–2009	99,879	108,613	60,941		269,433	37.1	40.3	22.6	
2009–2010	83,324	102,991	58,422		244,737	34.0	42.1	23.9	
2010–2011	135,813	137,701	71,016		344,530	39.4	40.0	20.6	
2011–2012	149,328	144,901	97,509		391,738	38.1	37.0	24.9	
2012–2013	165,346	175,845	132,601		473,792	34.9	37.1	28.0	
2013–2014	172,085	169,455	154,778		496,318	34.7	34.1	31.2	
2014–2015	188,016	188,128	167,969		544,113	34.6	34.1	30.9	
2015–2016	210,338	288,073	211,414		709,825	29.6	40.6	29.8	
2016–2017	225,370	381,756	254,499		861,625	26.2	44.3	29.5	
2017–2018	129,030	259,431	81,228	442,562	912,251	14.1	28.4	8.9	48.5
2018–2019 RE	130,038	259,612	9,283	643,900	1,042,833	12.5	24.9	0.9	61.7
2019–2020 BE[25]	155,904	300,000		663,343	1,119,247	13.9	26.8	0.0	59.3
Average	86,466.74	119,530.9	48,391.37	583,268.3	309,433.4	36.0	47.9	10.5	56.5

Sources: 1989–1990 to 1991–1992, Receipts Budget 1998–1999; 1992–1993 to 1999–2000, Receipts Budget 2001–2002; 2000–2001 to 2004–2005, Receipts Budget 2009–2010; 2005–2006 to 2009–2010, Receipts Budget 2014–2015; 2010–2011 to 2019–2020, Receipts Budget 2019–2020.

Note: [a] GST introduced since 1 July 2017.

[25] BE is the budgeted estimates. It is a budget allocation announced by GoI at the beginning of each financial year. RE is revised estimates. It refers to estimates of projected amounts of receipts and expenditure until the end of the financial year. Actual amounts are audited accounts of expenditure and receipts in a year.

entertainments, amusements, betting and gambling.[26] CST which has been now subsumed under GST was an important source of revenue for states, although it was levied by the union.

The local governments such as municipal corporations and gram panchayats levied duty on entry of goods in their jurisdiction. The levy was based on a physical control mechanism, where every transport vehicle was required to pay the tax and submit the relevant documents at the time of entry into the area. Octroi[27] holds the same importance for the local governments as sales tax for the states and excise for the centre.

Tax Structure

The taxation system of the country comprises direct and indirect (now known as GST) taxes. Indirect tax means tax on goods and services which are paid by a person to the service provider, producer or seller who is liable to pay the same to the government.

Total Tax

The total tax collection in 1990–1991 was ₹57,579 crore which moved to ₹186,516 crore in 2001–2002 and to ₹792,063 crore in 2010–2011 that further improved to ₹1,711,676 crore in 2016–2017. It is expected that it will be ₹2,266,000 crore in 2018–2019. The average annual growth of total taxes of the economy since 1990–1991 to 2018–2019 is 14.2 per cent.

Total Direct Tax

The proportion of direct taxes out of total tax collection was ₹12,418 crore in 1990–1991, which moved to ₹69,198 crore in 2001–2002 and to ₹849,713 crore in 2016–2017. As per the expectations, it will be ₹1,150,000 crore in 2018–2019. The average annual growth of

---

[26] Entry 62 of the State List.

[27] A duty levied in some countries on various goods entering a town or city.

direct taxes of the economy since 1990–1991 to 2018–2019 is 17.7 per cent.

Total Indirect Tax

The proportion of indirect taxes out of total tax collection was ₹45,161 crore in 1990–1991, which increased to ₹117,318 crore in 2001–2002 and to ₹861,963 crore in 2016–2017. It is expected to be ₹1,116,000 crore in 2018–2019. The average annual growth of indirect taxes of the economy from 1990–1991 to 2018–2019 is 12.6 per cent.

Proportion of Direct Tax and Indirect Tax

The statistics of Table I.2 depict that the proportion of indirect taxes in the total tax revenue of the country is on average of 57.6 per cent from 1990–1991 to 2018–2019. Indirect taxes accounted for 56.6 per cent of the total central taxes and 2.45 per cent of the GDP in 1950–1951; whereas, in 2015–2016, the proportion to total tax revenue had gone up to 48.9 per cent and that to the GDP had reached 7.9 per cent. The trend of the proportion of indirect taxes is decreasing from 1989–1990 to 2010–2011 except for 1998–1999. After that, it has increased during 2011–2012 and 2012–2013, and again decreased in 2013–2014. During 2014–2015 and 2015–2016, it was increasing. It was expected to be 49.2 per cent for the year 2018–2019 (BE).

Since the 1990s, the average contribution of direct tax is 42.4 per cent and indirect tax is 57.6 per cent to the economy. The proportion of direct tax, which was 23.2 per cent in 1991–1992, increased to 60.6 per cent in 2009–2010, but after that it moved more than 50 per cent except in 2016–2017 when it was 49.6 per cent. India's direct-to-indirect tax ratio is roughly 51:49. This contrasts with most OECD economies where the ratio is the exact opposite (67:33) and in favour of direct taxes. In the 50-year period, India's direct-to-indirect tax ratio has swung from a low of 13:87 to its current high of 31:49. 'For the OECD nations, throughout this 50-year period, the direct-to-indirect

Table 1.2 Revenue Realization from Direct and Indirect Taxes (in Rupees Crore)

Year	Total Revenue Realization from			Annual Growth (%)			Share in Total Taxes (%)	
	Direct Tax	Indirect Tax	Total	Direct Tax	Indirect Tax	Total	Direct Tax	Indirect Tax
1989–1990	11,194	40,442	51,636	–	–	–	21.7	78.3
1990–1991	12,418	45,158	57,576	10.9	11.7	11.5	21.6	78.4
1991–1992	16,994	50,367	67,361	36.8	11.5	17.0	25.2	74.8
1992–1993	20,029	54,608	74,637	17.9	8.4	10.8	26.8	73.2
1993–1994	21,853	53,890	75,743	9.1	–1.3	1.5	28.9	71.1
1994–1995	27,751	64,543	92,294	27.0	19.8	21.9	30.1	69.9
1995–1996	34,418	76,806	111,224	24.0	19.0	20.5	30.9	69.1
1996–1997	39,844	88,918	128,762	15.8	15.8	15.8	30.9	69.1
1997–1998	49,479	89,741	139,220	24.2	0.9	8.1	35.5	64.5
1998–1999	47,926	95,871	143,797	–3.1	6.8	3.3	33.3	66.7
1999–2000	59,311	112,449	171,760	23.8	17.3	19.4	34.5	65.5
2000–2001	69,922	118,681	188,603	17.9	5.5	9.8	37.1	62.9
2001–2002	70,935	116,125	187,060	1.4	–2.2	–0.8	37.9	62.1
2002–2003	84,982	131,284	216,266	19.8	13.1	15.6	39.3	60.7
2003–2004	107,054	147,294	2,54,348	26.0	12.2	17.6	42.1	57.9
2004–2005	134,022	170,936	304,958	25.2	16.1	19.9	43.9	56.1
2005–2006	168,126	199,348	367,474	25.4	16.6	20.5	45.8	54.2

(continued)

(continued)

Year	Total Revenue Realization from			Annual Growth (%)			Share in Total Taxes (%)	
	Direct Tax	Indirect Tax	Total	Direct Tax	Indirect Tax	Total	Direct Tax	Indirect Tax
2006–2007	231,974	241,538	473,512	38.0	21.2	28.9	49.0	51.0
2007–2008	314,116	279,031	593,147	35.4	15.5	25.3	53.0	47.0
2008–2009	335,866	269,433	605,299	6.9	-3.4	2.0	55.5	44.5
2009–2010	379,791	244,737	624,528	13.1	-9.2	3.2	60.8	39.2
2010–2011	448,542	344,530	793,072	18.1	40.8	27.0	56.6	43.4
2011–2012	497,439	391,738	889,177	10.9	13.7	12.1	55.9	44.1
2012–2013	562,443	473,792	1,036,235	13.1	20.9	16.5	54.3	45.7
2013–2014	642,415	496,318	1,138,733	14.2	4.8	9.9	56.4	43.6
2014–2015	700,773	544,113	1,244,886	9.1	9.6	9.3	56.3	43.7
2015–2016	745,823	709,825	1,455,648	6.4	30.5	16.9	51.2	48.8
2016–2017	854,197	861,625	1,715,822	14.5	21.4	17.9	49.8	50.2
2017–2018	1,007,355	911,653	1,919,008	17.9	5.8	11.8	52.5	47.5
2018–2019 RE	1,205,342	1,042,833	2,248,175	19.7	14.4	17.2	53.6	46.4
2019–2020 BE	1,385,943	1,166,188	2,552,131	15.0	11.8	13.5	54.3	45.7
Average	331,879.9	310,768.2	642,648.1	17.9	12.3	14.2	43.1	56.9

Sources: 1989–1990 to 1991–1992, Receipts Budget 1998–1999; 1992–1993 to 1999–2000, Receipts Budget 2001–2002; 2000–2001 to 2004–2005, Receipts Budget 2009–10; 2005–2006 to 2009–2010, Receipts Budget 2014–2015; 2010–2011 to 2019–2020, Receipts Budget 2019–2020.

Note: FTT/IATT abolished since 9 January 2004.

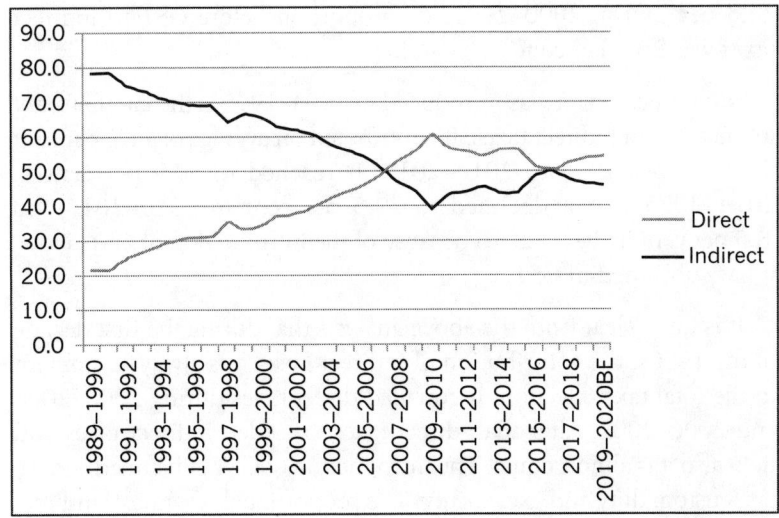

Figure I.1 *Comparative Picture of the Revenue from Direct Tax and Indirect Tax*

tax ratio has remained roughly constant in the range of 65:35.'[28] The recent decline in the ratio of direct taxes is however a matter of concern (Figure I.1).

Composition of Indirect Taxes

The composition of indirect taxes has undergone changes since Independence. In 1950–1951, excise duties contributed 29.2 per cent of the total central indirect taxes. The share almost doubled to reach 52.3 per cent by 1995–1996. After that, it increased to 61.1 per cent in 2003–2004. It was 44.3 per cent of total indirect tax prior to the introduction of GST.

Among the customs duties, the proportion of import duties to the total was 70 per cent in 1950–1951 and increased gradually to 99.6 per cent in a decade and a half. After that, it is showing decreasing trends. In 1990–1991, it decreased to 45.7 per cent and

[28] Chakravarty and Dehejia, 'India Is an Outlier'.

34.3 per cent in 2000–2001. Its proportion before GST to indirect taxes was 26.2 per cent.

Service tax which was introduced in 1994–1995 is the latest entrant to the arena of indirect taxes. It contributed on average of 11.2 per cent during 1994–1995 to 2016–2017. It reached to 30.9 per cent in 2014–2015, but it declined to 29.5 per cent in 2016–2017 and 8.5 per cent in 2017–2018 because of the introduction of GST. Now, it has subsumed in GST.

It is quite clear from the above analysis that during the first decade of the 1990s, the contribution of indirect taxes was always dominant in the total tax collection. It equalled direct taxes during 2005–2006 and 2006–2007. After that, direct taxes exceeded indirect taxes and now also it is almost equal. The introduction of GST subsumed service tax, custom duty and excise duty. The proportional revenue of indirect taxes will depend on the government policy, regulation and proper implementation of GST in due time. But in most developed economies, the share of direct taxes is higher than indirect taxes and that is how it should be even in India.

Indirect Tax Reforms after Independence

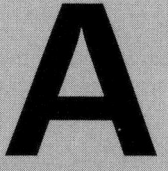

Tax Reform Committees over the Decades

Background

The ratio of tax revenue to the GDP in the developed countries is around 30 per cent, but, in India, it has hovered around 16 per cent. The celebrated French economist Thomas Piketty and others have said that the tax to GDP ratio in India is very low.[1] To improve the tax intake, a series of tax reforms have been discussed in India from time to time. The tax policy of a country plays a crucial role in the growth of the country. The Government of India (GoI) has also appointed a number of committees from time to time to suggest reforms in the tax structure. This was started when the first committee for reforms in taxes was set up under the chairmanship of John Matthai in 1953–1954. 'Domain experts like L. K. Jha, Raja Chelliah, Amaresh Bagchi, Govinda Rao and Vijay Kelkar have headed committees that have given critical inputs for more indirect tax reforms'.[2] The first report on tax reforms came out in the 1950s by the John Matthai Commission. Tax reforms have however moved forward significantly since the mid-1980s.

The report of Indirect Taxation Enquiry Committee (ITEC) in 1978 was the first in-depth report on indirect taxes. Besides ITEC, other reports of different committees and a number of studies by scholars have contributed to the reform process since Independence and especially in the last two decades. The reports of the tax reforms

---

[1] Chakravarty and Dehejia, 'India Is an Outlier'.

[2] Rajagoplan, 'It Took Three Decades'.

committees (1953, 1991, 1992 and 1993) paved the way for reforms in the taxation system. Several tax experts have made important contributions in this regard.

Taxation Enquiry Commission, 1953–1954

The reform process was started with the formation of first committee, Taxation Enquiry Commission, under the chairmanship of John Matthai on 1 April 1953.[3] The committee was formed to conduct a comprehensive enquiry into taxation. The appointment of the committee was announced by the then finance minister in his budget speech.[4] The terms of reference (ToR) of the committee were as follows:

- To examine the central, state and local taxation on the different classes of people and in different states
- To examine the suitability of existing taxation system of central, state and local government
- To examine the effects of the structure and level of taxation of income on capital formation and maintenance and development of productive enterprise
- To examine the use of taxation as a fiscal instrument in dealing with inflationary or deflationary situations
- To consider other relevant matters
- To make recommendations, in particular, regarding (a) modification required in the present system of taxation and (b) fresh avenues of taxation

Report

The commission examined in detail the whole system of central, state and local taxation and submitted its report in three volumes.[5] The

---

[3] The other members were V. L. Mehta, ex-member of Finance Commission; V. K. R. V. Rao of Delhi School of Economics; K. R. K. Menon, secretary, Ministry of Finance; B. Venkatappiah, a former finance secretary of the Bombay Government; and B. K. Madan, economic adviser to the RBI.

[4] GoI, *Budget for the Year 1953–1954*, 14.

[5] *Taxation Enquiry Commission Report 1953–54*, Vol. I, 216.

report dealt with all aspects of the system, rate of tax, structure, development finance, etc. Volume I depicts the whole tax system, central taxes, state taxes and local taxes. Volume II discusses central taxes, direct and indirect, principally income tax, excise, and custom and estate duties. Volume III gives the position of state taxes with reference to land and agriculture, sales tax and miscellaneous taxes.

Recommendations

The commission suggested the necessary measures which could be implemented as early as possible. It came forward with a set of recommendations to remove the shortcomings of the tax system. The commission was of the opinion that there was a scope for widening the base for taxation. The commission recommended that indirect taxes could be used as a means of progressive tax only in a limited manner. Sales tax was a source of revenue specifically for the states. It should continue to be levied and monitored by the states. The central government could intervene in the case of inter-state sales and specific intra-state sales. The levy of inter-state sales should be subject to a ceiling of 1 per cent. The same should be monitored and retained by the states. 'The power to levy taxes on sale and purchase of goods in the course of inter-sate trade and commerce was assigned to the Union by the Constitution (Sixth Amendment) Act, 1956.'[6]

Fourth Finance Commission, 1965

The GoI constituted the Fourth Finance Commission on 5 May 1964. P. V. Rajmannar was the chairman, Mohan Lal Gautam, D. G. Karve (part time) and Bhabatosh Datta were members, and P. C. Mathew was member secretary of the commission. It was the second step taken by the government towards tax reforms. The commission was asked to make recommendations on the effect of the combined incidence of states sales tax and central excise duty (CED) levied on the production, consumption or export of commodities/products.[7] The commission

---

[6] GoI, *CBIC, Goods and Service Tax (GST)*, 4.

[7] GoI, *Report of Fourth Finance Commission*, 1965, 1.

examined the way in which better coordination between union excise duties and states sales tax could be brought about.

Recommendations

The recommendations of the commission covered a period of five years commencing from 1 April 1964. The commission recommended a mean for the apportionment of estate duty, union excise and additional duties of excise. The commission also recommended following measures for improvement of taxation system:

- The revenue resources of states for five years ending with 1970–1971 on the basis of levels of taxation likely to be reached at the end of 1965–1966
- Creation of fund out of state duty proceeds over a specified limit for repayment of state's debt to the centre
- Scope for economy with efficiency in states' administrative expenditure

Central Excise (SRP) Review Committee, 1971

The government appointed Central Excise (Self Removal Procedure) Review Committee under the chairmanship of B. Venkatappiah on 11 October 1971 to examine the organizational and administrative setup of central excise.[8] The committee submitted its report in two volumes. Volume I dealt with the procedure and Volume II with organization. The committee made the following recommendations:

- It recommended that central excise administration should exercise three patterns of control, namely accounts-based control (ABC), production-based control (PBC) and clearance-based control (CBC).
- The classification lists should be required to be approved within a stipulated period. The stipulated period should ordinarily be a matter of days and in no case more than three months. If the list

[8] Kumar, *Committees and Commissions in India*, 38.

is not approved in the stipulated period, it should be deemed to have been accepted.

- There has been a continual modification of the tariff structure with a view to achieve certain objectives. There is a need to take stock of exemptions and remove those which are not serving any useful purpose like the end use based notifications.
- The underlying purpose for grant of licence is to regulate an activity rather than the scale of that activity. Excise license should be issued and renewed to all manufacturers for the full period of three years.
- The committee studied in detail the organizational setup and suggested a new organizational structure taking into consideration the administrative needs.

Indirect Taxation Enquiry Committee, 1976–1978

The government took the next major step in the 1970s for reforms in indirect tax system. The ITEC was formed in July 1976 under the chairmanship of the former RBI governor L. K. Jha who enjoyed a formidable reputation in the financial and economic sphere. The committee was asked to review the existing structure of indirect taxes in India and suggest policy reforms. The committee, however, devoted much of the time and attention to the scrutiny of indirect tax laws, specifically, union excise duties. 'L. K. Jha, [was] perhaps the most accomplished econocrat of his generation of ICS officials.... His report of 1978 laid the foundation of the MODVAT reforms implemented in V. P. Singh's time.'[9] The committee submitted its report in two volumes. The first volume[10] was submitted in 1977 and the second volume[11] in 1978.

The ToRs were as follows:

- To review the existing indirect tax structure of—union, state and local governments, in all its aspects
- To inspect the role of indirect taxes in boosting economic use of scarce resources

---

[9] Acharya, 'India's Tax Reforms'.

[10] GoI, *Report of the Indirect Taxation Enquiry Committee* (October 1977), Part I.

[11] GoI, *Report of the Indirect Taxation Enquiry Committee* (January 1978), Part II.

- To examine the structure and levels of excise duties, the impact of excise duties on prices and costs, the cumulative effect of such duties, their incidence on various expenditure groups, the scope for widening the tax base and increasing the elasticity of the system
- To examine the feasibility of adopting some form of value added tax (VAT) in the field of indirect taxation
- To examine structure and levels of import duties
- To advise the government on steps to be taken to implement the recommendations made
- To suggest changes, if any, required in the Constitution and in the related taxation statutes
- To examine the proper balance between indirect and direct taxes in the tax structure
- To make any other recommendations germane to the enquiry

Recommendations

ITEC was in favour of reforms to ensure sufficient availability of resources to the government on the one hand and develop a result-oriented, efficient and equitable system of taxation on the other. The committee recommended both short-term and long-term plans for reforms. As per the budget speech for 1978–1979,[12] the major recommendations of the committee were restructuring of the pattern of central excise and custom duties, desirability of the introduction of VAT to remove cascading effect of taxes, measures to assist small-scale industry (SSI) and reorientation of the tariff to make it income elastic. The committee also made suggestions regarding indirect taxes levied by the states and local authorities.

Let us discuss a few recommendations of the committee under the following sub-headings.

Excise Duties

The committee recommended the rationalization of excise duty right from the first stage of production to the final stage and the abolition

---

[12] GoI, *Finance Minister Budget Speech 1978–79*, 18.

of the input taxes. It also recommended that the procedure of collection and assessment of excise duty must be simplified.

Sales Tax

The committee recommended that state governments should move to a single point tax at the last stage. The committee further suggested that there should be a central legislation to bring about uniformity in the structure of sales tax among the states. Inter-state sales tax must be reduced to 1 per cent from 4 per cent.

Value Added Tax

The committee recommended that a collective effort should be started at centre to minimize the problem of cascading and overlapping of excise and sales taxes. In this connection, the committee recommended to adopt VAT at the manufacturing stage (MANVAT). The committee recommended a long-term move towards VAT system right through the indirect system at both centre and state levels together. This important recommendation of the committee led to the implementation of Modified Value Added Tax (MODVAT) in 1986.

Import Duties

The committee recommended that there was a need of gradual reduction in import duty rates of those goods which would reduce the prices of essential goods, promote exports and improve the balance of payments.

Tax Reform Committee, 1991

The government started economic reforms in 1991 and introduced a new economic policy. Accordingly, the government constituted the Tax Reform Committee (TRC) in 1991 to study the direct and indirect tax structure of the country. A seasoned economist Raja Jesudoss Chelliah was appointed the chairman of the committee.[13] 'India is

---

[13] The chairman of National Institute of Public Finance and Policy (NIPFP).

fortunate to have been able to call upon Raja Chelliah, one of the world's most experienced fiscal experts, to offer guidance.'[14] The ToR of the committee were to examine and give recommendations on the following:

- Ways and means of increasing the elasticity of tax revenues both direct and indirect, and increasing the share of direct taxes as a proportion of total tax revenues and of GDP
- Making the tax system fairer and broad based with necessary rate adjustments, particularly with regard to commodity taxation and personal taxation
- Rationalization of existing system of direct taxes with a view removing anomalies, improving equity and sustaining economic incentives
- Simplification and rationalization of customs tariffs with a view to reducing the multiplicity and dispersion of rates and eliminating exemption that have now become necessary
- Identifying new areas of taxation
- Ways and means of improving compliance of direct taxes and strengthen their enforcement
- Reducing the level of tariffs rates, keeping in view the need of mobilizing the resources to facilitate fiscal adjustment and the objective of promoting international competitiveness
- Extending the scope of MODVAT scheme
- Simplification and rationalization of structure of excise duty for better tax compliance and administration
- To make recommendations on any other matter relating to the above ToR

Recommendations

The committee came up with three reports: (a) Interim Report in December 1991, (b) Final Report I in August 1992 and (c) Final Report II in December 1992. The committee recommended several measures in its report. The interim report discussed principles of reforms and

---

[14] Bird, 'Tax Reforms in India', 2721.

applied them to the basic taxes such as income tax, wealth tax, tariffs and consumption tax. The major recommendation in interim report for indirect taxes was to move towards VAT covering services as well as commodities.

Part I of the final report dealt with both direct and indirect tax reforms. The Part II of the final report contained a discussion of proposed restructuring of the tariff structure. The committee recommended in the final report that the two boards: Central Board of Direct Taxes (CBDT) and Central Board of Excise and Customs (CBEC, now known as Central Board of Indirect Taxes and Customs [CBIC]) should be given financial autonomy. The committee suggested measures for effective tax collection and efforts to combat tax evasion through better audit.

The government implemented many of the recommendations of the committee. It merged the tax rates of MODVAT into three rates (8%, 16% and 24%) in 1999–2000, with additional rates on some goods. Further, three rates were merged into one rate with the new name Central Value Added Tax (CENVAT) in 2000–2001 with some commodities subject to special excise duty (SED).

Chelliah's recommendations provided the basis for the direct taxes emerging as the major component of tax revenues (a position occupied by customs and excise duties) and, as a consequence, the tax system becoming less regressive. By pushing for a slashing of the tax rates and the number of slabs in respect of corporate as well as personal incomes, he got the system modified to encourage tax payment rather than tax avoidance. He not only visualised and concretised VAT (Value Added Tax) but also negotiated with the State governments for adopting it.[15]

Committee on Indirect Taxes, 1992

A high-level committee was appointed by GoI in 1992 to evolve a common code of indirect taxes with a view to simplifying and streamlining procedures of both the customs and excise duties. The

---

[15] Rao, 'Father of Tax Reforms'.

chairman of the committee was K. L. Rekhi,[16] former chairman of CBEC. The committee submitted its report in 1993 and the recommendations of the committee were almost on the lines of TRC. The focus of the committee's report was on the procedures for tax management. The major recommendations were as follows[17]:

- The committee recommended that there should be a common integrated tariff for both the customs duties and excise duties based upon a harmonized system of nomenclature.
- The committee recommended continuing the internationally adopted harmonized system of nomenclature, especially in the context of globalization of the economy and international trade practices.
- The committee observed that most of the classification disputes arise because of a very large number of exemption notifications and thus there was a need to reduce the number of notifications, especially after the annual budget.
- The input duty relief should be extended to all inputs used whether directly or indirectly and whether contained physically in the final product or not.
- The committee sought to strengthen the appellate system so that it was able to tender quick and effective justice to assesses.
- The committee recommended a single, high-powered tribunal under the law ministry on the pattern of the central administrative tribunal with 1 president, 8 vice presidents and 32 members spread over 20 two-member benches.
- The committee had proposed the constitution of an independent, high-powered advance ruling committee for giving its rulings on the classification of a commodity.
- It had recommended a time-bound decision on price list and classification list, but they should be deemed to have been approved after the expiry of one month from the date of filing.

---

[16] Murty, *Structural Transformation*, 105.

[17] Lekhi, *Public Finance*, 233.

Reform of Domestic Trade Taxes in India, 1994

A team led by Amaresh Bagchi, Professor Emeritus of National Institute of Public Finance and Policy (NIPFP),[18] carried out a study with the title 'Reform of Domestic Trade Taxes in India' in 1994 on reforms in indirect tax, specially sales tax. The aim of the study was to design a possible system of VAT for India on which there could be a broad agreement between union and states.

The report was an important step towards reforms in indirect taxes. The report 'became a key report guiding the reform of state sales taxes and exploring the VAT options available under India's Constitution'.[19] The team acknowledged the fact that trade tax of the country needs an urgent reform because the system that was operating then was archaic and irrational. It was the most complex in the world.

Reform Measures

The team was of the opinion that the government must take action to solve the problem at their roots and not the symptoms alone, if the ills of the present system were to be remedied. The guiding principles must be simplicity, neutrality and equity. A new system of tax, VAT, could help to stabilize the economy and free it from the clutches of a complex and outdated system of taxation. The report recommended the following[20]:

1. Convert sales taxes into VAT by moving over to a multistage system of sales tax with rebate for tax on all purchases with only minimal exceptions.
2. Extend the tax base to include all goods sold or leased with minimal exceptions, and services which were integral to the sale of goods. The base should also include services which were predominantly of a consumption nature and could be taxed conveniently by the states.

---

[18] NIPFP, *Reform of Domestic Trade Taxes*.

[19] Acharya, 'India's Tax Reformers'.

[20] NIPFP, *Reform of Domestic Trade Taxes*, 61.

3. To allow input tax credit (ITC) to all raw materials and parts, consumables, goods for resale and production machinery and equipment.
4. To replace the existing structure of tax rates with two or three rates within specified bands, applicable in all states and union territories.
5. Remove the exemptions except for a basic threshold limit and items like unprocessed food and withdraw other concessions like tax holiday, etc.
6. Zero-rate exports out of the country and inter-state sales and consignment transfers to registered traders with suitable safeguards against misuse.
7. Tax inter-state sales to non-registered persons as local sales.
8. Modernize tax administration, computerize operations and the information system and simplify forms and procedures.

Task Force on Indirect Taxes, 2002

An important committee towards the indirect tax reforms was Task Force on Indirect Taxes. In July 2002, the then Finance Minister Jaswant Singh had proposed setting up two task forces to recommend measures to simplify and rationalize direct and indirect taxes. Subsequently, on 3 September 2002, a 12-member task force was formed under the chairmanship of the then Advisor to Ministry of Finance and Company Affairs Vijay Kelkar. The task force had wide representation of industry that included[21] S. K. Munjal from CII, K. S. Suresh from FICCI, N. Kothari (ASSOCHAM), H. S. Bhatia (PHDCCIS), Y. P. Suri (FASSI), K. S. Ravishankar (NASSCOM) and D. Puri from ESEPC. The objective of task force was to bring indirect tax structure and procedure at international level with the help of information technology (IT) to reduce transaction cost.

Recommendations

Kelkar Committee Report is known as the task force on direct and indirect taxes. The task force submitted its report to the government on

---

[21] *Financial Express,* 'Kelkar heads the Task Force'.

25 November 2002. The committee had made various suggestions on toning up tax administration to make it effective and simple. The task force recommendations can be bifurcated into two groups: tax administration and central excise. The major recommendations are as follows[22]:

Tax administration

- Customer clearance should be based on trust and be uniformly spread to all exporters and importers. A new mechanism should be introduced by the importer for self-assessment of bill of entry.
- The inter-agency issues should be settled by a high-level inter-ministerial committee.
- There should be a time limit for processing of export and import document.
- The central excise levy should be based on value addition.
- A guideline for determination of cost of production should be issued soon.
- The levy based on MRP should be lengthened.
- The distinction between capital goods and inputs should be abolished and CENVAT Credit Rules should be amended.
- Central excise and custom rates should be made fully automatic.

Central excise

- CENVAT should replace all the levies.
- There should be four rates: 0 per cent, 6 per cent, 14 per cent and 20 per cent.
- The 0 per cent should be for life saving drugs and equipment, 6 per cent for matches and processed food products, 14 per cent for all items not mentioned against other rates, and 20 per cent for air conditioners, motor vehicles and aerated waters.
- There should be a separate rate for tobacco products.
- The exemption duty for small-scale sector should be extended to only small units with turnover of ₹50 lakh.

---

[22] GoI, *Economic Survey 2002–2003*.

- The procedure, legislation and documentation of state VAT should be uniformed.
- A separate service tax legislation to be integrated with the central excise law.
- The service tax should increase on all services except a few that are in negative list.

Task Force on Implementation of FRBMA Act, 2002

The Fiscal Responsibility and Budget Management Act (FRBMA), 2002 although approved by the Parliament was not notified. Finance Minister Jaswant Singh, who had swapped places with Yashwant Sinha in June 2002, constituted a task force on the implementation of FRBMA 2003 to chalk out legislation for fiscal policy to achieve FRBMA targets. The task force was led by economist Vijay Kelkar. Kelkar, along with Ajay Shah, advisor in the Ministry of Finance and an IRS officer Arbind Modi, who was on special duty in the ministry, started work on a report of the task force. The Kelkar-led task force submitted its report on 16 July 2004. The report comprised seven chapters followed by appendices. It was the first report on the design of Goods and Services Tax (GST), which suggested a single rate: 7 per cent for states and 5 per cent for the centre.

Task force suggested a way of fiscal adjustment. It was revenue-led reforms on revenue expenditure and enhanced capital expenditure to counteract the contractionary effects of fiscal correction. As per the economic survey 2004–2005,[23] task force expected that with the implementation of reforms, the union tax to GDP ratio would improve from 9.2 per cent in 2003–2004 (RE) to 13.2 per cent in 2008–2009. The total expenditure of union would come down from 15.4 per cent of GDP in 2003–2004 (RE) to 14.3 per cent of GDP by 2008–2009. They estimated that there will be a revenue surplus of 0.2 per cent of GDP in 2008–2009 and fiscal deficit would come down to 2.8 per cent of GDP in 2008–2009 from 4.8 per cent in 2003–2004.

The task force led by Kelkar recommended that the existing system of taxation of goods and services suffered from many problems. The

[23] GoI, *Economic Survey 2004–2005*, 40.

task force also said that the indirect tax policy of the country was steadily progressing towards VAT since 1986. The task force suggested some strategies for fiscal policy. Let us look at them.[24]

Tax Reforms Strategy

The task force suggested the following:

- Widening the tax base via elimination of exemptions and 'grandfathering'.
- Enhancing equity of the taxation system at both vertical and horizontal.
- Moving towards non-distortionary consumption tax.
- Enhancing the neutrality of present and future consumption.
- Constituting an effective and efficient compliance system.

Tax Measure Proposals

The task force suggested the following:

- Moving towards GST.
- Increasing income tax exemption limit to ₹100,000.
- A two-tier rate structure for individuals. Of the total, 20 per cent tax for income of ₹100,000–₹400,000 and 30 per cent for income above ₹400,000.
- Eliminating standard deduction that was available to salaried class.
- Reducing income tax for corporate to 30 per cent for domestic companies and reducing the deprecation rate to 15 per cent from 25 per cent.
- Three-tier custom duty rates of 5 per cent, 8 per cent and 10 per cent to reduce tariffs to ASEAN levels.
- Reducing threshold exemption limit for small-scale industries from ₹1 crore to ₹40 lakh.
- Converting the ad valorem excise rates to specific rates for petroleum products.

[24] Strategy for Tax reforms and Proposal for Tax measures is extracted from GoI, *Economic Survey 2004–2005*.

Thirteenth Finance Commission Report (2010–2015)

The Thirteenth Finance Commission was constituted by the President of India on 13 November 2007 under Article 280 of the Constitution of India. The chairman of the commission was Vijay Kelkar, and other members were Indira Rajaraman, Atul Sharma, Sanjiv Mishra and B. K. Chaturvedi (part-time member). The commission submitted its report to the Parliament on 15 December 2009. As government wanted to implement GST from 1 April 2010, the commission studied Indian tax structure in depth. The report included a detailed study on GST as Chapter 5 of Volume I. The commission formed a task force under Arbind Modi, then joint secretary in the Department of Revenue. The members of the task force were V. Bhaskar, Shri B. S. Bhullar (both were joint secretaries) and Rathin Roy (economic adviser) and Ritvik Pandey (deputy secretary). The task force was constituted to assist the Finance Commission on issues related to the proposed implementation of GST from 1 April 2010.[25]

Term of Reference

The task force was asked by Finance Commission to conduct a study on 'the impact of the proposed implementation of Goods and Services Tax with effect from 1 April 2010 including its impact on the country's foreign trade'.[26] Three other items of consideration in the ToR were as follows[27]:

- To estimate the resources of central and state governments
- To generate surpluses in the capital account not only balancing the receipts and expenditure on the revenue account
- To improve tax to GDP ratio of the centre and the states

---

[25] GoI, *Thirteenth Finance Commission*, 19.

[26] Ibid., 63.

[27] Ibid., Chapter 5.

Recommendations

The task force studied all aspects of GST. The report of the task force is included as Chapter 5 in the report of Finance Commission. The report of the Thirteenth Finance Commission's task force on GST is indeed a visionary document and makes comprehensive recommendations for the implementation of GST in India. The report is on the lines of Kelkar's concept which he had outlined in his earlier report, *Report on Implementation of the Fiscal Responsibility and Budget Management Act (FRBMA)*. The task force recommended the adoption of the 'flawless' GST. They also suggested a model GST. The recommendations of the task force are as follows[28]:

- GST should be levied on consumption and computed on the basis of the invoice credit method.
- The proposed GST will subsume all major indirect taxes (specifically stamp duty, taxes on vehicles, taxes on goods and passengers and taxes and duties on electricity) excluding customs and all cesses and surcharges.
- Transmission fuels, high-speed diesel, motor spirit and aviation turbine fuel should be brought under a dual levy—GST and an additional levy without ITC. However, all other petroleum products should be brought under the ambit of GST, as should natural gas.
- The sumptuary goods of tobacco and alcohol should be taxed through GST as well as an additional levy, with no ITC being provided on the additional levy.
- GST should include transportation sector and subsumed taxes on vehicles, goods and passengers.
- The power sector should be included in the tax base and electricity duty subsumed.
- GST should include real estate sector in the tax base and subsume stamp duty levied by state governments.
- The financial service sector should be brought under the GST tax base.

---

[28] Ibid., 66–67.

- Capital goods should be treated as other goods and services.
- The 'place of supply' rules should be based on international best practices for goods and services.
- The threshold of ₹10 lakh should be adopted with a composition limit of ₹40 lakh, above which GST would be mandatorily applicable.
- The exemptions on the basis of area should be withdrawn and the tax paid reimbursed wherever considered necessary.
- Inter-state transactions should be treated through a mechanism which permits sellers in one state to charge SGST from buyers in another state.
- There should be harmonization in registration, return filing, assessment and audit across states.
- The Revenue Neutral Rate (RNR) would be 11 per cent (5% for CGST and 6% for SGST).

There is a common practice around the world that the report of any committee/commission is implemented quickly with or without change. But in India, the recommendations of the various committees/ commissions even if accepted are implemented tardily, if at all leading to the avoidable wastage of resources and ignoring the hard work of many eminent persons. Sometimes, the national loss is incalculable. The way Kelkar's report on GST was treated is a classic example of this approach.

Modified Value Added Tax: 1986 to 2000

Most economists generally agree that modern tax reforms in India were really initiated by V. P. Singh during his two-year tenure as finance minister in Rajiv Gandhi government in the 1980s. The introduction of MODVAT has been considered as a major step in the reform process of indirect tax system. It was called 'modified' as it was restricted only up to the manufacturing stage. The reform in the system of indirect taxes was an important item in the agenda of the union budget of 1986–1987. The government took the first step with the introduction of new tariff for customs and excise on the basis of harmonized system of classification.

In the second stage, the tariff structure with such amendments of duties as necessary, replaced the old customized system. Under excise, the irritating question of taxation of inputs and its cascading effect on the final product was a major problem. Introduction of MODVAT was an attempt to remove this problem.

V. P. Singh introduced MODVAT in the union excise duties on 28 February 1986 in his second budget speech for 1986–1987. This budget was a modest beginning of a major indirect tax reform that led to the introduction of CENVAT and finally to GST. The scheme came into force on 1 March 1986 through the budget of 1986–1987.[1] The credit for the payment of excise duty on manufactured products was

---

[1] The MODVAT scheme was inserted by notification 176/86 dated 1 March 1986 as Section AA.

available under the new system. The operation of MODVAT had the following three effects[2]:

1. An increase in transparency of the tax burden under the UEDs
2. A reduction in the cascading effect of input taxation
3. The generation of a mechanism to check tax evasion through self-policing

The aim of the introduction of MODVAT was to reduce the cascading effect of taxes on the final price of goods through availability of immediate credit of excise duty paid on inputs and reduction of interest cost. MODVAT allowed manufacturers to get immediate reimbursement of excise duty paid on raw materials and components. It was introduced with the hope that it will reduce the cost of the final product. It brought in rationalization in tax structure. It ensured revenue of the same order and at the same time maintaining if not reducing the price of the product.

The government implemented the MODVAT scheme in stages. In the beginning, it was implemented only for select commodities and was extended to a larger number of commodities later. In the first instance, MODVAT was introduced for all goods covered under 37 specified chapters of Central Excise Tariff Act, 1985. The scheme covered the products of paints and packaging materials, rubber products, chemical and allied industries, base metals/articles of base metals, motor vehicles, plastics, glass and glassware, machinery and mechanical appliances along with electrical equipment, and certain miscellaneous manufactured products.

By the end of the year, MODVAT covered 38 chapters of the Excise Tariff.[3] The exemptions were significant including as they did petroleum products, textiles, and tobacco products.[4]

---

[2] Aggarwal, *Modified Value Added Tax (MODVAT)*.

[3] GoI, *Budget Speech, 1987–88*, Para 103.

[4] Purohit, *Problems of Introducing Value Added Tax in India*.

T. N. C. Rajagopalan in his article in Business Standard wrote that 'over a period, the MODVAT scheme was extended to cover all items. Its scope was enlarged to many other chapters later on; barring a few the central excise rules were also suitably modified. Service tax was also enlarged'.[5] Thus, we can say that the full coverage of MODVAT was achieved by 1996–1997 when it was extended to cover all items.

Rajiv Gandhi presented the budget for 1987–1988 as finance minister. He was the third Prime Minister of India who presented a union budget after Indira Gandhi and Jawaharlal Nehru. He introduced the concept of zero-based budgeting. He extended MODVAT to the remaining chapters except those related to tobacco, textile and petroleum sectors. The tax was extended to cover leather and travel goods, food products, paper and paperboard, asbestos cement products, footwear, wood and cork products, precious metals, and mineral products.[6]

The Finance Minister Narayan Dutt Tiwari made some corrections in MODVAT scheme in his budget speech for 1988–1989. He rationalized rates of excise duty in respect of a few commodities. The procedural problems of MODVAT that government faced in the initial stages had been sorted out.

The MODVAT scheme was appreciated by industry and they had been asking for the extension of the new scheme to other sectors as well. In the budget speech for 1991–1992, Manmohan Singh reintroduced MODVAT scheme in aerated water and extended it to filament yarns and manmade fibres in respect of their inputs.

As per the provision, the buyers of goods from small-scale manufacturers were getting a notional credit under MODVAT which was five percentage points more than the CED actually paid by the latter. The Public Accounts Committee (PAC) found irregularities in the operation of this facility. The TRC was also not in favour of this scheme. Hence, the government withdrew the higher notional scheme which buyers were getting for the purchase of goods from small-scale

---

[5] Rajagoplan, 'It Took Three Decades'.

[6] GoI, *Budget Speech, 1987–88.*

units. In his budget speech for 1993–1994, the finance minister abolished this scheme and announced that buyers would receive MODVAT credit only on the basis of excise duty actually paid.

The subsequent extension of MODVAT reduced the cascading effect of input taxes. But the coverage was limited. Matches, capital goods, petroleum products, tobacco products and textiles were not under the scheme. Industry was demanding increase in its coverage. Hence, the government extended the coverage of MODVAT to two important sectors, namely capital goods and petroleum products.[7] This was a long-standing demand of all sectors of Indian industry.

The MODVAT scheme covered all yarns after including yarns made from fibres. The objective was to broaden the base, shift to ad valorem rates as soon as possible, simplify the tax structure, reduce the high rate of duty in order to reduce evasion and extend the coverage of MODVAT. The changes were evident in terms of growth of excise revenue in FY 1994–1995.

The manufacturers of plastic woven bags were demanding the extension of MODVAT to the users of such bags. The government allowed full credit of excise duty paid to the users of plastic bags and jute bags. There were requests from trade and industry for the further liberalization and simplification of MODVAT scheme. Therefore, the government relaxed the following MODVAT rules:

- Allowed credit for pollution control, testing, R&D equipment and specified quality control
- Allowed credit for low sulphur and furnace used for power generation in a factory that manufacture excisable goods
- The use of MODVAT credit for payment of duty on any goods that notified under the MODVAT scheme

Some major changes were introduced in the budget for 1995–1996. The government extended MODVAT scheme to tyre yarn used tyres by imposing excise duty of 20 per cent on intermediate tyre cord fabrics. The specific rates of duty on tyres were raised by 8 per cent to

---

[7] GoI, *Budget Speech, 1994–95.*

make up revenue loss. The duty on tyres for two and three wheelers was not raised.

The government further extended MODVAT scheme to industrial fabrics. In the case of woollen fabrics also, MODVAT was extended fully, as such fabrics already attracted basic excise duty and enjoyed limited MODVAT facilities.[8] Despite the changes of 1995–1996, there was a decline in the growth rate of revenue from union excise duties.

General elections were held for the eleventh Lok Sabha in 1996. The result of the election was a hung Parliament. No one national party got a majority to form the government. The BJP was invited to form the government but failed to prove its majority in Parliament. Thereafter, H. D. Deve Gowda of Janata Dal-led United Front formed the government with the outside support of Indian National Congress. The United Front made a Common Minimum Programme to run the government. Finance Minister P. Chidambaram in his budget speech for 1996–1997 said that the Common Minimum Programme mandated the government to continue with tax reforms.[9]

He told Parliament that the government has taken a number of steps to reform the structure of indirect taxes by switching over to ad valorem rates, reducing the number of rates and removing exemptions. The union excise duty was revamped and moved closer to VAT. MODVAT was introduced for capital goods. The facility of input credit was extended to all items necessary for manufacturing. The changes resulted in the growth of industrial production which led to growth in revenue. The collection of indirect tax was increased by 19 per cent.

He said that some state governments are moving towards the VAT system.[10] The union government also wanted to adopt a central VAT but there were some legal obstacles. The union excise structure had 11 ad valorem rates varying from 0 per cent to 50 per cent. Finance minister said, 'Ideally there should have been only 3–4 rates of excise duties Ñ

---

[8] GoI, *Budget Speech, 1995–96.*

[9] GoI, *Budget Speech, 1996–97,* Para 102, 121–122.

[10] GoI, *Budget Speech, 1996–97,* Para 121.

zero, a lower rate of excise duty on goods of mass consumption, a single normal rate on all other goods and a higher rate on luxury items'.[11]

Yashwant Sinha came back to North Block in 1998 as union finance minister. In his maiden budget for 1998–1999, he proposed to make amendments with reference to treatment of MODVAT credit in the valuation of inventory and capital assets, and block assessment procedure as further rationalization measure. The government restricted the availability of credit to 5 per cent of excise duty paid in the case of inputs used in the manufacturing of excisable goods. This restriction was not applicable in capital goods.

Yashwant Sinha also announced in Parliament that the medium-term objective of the government was to increase the tax to GDP ratio. He said,

> Until a few years ago the regime was characterized by a multiplicity of rates and punctuated with numerous ad hoc exemptions. As a result, the tax structure was opaque. It is the objective of the present proposals to introduce greater transparency in the system through a significant rationalization of rates. The ultimate objective of this process is to move towards a Central Value-Added Tax (VAT) system which can then be merged with a generalized VAT.[12]

Under MODVAT, manufacturers were claiming a higher refund of excise paid by them on inputs, claiming that they had used a certain variety of inputs. It made it difficult for the authorities to verify this claim leading to disputes. As both the centre and the states depended heavily on indirect taxes, it was the need of the time to restructure tax rate, reduce compliance cost, rationalize and simplify procedure.

The major changes introduced in the budget for 1999–2000 were rationalization of rate structure to reduce multiplicity of rates and converge it with a central rate with a merit rate and a demerit rate. Yashwant Sinha proposed the reform of excise taxes in the budget. He said that, in the medium-term, we would move to a single rate and a full-fledged VAT system. The government reduced the 11 ad valorem

[11] GoI, *Budget Speech, 1996–97*, Para 122.

[12] GoI, *Budget Speech, 1998–99*, Para 117–118.

rates to three rates[13]—a central rate of 16 per cent, a merit rate of 8 per cent and a demerit rate of 24 per cent. The three rates were achieved with the following formula:

- The existing rates of 5 per cent, 10 per cent and 12 per cent merged with 8 per cent
- The existing rates of 13 per cent, 15 per cent and 18 per cent merged with a new rate of 16 per cent
- The existing rate of 25 per cent sifted to a new rate of 24 per cent

The government announced to lift the cap on MODVAT claims and restored it to 100 per cent.

> Last year government made a cap of 75% for the same. Yashwant Sinha told Parliament, 'there is [was] also a happy coincidence that this rate is [was] almost identical to the rate of one-sixth (Shadbhaga) advised by Kautilya, the noble sage of Pataliputra, which also happens to be my birthplace'.[14]

In the budget speech for 2000–2001, Finance Minister Yashwant Sinha said that the dispute between the department and assesses on the interpretation of MODVAT rules and procedure plagued the system in the initial years. The existing rules were replaced by simple and transparent rules with effect from 1 April 2000. The new rule reduced disputes to a minimum. The MODVAT credit on capital goods was allowed to be spread over a period of two years. He extended MODVAT scheme to cigarettes for the first time. He enhanced the rates of excise duty on all categories of cigarettes by 5 per cent.[15]

In the budgets from 1991–1992 to 1999–2000, serious efforts were made to restructure the excise duty in such a way that it encouraged the industry and made it more competitive. Introduction of MODVAT was a means to remove the problems of indirect taxes. There were a very large number of rates for MODVAT in the initial stage. Throughout the 1990s, the rate brackets of MODVAT had been

[13] GoI, *Budget Speech, 1999–2000*, Para 61.

[14] GoI, *Union Budget of 1999–2000*, Para 61.

[15] GoI, *Budget Speech, 2000–01*, Para 89–90.

reduced and rates were rationalized. A number of specific rates were converted into ad valorem rates. While the number of rates had been reduced over the years, the rates of MODVAT had 10 categories of rates (i.e., 0, 5, 10, 15, 20, 25, 30, 35, 40 and 50).

There were exceptions at higher and lower rates. The higher rate of 225 per cent was levied on luxury goods and lower rates of 1–8 per cent were levied on a few necessity goods which were still high by international standards. The multiplicity of rates was creating the problems of tax evasion, misclassification and cumbersome litigation. It also encouraged inefficient allocation of resources. Where India was struggling with a number of problems due to multiplicity of rates on the one hand, on the other more than 100 countries in the world were enjoying the benefits of VAT with a small number of rates.

Central Value Added Tax: 2000 to 2017

The introduction of CENVAT was the second crucial step towards reforms in indirect taxes in the country. It was Yashwant Sinha who introduced a single rate CENVAT at the centre in the budget speech for 2000–2001. He converted MODVAT scheme into CENVAT scheme.[1] It came into existence from 1 April 2000 vide new set of rules 57AA–57AK. The new system was introduced to give long-term stability, abolish uncertainties in the mind of businessman, and eliminate disputes of taxation classification.

Robin Burgess, Stephen Howes and Nicholas Stern wrote in their paper that the advantages of the new tax were clear.[2] The single rate tax avoided all the complexities that would arise if different states had different VAT rates.[3] Jayashree Parthasarathy and P. C. Anand however in their article wrote that the CENVAT rules were hastily withdrawn and replaced with a new and improved set of rules for the simplification of credit procedure.[4]

CENVAT was the predecessor of the present-day GST, and it was almost the same as MANVAT suggested by L. K. Jha. Under the new scheme, a final product manufacturer could take credit for excise duty on any input received in the factory, and taxable service provider could take credit for service tax paid of any input service received by manufacturer of the final product.

[1] GoI, *Union Budget, 2000–01*, Para 87.

[2] Burgess, Howes, and Stern, 'Value-Added Tax Options for India', 119.

[3] Ibid.

[4] Parthasarathy and Anand, 'The New Set of CENVAT Rules'.

Yashwant Sinha brought about significant changes in the central excise laws: introducing new valuation rules in 2000, new central excise rules in 2001 and replacing the MODVAT scheme and capital goods credit scheme with the CENVAT scheme. Three ad valorem rates (8%, 16% and 24%) of MODVAT were converged in to a single rate of 16 per cent CENVAT. A few commodities were subject to special duty. The 8 per cent excise rate was therefore abolished and most of the items at this rate were moved to 16 per cent. However, certain items—essentially covering medicare and items of use by the common man—were exempted from the excise duty. Besides 16 per cent, there were three special excise rates of 8 per cent, 16 per cent and 24 per cent. These three special excise duties were not MODVAT-able and users were not able to avail MODVAT credit for these duties. In addition, the duty on a few other products, charged at the rate of 24 per cent, was reduced. Shankar Acharya in his article in *Business Standard* praised Yashwant Sinha for the major breakthrough in reforming excise rates and bringing 11 excise rates to 3 in 1999–2000, and finally to the single rate of 16 per cent in 2000–2001.[5]

The scope of the MODVAT scheme was expanded and rationalized. All the inputs and capital goods were included in the eligible list of MODVAT. High-speed diesel and petrol were the only exceptions. The availability of MODVAT credit on capital goods was allowed for the period of two years with effect from 1 April 2000.

In the budget speech for 2001–2002, Yashwant Sinha announced in Parliament his intent to reduce the three rates of SED to a single rate of 16 per cent. According to him, the single rate of CENVAT was contributing to about 68 per cent of total excise revenue from ad valorem duties.[6]

Mr Sinha abolished 8 per cent SED on mattresses and articles of bedding, glazed tiles, scooters and motorcycles, and taxis, carpets and floor coverings, studio back cloth, painted canvas, linoleum, and textile wall covering.

[5] Acharya, 'India's Tax Reformers'.

[6] GoI, *Budget Speech, 2001–02*.

This scheme shall work as follows:

Mr Ram manufactures product X in his factory and the assessable value of one X is as under:

Assessable value of product X = ₹100
Excise duty on ₹100 @ 12.36% = ₹12.36

However, Ram has to use product Y as raw material to manufacture product X, which he buys from his supplier Mr Shyam.

Assessable value of product Y = ₹50
Excise duty paid by Mr Shyam on ₹50 @ 12.36% = ₹6.18

Now while making payment to Mr Shyam for product Y, Mr Ram has to pay him ₹50 for product Y along with ₹6.18 as reimbursement of excise duty borne by Mr Shyam.

Since product Y is being used to manufacture product X, one may say that the assessable value of ₹100 of product X (₹50 of product Y) is included on which Mr Shyam has already paid the excise duty to the government. Therefore, if we tax ₹100 once again, there will be double taxation of excise. One may call it cascading effect of duty. To avoid this, MODVAT/CENVAT scheme is introduced.

Now, final duty at the time of removal of product X will be as under in MODVAT/CENVAT scheme:

Excise duty on product X = ₹12.36
Less: CENVAT of duty paid for raw material Y = ₹6.18
Net excise payable by Mr Ram on product X = ₹6.18

Now, there is no double taxation of duty by applying the MODVAT/CENVAT system.

In the budget speech for 2002–2003, Yashwant Sinha abolished the rate of 16 per cent SED on a number of items.[7]

The abolition had reduced disputes and litigation and assesses' compliance cost. SED was narrowed to only eight items: motor cars, polyester filament yarn, tyres for replacement, air conditioners, aerated soft drinks and soft drink concentrates, multi-utility vehicles, pan masala, and chewing tobacco and miscellaneous tobacco preparations. The concessional rate of 8 per cent was increased to 16 per cent in 2002. A separate CENVAT Credit Rule which was introduced since 1 July 2001 was replaced by CENVAT Credit Rule 2002.

In 2003, Jaswant Singh became the finance minister, and, in his maiden budget speech for 2003–2004, he reduced excise duty from 32 per cent to 24 per cent on polyester filament yarn, from 16 per cent to 12 per cent on all spun and other filament yarns, from 12 per cent to 8 per cent on all knitted cotton fabrics and garments, from 12 per cent to 10 per cent on all woven fabrics and other knitted fabrics, and from 10 per cent to 5 per cent on paraxylene. The government retained pure cotton yarn at 8 per cent excise duty and withdrew exemption from all knitted and unprocessed woven fabrics, and a few exempted items were brought under the tax net. But this playing with rates seriously disturbed Yashwant Sinha's vision to limit the rates to three and ultimately bring them to one rate of 16 per cent.

The government received a number of representations for full exemption for items of the common man's use. These items—registers and account books, kerosene pressure lanterns, articles of wood, adhesive tapes, walking sticks, unbranded surgical bandages, tubular knitted gas mantle fabrics, bicycles and parts, umbrellas, articles of mica, imitation zari, mosaic tiles, utensils and kitchen articles, glasses for corrective spectacles, knives, toys, spoons and similar kitchenware/tableware—were attracting 4 per cent excise duty. The remaining items that were attracting 4 per cent excise duty without CENVAT were taxed at 8 per cent rate with CENVAT. The non-merchandized

[7] The three rates of SED were reduced to a single rate of 16 per cent.

matches were fully exempted from excise duty. However, semi-merchandized matches and mechanized sector was charged ad valorem duty of 8 per cent without CENVAT.

Yashwant Sinha wanted most exempted items to be brought under CENVAT. But he wanted to do it gradually. So he introduced an escalator formula under which the exempted items were brought under the tax net by charging a low rate of 4 per cent to begin with, without the benefit of refund. It was to be raised to 8 per cent the next year again without the benefit of refund. The escalator was supposed to ultimately climb to 16 per cent with full refund benefit. This was not followed up by his successors and therefore remained on paper.

In the 2004 general elections, Congress came back to power and P. Chidambaram became the finance minister. In his budget speech for 2004–2005, he levied excise duty on playing cards and contact lenses. He increased excise duty from 8 per cent to 16 per cent on a few items: imitation jewellery, plastic insulated ware, prefabricated buildings, laboratory glassware, vacuum flasks, populated PCBs, candles and parts of clocks, scented supari, black and white television sets, and watches. He also increased excise duty from 8 per cent to 16 per cent with CENVAT credit on merchandized/semi-merchandized matches.

In 2004, the central government had taken a major step to unify the credit regime for goods under CENVAT Credit Rules 2002 and services covered under service tax credit rules 2002. The CENVAT Credit Rules that was introduced on 1 July 2001 was replaced by CENVAT Credit Rules 2002. The CENVAT Credit Rules 2002 was further replaced by CENVAT Credit Rules 2004 on 10 September 2004.

Introduction of CENVAT Credit Rules 2004 was instrumental in codifying the credit mechanism into a single law for availing and utilizing credit of taxes paid on goods as well as services for both the manufacturers and the service providers. Over the years, the government has made several changes to the CENVAT Credit Rules, considering representations from the industry as well as to prevent misuse of the scheme. Noteworthy changes were made during 2011 and 2012 to the definitions of inputs, input services as well as capital goods. Primarily, the changes related to extending the list of exclusions from the pool of eligible credits such as restricting the credit with respect to inputs and input services for construction and/or execution of works of building/civil structure, input service of renting a motor vehicle, input services relating to outdoor catering, life insurance, health insurance, etc., when such services are primarily used for personal use or consumption of any employee, any goods used in a guest house and residential colony, etc., and input services related to setting up of a factory in the premises of a service provider.[8]

P. Chidambaram in his budget speech for 2005–2006 announced in Parliament that 'the country has VAT at central level with the name CENVAT for goods only'. He emphasized that 'the entire production–distribution chain should be covered by a national VAT, or even better, a goods and services tax, encompassing both the centre and the states'.[9] He wanted to bring as many goods as possible to CENVAT rate of 16 per cent. At that time, five items attracted the duty of 24 per cent, and, out of five, three (polyester filament yarn, tyres and ACs) were picked out and excise duty on them was reduced to 16 per cent. The other two items—motor cars and aerated drinks— were left to wait for some more time. SSI got some tax relief too. Hence, the ceiling for SSI exemption, which was based on turnover, was increased from the level of ₹3 crore to ₹4 crore per year.

P. Chidambaram reiterated that he intended to converge all rates at the CENVAT rate of 16 per cent. At that time, only two items, aerated drinks and cars, were attracting the higher rate of 24 per cent. The excise duty on aerated drinks and cars (only small cars) was reduced to 16 per cent.

A small car, for this purpose, meant a car of length not exceeding 4,000 mm and with an engine capacity not exceeding 1,500 cc for diesel cars and not exceeding 1,200 cc for petrol cars. The government was

[8] Menon, 'Indirect Taxes'.

[9] GoI, *Budget Speech, 2005–06*, Para 94.

confident that industry will seize the opportunity to make India a hub for the manufacture of small and fuel-efficient cars.[10]

An 8 per cent excise duty was imposed on packaged software sold on the counter. The customized software, software packages downloaded from the Internet, DVD drives, flash drives and combo drives were exempted from excise duty.

There was no tax on many food items, including packaged items. The food processing industry, condensed milk, ice cream, preparation of meat, fish and poultry, pectin, pasta and yeast were fully exempted from excise duty. The excise duty on ready-to-eat packaged foods and instant food mixes such as dosa and idli mixes was reduced from 16 per cent to 8 per cent.

P. Chidambaram said, 'It is my sense that there is a large consensus that the country should move towards a national level Goods and Services Tax (GST) that should be shared between the centre and the states'. He set 1 April 2010 a date for the introduction of GST. He said, 'World over, goods and services attract the same rate of tax. That is the foundation of a GST. People must get used to the idea of a GST. Hence, we must progressively converge the service tax rate and the CENVAT rate'. The service tax rate was increased from 10 per cent to 12 per cent. The finance minister reduced ad valorem component of excise duty on petrol and diesel from 8 per cent to 6 per cent in his budget speech for 2007–2008. Water purification devices operating on specified technologies as well as domestic water filters not using electricity were fully exempted from excise duty. The excise duty on cigarettes and bidis was increased by 5 per cent.

P. Chidambaram reduced CENVAT rate on all goods from 16 per cent to 14 per cent in his budget speech for 2008–2009. He reduced excise duty on all goods produced in the pharmaceutical sector from 16 per cent to 8 per cent, buses and their chassis from 16 per cent to 12 per cent, small cars from 16 per cent to 12 per cent and on hybrid cars from 24 per cent to the general revised rate of 14 per cent, two wheelers and three wheelers from 16 per cent to 12 per cent. Further,

---

[10] GoI, *Budget Speech, 2006–07.*

the excise dusty was reduced on paper, paperboard and articles manufactured out of non-conventional raw materials by units not having an attached bamboo/wood pulp making plant from 12 per cent to 8 per cent, with a further reduction on clearances up to 3,500 MT from 8 per cent to nil. Furthermore, excise duty on certain varieties of writing, printing and packing paper was reduced from 12 per cent to 8 per cent and from 16 per cent to nil on a few other items including composting machines, wireless data cards, packaged coconut water, tea and coffee mixes and puffed rice. The anti-AIDS drug, Atazanavir, as well as bulk drugs for its manufacturing were fully exempted from excise duty. The refrigeration equipment (consisting of compressor, condenser units, evaporator, etc.) above 2 TR (tonne refrigeration) utilizing power of 50 KW and above were exempted from excise duty on end-use basis. Chidambaram also departed from the Yashwant Sinha formula of three rates and introduced other rates; thus, bringing back the old formula of multiple rates.

Finance Minister Pranab Mukherjee made some changes in central excise rate to pave the way for GST in his budget speech for 2011–2012. He exempted about 100 items from central excise as well as state VAT, reduced the standard rate of excise duty for non-petroleum goods from 14 per cent to 8 per cent, and raised the standard rate from 10 per cent to 12 per cent, merit rate from 5 per cent to 6 per cent, and lower merit rate (demerit rate) from 1 per cent to 2 per cent. However, the lower merit rate for coal, fertilizers, mobile phones and precious metal jewellery was retained at 1 per cent.[11]

In 2014, BJP-led National Democratic Alliance (NDA) II came to power and Arun Jaitley became the finance minister. In his maiden budget speech for 2014–2015, he withdrew the concessional excise duty on smart cards and levied a uniform excise duty at 12 per cent.[12] The excise duty on specified food processing and packaging machinery was reduced from 10 per cent to 6 per cent. The duty on footwear of retail price exceeding ₹500 per pair but not exceeding ₹1,000 per pair was reduced from 12 per cent to 6 per cent. Arun Jaitley in his budget

[11] GoI, *Budget Speech, 2012–13.*

[12] 2 per cent without CENVAT benefit and 6 per cent with CENVAT benefit.

speech for 2015–2016, increased the time limit for taking CENVAT credit on inputs and input services from six months to one year as a measure of business facilitation.

CENVAT played a crucial role in the reform of indirect taxes in India. It removed cascading burden to a great extent through enlarging the coverage of input credit for all inputs including capital goods. Later, it allowed input credit to services. It reduced disputes. GST subsumed CENVAT.

Service Tax and Related Issues

There was a long debate on levying tax on services. Several countries were and are levying taxes on services. But India was taxing only goods and exempting services from taxation even though the service sector was showing strong growth. It was contributing about 60 per cent to the GDP. The government was making every effort to improve the tax structure and increase the tax base. In this backdrop, government constituted a number of TRCs. A TRC led by Raja Chelliah had recommended imposing tax on services to broaden the base of indirect taxes. The committee suggested levying service tax on selected services that will widen the indirect tax net. It was the first committee that recommended the inclusion of services in the tax net.

The government decided to include services in the tax net in 1994. Therefore, taxation on services was introduced by the then Union Finance Minister Manmohan Singh in his budget of 1994–1995. Service tax was the only one that was introduced through finance act. He included three services in the preview of tax. Earlier all the taxes were introduced through a special legislation/act. Service tax was introduced with the aim of reducing the tax burden on the core business, trade and industry without impacting government's earnings. Liberalization saw a fast growth in the service sector, where government saw immense potential to increase its revenue.

The provisions of service tax were brought into force with effect from 1 July 1994 vide Chapter V of the Finance Act, 1994. It was extended to the whole of India except Jammu and Kashmir. Entry 97, Schedule VII of the Constitution of India gave the constitutional right to GoI to levy service tax. The department of revenue on behalf of the government administered the levy and collection of service tax. Service tax was an indirect tax and its administrative control was vested with Central Board of Excise and Customs (CBEC). The CBEC is now known as CBIC.

After the introduction of service tax in 1994, all successive finance ministers widened the service tax net in their budgets. P. Chidambaram, the successor of Manmohan Singh, levied service tax on a number of well-known services in his budget speech for 1997–1998.[1] These services were transportation of goods by road, custom house, air travel agents, agencies for manpower recruitment, consulting engineers, steamer, tour operators and car rental agencies, clearing and forwarding agents, mandap keepers, outdoor caterers, and pandal contractors. The levy of tax on services yielded revenue of ₹100 crore in that year. The proceeds of tax on transportation of goods were utilized to increase the resources of national highway authority.

The inclusion of a number of services in service tax by P. Chidambaram in 1997–1998 spread resistance and protests. In the budget speech for 1998–1999, Finance Minister Yashwant Sinha told Parliament that government had decided to abolish the service tax on transportation of goods by road and service tax payable by outdoor caterers and pandal contractors. He also proposed to tax some new services.[2] These services were provided by chartered accountants, cost accountants, company secretaries, management consultants, interior decorators, private security services, market research agencies, credit rating agencies, underwriting agencies, architects, real estate agents and real estate consultants, and slaughter houses using mechanized means for large animals.

The tax experts were of the opinion that service tax should be made applicable to all services in one go. There were others who suggested for basic changes in the service tax structure. In the budget speech for 2000–2001, Finance Minister Yashwant Sinha said that 'service tax is emerging as an area of promise as well as problems'.[3] He constituted

---

[1] GoI, *Budget Speech, 1997–98*, Para 146–147.

[2] GoI, *Budget Speech, 1998–99*, Para 169.

[3] GoI, *Budget Speech, 2000–01*, Para 126.

an expert group to look into the matter, review and give him advice. Earlier, service tax was applied to specified services of banks and non-banking companies. Sinha extended it to corporate bodies that were providing similar services.

Structural changes were taking place in the economy as the service sector was growing faster than other sectors. Encouraged by it, the government decided to expand the net of service tax. Yashwant Sinha in his budget speech for 2001–2002 added new services to the list of taxable services. These services were port services, telex services, facsimile services, broadcasting services, telegraph services, convention services, sound recording services, photographic services, services auxiliary to insurance, specified banking and financial services, scientific and technical consulting services, video tape production services, authorized service stations for servicing of vehicles including two wheelers, on-line information and database retrieval services, and service provided to lease circuit line holders.[4]

Service tax, which was confined to limited number of services to begin with, was gaining ground. In the budget speech for 2002–2003, Finance Minister Yashwant Sinha extended the service tax to the following services: inland cargo handling, fashion designers, dry cleaning services, event management, beauty parlours, rail travel agents, health clubs and fitness centres, cable operators, storage and warehousing services (except agriculture produce and cold storages), and life insurance (including insurance auxiliary services).

In his budget speech for 2003–2004, Finance Minister Jaswant Singh suggested a constitutional amendment in service tax. The aim of the amendment was to enable levy of service tax as an important and specific source of revenue. He told the Parliament that constitutional amendment and the following legislation would give power to the union 'to levy the tax and both the central and the state governments sufficient powers to collect the proceeds'.[5]

P. Chidambaram again became the finance minister in 2004. In his budget speech for 2004–2005, he told the Parliament that he was

---

[4] GoI, *Budget Speech, 2001–02,* Para 119–120.

[5] GoI, *Budget Speech, 2003–04,* Para 134.

committed to expanding the service tax net because service sector was accounting for 51 per cent of GDP. He extended credit of service tax across services. He also enhanced service tax rate from 8 per cent to 10 per cent to neutralize the revenue impact. He also levied a cess of 2 per cent on service tax.

Since the contribution of the service sector was increasing year by year and in 2005 accounted for 52 per cent of GDP, the government decided to cast the net wide. P. Chidambaram included some additional services in the service tax net in his budget speech for 2005–2006. The new services included in tax net were site formation, survey services and map making services, pipeline transport of goods, membership fees (clubs and associations), packaging services and specialized mailing services, demolition and like services, dredging services (rivers and harbours), construction of planned residential complexes, (with more than 12 dwelling units and developed by builders), and cleaning services (for commercial buildings and similar premises).[6]

The contribution of the service sector increased to 54 per cent of GDP in 2006. The government was looking to increase its revenue from this sector with hope. In the budget speech for 2006–2007, P. Chidambaram increased the service tax rate to 12 per cent. The government expanded the number of services in the service tax net. The new services were ship management services, travel on cruise ships services, ATM operations, sale of space/time for advertisements (other than in the print media), auctioneering, share transfer agents, registrars and bankers (to an issue), recovery agents, sponsorship of events by companies (other than sports events), maintenance and management, international air travel (excluding economy class passengers), business support services, public relations management services, and container services on rail (excluding the railway freight charges).[7]

The government decided not to change the service tax rate for 2007–2008. It also increased exemption limit for small service

[6] GoI, *Budget Speech, 2005–06*, Para 146.
[7] GoI, *Budget Speech, 2006–07*, Para 152.

providers from ₹400,000 to ₹800,000. As a result, some 200,000 out of 400,000 assessees went out of the tax net. To compensate the loss due to this move, government extended service tax on the following services: asset management by individuals, design services, renting of immovable property for commerce/business use, supply and development of content to be used in advertising and telecom, outsourcing of services for mining of mineral, oil and gas.[8] Finance Minister P. Chidambaram also included services involved in the execution of works contracts with an optional composition scheme under which service tax was levied at 2 per cent of the total value of the works contracts. The government exempted services provided by resident welfare associations to their members who were contributing less than or equal to ₹3,000 per month.

The contribution of service sector in GDP increased to 55 per cent in 2008. To increase the contribution of service sector to the government exchequer, P. Chidambaram in his budget speech for 2008–2009 brought the following services in the service tax net[9]:

1. The services of clearing houses, stock exchange and commodity exchange
2. Asset management service under ULIP
3. Right to use goods (if VAT is not payable)
4. Customized software

A few doubts were raised in respect of certain services at this stage. Finance minister removed those doubts and clarified that services liable to service tax were tour operators using contract carriage vehicles, money changers and persons running games of chance.

Pranab Mukherjee took charge as finance minister in 2009. He included advice services, consultancy/technical assistance services (in the field of law) in service tax net in his budget speech for

---

[8] GoI, *Budget Speech, 2007–08*, Para 153.
[9] GoI, *Budget Speech, 2008–09*, Para 156–157.

2009–2010.[10] He also announced in his budget speech for 2010–2011 that the service sector was contributing nearly 60 per cent of GDP but service tax to GDP ratio was only around 1 per cent.[11] Service sector had the potential to increase the revenue of the government. But the government was in the process of implementing GST. The finance minister said that he had the option to raise service tax rate to 12 per cent as it was before, but decided to retain it at 10 per cent to pave the way for GST.

The government was not happy with the actual collection of service tax because it was not reflecting the full potential of this sector. The tax rate was retained at 10 per cent because the government was moving towards GST. But, to compensate for the loss, government included hotel accommodation service and service provided by AC restaurants in the service tax net.[12] Finance Minister Pranab Mukherjee raised service tax on air travel by ₹50 for domestic travel and ₹250 for international journey. He also brought the services of life insurance companies' investments in ULIPs in tax net. A net revenue gain of ₹4,000 crore was expected in 2011–2012 as a result of the inclusion of these new services in the tax net.

The year 2012 was a historic year in the history of service tax. In the month of June that year, service tax attained adulthood by completing 18 years. A debate among experts was also going on since long that service tax should be based on a small negative list. The government decided to move via negative list for service tax. Pranab Mukherjee announced in Parliament that all services except those which were in the negative list in the budget speech for 2012–2013 were liable to tax. The service sector's contribution stood at 59 per cent of GDP. But the share of service tax in overall taxes was far below its potential. Therefore, the government decided to shift gear and accelerate. The government raised service tax rate from 10 per cent to 12 per cent to generate additional revenue of ₹18,660 crore. The finance minister

---

[10] GoI, *Budget Speech, 2009–10*, Para 133.

[11] GoI, *Budget Speech, 2010–11*, Para 166, 179.

[12] GoI, *Budget Speech, 2011–12*, Para 185, 187, 188.

also announced the setting up of 'a study team to examine the possibility of common tax code for service tax'.[13]

In July 2012, P. Chidambaram returned to the North Block as Pranab Mukherjee became the thirteenth President of India. Chidambaram announced in his budget speech for 2013–2014 that he would not change the service tax rate and keep it at 12 per cent. He followed the negative list of services that was made by his predecessor. He only included two services—agriculture produce and vocational courses related to agriculture—in the negative list. The government granted full exemption from service tax on copyright and cinematography.

In the general elections of 2014, the BJP-led NDA came back to power under the leadership of Narendra Modi, and Arun Jaitley became his finance minister. In his maiden budget speech for 2014–2015, he announced that service tax had shown the highest rate of growth. He said that as government was moving towards GST, changes in service tax should be minimal. He made certain changes in the Finance Act, 1994, that was related to service tax.

The NDA II government's main focus was on the ease of doing business. For that, they decided that service tax registration would be done in two working days. In the budget speech for 2015–2016, finance minister announced increase in service tax rate and education cess from 12.36 per cent to a consolidated rate of 14 per cent. The government reviewed negative list and withdrew certain exemptions to widen the tax base.

In the budget speech for 2016–2017, finance minister announced in Parliament that the government was amending Section 73 of Finance Act, 1994 to increase the limitation period from 18 months to 30 months for the refund of service tax. The government made a number of changes in service tax structure that may be seen in the budget speech for 2016–2017. In the budget speech for 2017–2018, finance minister announced that he would not change the current regime of service tax as the same was to be replaced by GST.

---

[13] GoI, *Budget Speech, 2013–14*, Para 172.

Revenue, Services under Tax and Assessees

There has been tremendous growth in service tax collection since its inception. The average collection of service tax has been ₹58,070 crores during 1994–2019. The average growth for the same period has been 27.03 per cent. Total tax collection was only ₹407 crore in 1994–1995. It increased to ₹14,200 crores in 2004–2005 and to ₹167,969 crores in 2014–2015 and, in 2016–2017, it was ₹254,499 crores. The number of taxable services has also increased year by year. While it was three in 1994, it increased to 119 in 2012–2013. Since 1 July 2012, the concept of negative list regime has been introduced to levy service tax. The number of assessees had also increased. It was only 3,943 in 1994, but, in 2013, it was 1,712,617. The budgetary target of revenue collection in the FY 2016–2017 is ₹231,000 crores which is about 14 per cent of the total tax collection target of GoI. The revenue, number of services under tax and assessees data from 1994 onwards can be seen in Table 4.1.

Table 4.1 *Service Tax Revenue*

Financial Year	Revenue (₹ crores)	Growth	Number of Services	Assesses Number	Growth
1994–1995	407	–	3	3,943	–
1995–1996	862	111.8	6	4,866	23.41
1996–1997	1,059	22.9	6	13,982	187.34
1997–1998	1,586	49.8	18	45,991	228.93
1998–1999	1,957	23.4	26	107,479	133.7
1999–2000	2,128	8.7	26	115,495	07.45
2000–2001	2,613	22.8	26	122,326	05.91
2001–2002	3,302	26.4	41	187,577	53.34
2002–2003	4,122	24.8	52	232,048	23.71
2003–2004	7,891	91.4	62	403,856	74.04

(continued)

(continued)

Financial Year	Revenue (₹ crores)	Growth	Number of Services	Assesses Number	Growth
2004–2005	14,200	80.0	75	774,988	91.89
2005–2006	23,055	62.4	84	846,155	09.18
2006–2007	37,598	63.1	99	940,641	11.17
2007–2008	51,301	36.4	100	1,073,075	14.08
2008–2009	60,941	18.8	106	1,204,570	08.78
2009–2010	58,422	–4.1	109	1,307,286	08.53
2010–2011	71,016	21.6	117	1,372,274	04.97
2011–2012	97,509	37.3	119	1,535,570	11.90
2012–2013	132,601	36.0	Negative list regime	1,712,617	11.53
2013–2014	154,778	16.7		–	–
2014–2015	167,969	8.5		–	–
2015–2016	211,414	25.9		–	–
2016–2017	254,499	20.4		–	–
2017–2018*	81,228	–68.1		–	–
2018–2019 RE	9,283	–88.1		–	–
Average	**58,070**	**27.00**		–	–

Source: www.cbic.gov.in; *GoI, Receipt Budget 2019–2020, p. 21.

Service tax was introduced with three services: telephone services, non-life insurance services and stock brokers' services. In the meanwhile, the list of services on which service tax was levied went on expanding. It had gradually increased from 3 to 119 services. The concept of 'negative list' instead of a 'positive list' of services was introduced on 1 July 2012. It changed the system of taxation from tax on specified services to tax on all services except those which were in the 'negative list' of services or which were exempted by a notification. Pranab Mukherjee introduced the negative list regime and taxed all services except 17 services which were out of taxation net.[14] P. Chidambaram included two new services in negative list. Arun Jaitley reviewed the negative list.[15] Now, the service tax has been subsumed in GST.

---

[14] GoI, *Budget Speech, 2012–13*, Para 158, 160.
[15] GoI, *Budget Speech, 2014–15*.

State VAT (State Value Added Tax): 2002 to 2017

5

VAT is a consumption tax. It is a multipoint destination-based tax. It is being levied on the value addition in the product at each stage of its manufacturing cycle and price paid by the final consumer. It starts from the purchase of raw materials and goes all the way to final retail purchase. It is a very efficient form of commodity taxation. It was France that first adopted VAT in 1954. It became one of the important fiscal innovations in the 20th century. VAT is the most radical fiscal reform of this century. It is a modern and transparent indirect tax system. It has been adopted by more than 160 countries in the world. It is known by different names in different countries. It is known as Tax on Value Added (TVA) in Germany and France, and Ad Valorem Taxes (AVT) in America. However, VAT is a popular nomenclature.

India was among one of the last countries in the world to introduce VAT in 2005. It replaced the erstwhile sales tax of states. The introduction of State VAT solved the problems of double taxation of commodities and multiplicity of taxes, and cascading tax burden. 'All other existing taxes such as turnover tax, surcharge, additional surcharge and Special Additional Tax (SAT) were abolished'.[1] It helped common people, traders, industrialists and also the government.

The Empowered Committee (EC) of State Finance Ministers had formulated the concept of VAT in its 'White Paper' on State VAT.

> The essence of VAT was in providing set–off for the tax paid earlier, and this has been given effect through the concept of input tax credit/rebate. This input tax credit in relation to any period means setting off the amount

[1] EC of State Finance Ministers, *A White Paper*, 12.

of input tax by a registered dealer against the amount of his output tax. The Value Added Tax (VAT) was based on the value addition to the goods, and the related VAT liability of the dealer was calculated by deducting input tax credit from tax collected on sales during the payment period.[2]

Let us understand the concept of VAT with the help of an example which was given by the Committee of State Finance Ministers in its concept paper on VAT in its 'White Paper'.

If, for example, input worth ₹100,000 is purchased and sales are worth ₹200,000 in a month, and input tax rate and output tax rate are 4 per cent and 10 per cent respectively, then ITC/set-off and calculation of VAT will be as shown below:

a. Input purchased within the month: ₹100,000
b. Output sold in the month: ₹200,000
c. Input tax paid: ₹4,000
d. Output tax payable: ₹20,000
e. VAT payable during the month: ₹16,000

After set-off/input tax credit: (d – c)

Source: GoI. A White Paper on State-Level Value Added Tax. January 17, 2005, pp. 6–7.

'India can be globally competitive as a fully integrated market in the Value-Added Tax regime.'

—Raja J. Chelliah

'A comprehensive VAT widens tax net, as it makes tax evasion difficult. Going by the experience of other countries, VAT has proved beneficial and leads to revenue buoyancy.'

—Michael Carter, World Bank Country Director

States had been levying sales tax since Independence. But it was plagued by some serious flaws. States levied it in an uncoordinated

[2] Ibid., 6.

manner. The country was struggling because of the double taxation system in vogue. There were different rates of sales tax for different commodities in different states. There was no harmony in the sales tax rates among the states. Sales tax rate was different for the same commodity in different states. There was a race to the bottom because each state wanted to be ahead of the others in the race in order to attract industries. There was a so-called 'rate war' among the states, resulting in revenue loss. Tax on goods was levied on both pre- and post-production stages, which had a negative impact on the economy.

The government decided to implement VAT throughout the country to solve the problems of multiplicity of tax rates, different procedures of tax collection, large number of concessions and exemptions, and lack of uniformity of tax across states. It was Manmohan Singh who first took the initiative to introduce State VAT in India. He stated in his budget speech for 1993–1994 that the rates of excise duty should be simplified.[3] In the long term, the government was to move towards the VAT system. He further told Parliament that a nationwide VAT could not be introduced overnight because introduction of the new tax system required a broad agreement between centre and the states on the structure of such system. He requested NIPFP to come out with a design of a possible VAT system.

The introduction of State VAT was a significant step in the reform of the indirect tax regime of India. It was the third most important step in this direction after the introduction of MODVAT and CENVAT. Later, it provided a basis for the introduction of GST. As State VAT was a state subject, introducing it was not easy. It required change in Entry 54 of the State List.

Yashwant Sinha, after assuming office, tried to push forward with VAT and put an end to the sales tax rate war among the states. At the central level, he introduced CENVAT in place of central excise by making tax refund fully available to traders and manufacturers. He established a single rate CENVAT at the centre.

---

[3] GoI, *Budget Speech, 1993–94*, Para 52.

The first discussion on State VAT had taken place in the meeting of chief ministers in 1995. The meeting was convened by the then Finance Minister Manmohan Singh. The basic issues of the new tax were discussed in this meeting. The meeting was followed up by periodic interaction of finance ministers of states, but the matter did not move forward in any significant way.

During his first tenure as finance minister, Yashwant Sinha remained completely preoccupied with tackling the adverse effects of the international sanctions imposed on India post the nuclear tests in May 1998 and other immediate issues. But he turned his attention to State VAT when he returned to North Block after the general elections of 1999. He called a meeting of chief ministers of all states which was held on 16 November 1999. After some general discussions in this meeting, the chief ministers, at the suggestion of Yashwant Sinha, agreed to form a committee of chief ministers under the chairmanship of Jyoti Basu, the then chief minister of West Bengal and the longest serving chief minister of India. This committee was charged with the responsibility of discussing all the concerned issues with regard to the speedy implementation of VAT and prepare a report for the next meeting of the chief ministers. Another meeting of the chief ministers was convened after the report of this committee was ready. Three important decisions were taken in the meeting[4]:

1. Prior to state-level VAT, the unhealthy practice of sales tax rate 'war' among the states would have to end and sales tax rates would need to be harmonized by implementing uniform floor rates of sales tax for different categories of commodities with effect from 1 January 2000.
2. In the interest of harmonization of sales tax, the sales tax related industrial incentive schemes would also have to be discontinued with effect from 1 January 2000.
3. After achieving the first two objectives, steps would be taken by the states for the introduction of state-level VAT after adequate preparation.

[4] EC of State Finance Ministers, *A White Paper*, 3.

It was in this meeting that Yashwant Sinha suggested the formation of a Committee of State Finance Ministers (EC) for implementing the decisions taken in the meeting of the chief ministers and preparing a blue print for the introduction of VAT. Thereafter, the EC started to meet on a regular basis. The committee took a period of one and half years to complete about 98 per cent of the work relating to the first two objectives.

EC took a number of steps for the introduction of State VAT. It made attempts to harmonize the State VAT design because every state had its own distinctive features that needed to be harmonized. The states collectively agreed to implement State VAT through discussions in the EC on certain points of convergence of VAT and certain flexibility for the local needs of the states. In course of time, again at the suggestion of Yashwant Sinha, the chief ministers agreed to convert the EC into an empowered group so that work could move faster and without bothering the chief ministers every now and then.

The preparatory work relating to the introduction State VAT was completed in due time and was ready for implementation from 1 April 2001. A meeting of state finance ministers was held in Delhi to give finishing touches to the introduction of VAT. The representatives of traders were also called to this meeting because their cooperation was essential for the introduction of State VAT. The traders' representatives present in the meeting opposed VAT tooth and nail and warned of dire consequences if it was introduced without adequate preparation on their part. In view of this very determined opposition of the traders, it was decided that the implementation of State VAT should be postponed by a year, and the intervening time should be used to hold meetings with the traders in the capitals of various states to prepare them for this change. This process could not be completed by the end of March 2002, and its implementation had to be postponed again. In the meanwhile, Yashwant Sinha moved to the Ministry of External Affairs, and Jaswant Singh became the new finance minister on 1 July 2002. The introduction of VAT was postponed as states were not ready to implement it at that time. Jaswant Singh proposed a new deadline to bring it up from 1 April 2003 at the state level, but it was put off yet again. The implementation of the VAT system from 1 April

2003 was deferred due to differences among the states, and a nationwide bandh was called by traders.[5]

A Conference of chief ministers of all states along with union finance minister was held on 18 October 2002. The meeting was convened by the then Prime Minister Atal Bihari Vajpayee. In the meeting, the then Union Finance Minister Jaswant Singh clearly stated his intention of introducing VAT from 1 April 2003. However, there were certain hassles that delayed the introduction of State VAT. In spite of these hassles, a number of states were interested to implement VAT. Haryana had already introduced VAT on its own with good results in revenue growth.

About 29 states and union territories prepared their State VAT legislations and sent the same to Union Ministry of Finance for prior scrutiny. The Ministry of Finance considered all the draft bills. The ministry sent its comments and suggestions to the states/union territories for incorporating the same in the bills to be placed in their respective legislative assemblies and further transmission to the central government for the assent of the President of India. The Madhya Pradesh VAT bill had already been accorded presidential assent in November 2002. The EC endorsed the suggestion on 8 February 2003 that the legislations of all states should have a minimum set of common features.

However, a large number of states had expressed their apprehension about the possible loss of revenue in the initial years of the implementation of the VAT. The central government agreed to compensate the states for their possible revenue loss due to the introduction of VAT. Finance minister Jaswant Singh in the budget speech for 2003–2004 announced that the government will 'compensate 100 per cent of the loss in the first year, 75 per cent of the loss in the second year and 50 per cent of the loss in the third year of the introduction of VAT as per an "agreed formula"'.[6] He said that

---

[5] *The Hindu*, April 2, 2003.

[6] GoI, *Budget Speech, 2003–04*, Para 131.

the government would assist the states to transit successfully from the erstwhile sales tax to a modern VAT.

After the change of government after the general elections of 2004, the new Finance Minister P. Chidambaram picked up the threads of tax reforms. He worked out the financial support to states and campaigned for the introduction of VAT. P. Chidambaram in the budget speech for 2004–2005 proposed a formula for determining the revenue loss due to the introduction of VAT.[7] He had offered states the services of a 'Technical Expert Committee'. The committee worked closely with states and helped them to move steadily towards the implementation of VAT.

The EC called a meeting on 18 June 2004 in which it invited the then Finance Minister of India P. Chidambaram as special invitee. All the states, except one, participated in the meeting. The meeting was chaired by the Chairman of EC Asim Das Gupta, the finance minister of West Bengal. The member states fixed a new deadline to introduce VAT from 1 April 2005.[8] All the goods, including declared goods, were covered under State VAT and would get ITC benefit.[9]

Meanwhile, the EC submitted a White Paper on State-level VAT on 17 January 2005. The White Paper was a basic design of State VAT that was prepared with the collective efforts of all states. The White Paper was in three parts. Part I stated the background and justification of State VAT. Part II gave the basic design of State VAT. Part III discussed other issues related to implementation of VAT. In the White Paper, the EC suggested that State VAT would cover about 550 goods at two basic rates of 4 per cent and 12.5 per cent. There were 270 items in the 4 per cent category which was common for all states. It included items of basic necessities such as medicines and drugs, agricultural and industrial inputs, capital goods and declared goods. The remaining items were under the general VAT rate of 12.5 per cent, again common for all states. They also suggested a special rate of 1 per cent for gold

---

[7] GoI, *Budget Speech, 2004–05*, Para 69.

[8] EC of State Finance Ministers, *Annual Report for 2005–06*, 29–30.

[9] EC of State Finance Ministers, *A White Paper*, 13.

and silver and precious stones and a specific category for tax exempted goods. The EC suggested abolition of the additional taxes such as surcharge, additional surcharge and turnover tax while continuing entry tax even under VAT.

The White Paper also suggested that AED items should not be taxed for one year after the implementation of State VAT because of the initial administrative difficulties.[10] It further suggested that till that time, existing arrangements should be continued. AED came into State VAT in addition to the levy of tax under Additional Excise Duty (Goods of Special Importance) Act, 1957. The rate of State VAT to be levied should not exceed 4 per cent. If it exceeded 4 per cent, the state might lose the share of revenue under the AED Act. This move, to be effective from a date to be notified, ostensibly was to help the states augment revenue and to integrate these goods in the VAT chain. At that time, states were getting merely 1.5 per cent of central excise revenue distributed to them as per the formula given by Finance Commission for giving up their right to levy sales tax on AED commodities. The major source of revenue for the states was petroleum products and liquor. Thus, alcohol, tobacco, textile, petrol, diesel and aircraft turbine fuel were given a one-year breather. The State VAT model asked all existing dealers to register themselves for VAT. The threshold limit was fixed at ₹50 lakh. The traders with income up to ₹5 lakh were out of the VAT net. An 11-digit Tax Identification Number (TIN) was made compulsory.

P. Chidambaram in the budget speech for 2005–2006 announced that all the states had agreed to introduce VAT from 1 April 2005.[11] He paid his tribute to the EC for working diligently through the last seven years and preparing a framework that was accepted by all states. At that time, more than 130 countries, from Sri Lanka to China, had adopted VAT. India also had VAT but at central level and only for goods, not for services.

---

[10] Textiles, tobacco and sugar, are commonly known as AED goods. AED was a revenue compensation package.

[11] GoI, *Budget Speech, 2005–06*, Para 9

However, after some resistance, it finally came into force on 1 April 2005. A majority of states switched over to State VAT from 1 April 2005 in place of sales tax despite protests from traders.[12] Finance minister requested the non-VAT states to join the mainstream because the next step of reform depended on the implementation of VAT by all the states.

Subsequently, Assam and Meghalaya joined the mainstream on 1 May 2005, followed by Uttaranchal (now Uttarakhand) and Chandigarh that introduced VAT from 1 October 2005 and 15 December 2005, respectively. 'In 2006, most of the states had adopted VAT in place of sales tax. But eight states, mostly those ruled by the BJP, had refused to implement the tax.'[13] However five states—Gujarat, Rajasthan, Madhya Pradesh, Jharkhand and Chhattisgarh—implemented State VAT with effect from 1 April 2006.

Tamil Nadu introduced VAT effective from 1 January 2007 followed by Puducherry from 1 July 2007. Haryana was the first state which implemented VAT on 1 April 2003. Finally, the last Indian state, Uttar Pradesh, switched from sales tax to VAT from 1 January 2008. Andaman and Nicobar and Lakshadweep did not accept VAT. Finally, all Indian states had implemented VAT as a part of domestic trade reforms being initiated in the country. But Mr L. K. Jha, the real architect of VAT, had died long ago in 1988.

The EC recommended that central sales tax (CST) should be phased out. It further requested the centre to compensate the states for the expected revenue loss. The central government promised to compensate the states through monetary and non-monetary measures which could be taken together.[14] P. Chidambaram in the budget speech for 2006–2007 announced that the government had

---

[12] Karnataka, Andhra Pradesh, Maharashtra, Odisha, West Bengal, Arunachal Pradesh, Himachal Pradesh, Kerala, Punjab, Sikkim, Goa, Jammu and Kashmir, Delhi, Nagaland, Tripura, Mizoram, Bihar, Dadra and Nagar Haveli, Manipur, and Daman and Diu.

[13] *The Hindu*, April 2, 2005.

[14] GoI, *Budget Speech, 2006–07*, Para 175.

made a provision of ₹3,000 crore towards compensation for VAT losses in the budget.[15]

The experience of introducing VAT was welcomed by all stakeholders. The growth in tax revenue had been reported by all states as compared to the tax collection during the same period in previous year. P. Chidambaram in his budget speech for 2007–2008 told Parliament that State VAT had proved to be an unqualified success. The revenue of states which had implemented VAT increased by 13.8 per cent in 2005–2006 and by 24.3 per cent in the first nine months of 2006–2007.

The introduction of the State VAT was a historic reform of our domestic tax system. It had replaced the erstwhile state sales tax. It had eliminated the cascading effect of sales tax through giving set-off for tax paid on inputs as well tax paid on previous purchases. It has been considered a major step in the sphere of indirect tax reforms in India.

In the beginning, most of the states were opposing the switchover from the existing sales tax to VAT because of their economic and political reasons. It was a challenging task in a federal country like India to get all the states to agree to it. Every state had the constitutional power to levy and collect the taxes assigned to it by the Constitution. But, Yashwant Sinha took the initiative of Dr Manmohan Singh forward and constituted the EC which created the political consensus leading to the final introduction of VAT at the state level. P. Chidambaram took up the baton and finished successfully the race initiated by Yashwant Sinha.

The new tax was consistently opposed by the traders. The Confederation of All India Traders (CAIT) observed 1 April 2005 as a 'black day' for the trading community. They continued their stir in many parts of the country. The state-level VAT was opposed by some other stakeholders also. There was a trade bandh. The then Secretary General of CAIT Praveen Khandelwal was leading the bandh. He said, 'We are continuing our strike against VAT, which will keep prices high and affect the poor'.[16]

---

[15] Ibid., Para 109.

[16] *The Economic Times*, 'VAT Implemented in 20 States'.

The reform that converted state-level sales tax into State VAT encouraged the government to move towards a national-level GST at a uniform rate throughout the country. The new tax was to cover both goods and services. P. Chidambaram in his budget speech for 2007–2008 fixed the deadline for the introduction of the new tax—1 April 2010. The GST which came into force from 1 July 2017 has subsumed all the indirect taxes. State VAT was also abolished.

Setting Up of the Empowered Committee of State Finance Ministers and Its Role

Inder Kumar Gujral was running the United Front coalition government at the centre with the outside support of the Indian National Congress. There were 14 parties in the coalition. The minority coalition government collapsed on 28 November 1997. The Congress Working Committee unanimously decided to pull the plug on the United Front government. The General Secretary of Congress Oscar Fernandes reached the home of I. K. Gujral with a letter to inform the withdrawal of support. Prime Minister Gujral submitted his resignation to the President. The then Congress President Sitaram Kesri wanted to form a Congress government at the centre and even wrote a letter to the President to stake his claim. He wrote, 'We are sure given the chance we will be able to prove our majority on the floor of the house'. But instead, President K. R. Narayanan dissolved Parliament on 4 December 1997 and called for fresh elections. The post-election manoeuvring gave the BJP-led NDA a working majority of 265 seats and Atal Bihari Vajpayee became the Prime Minister on 19 March 1998.[1] He appointed Yashwant Sinha as his finance minister On the taxation side, Yashwant Sinha's first priority was to introduce CENVAT and ultimately VAT as suggested by the L. K. Jha Committee in 1976.

---

[1] India: Parliamentary Chamber: Lok Sabha—Elections Held in 1998. http://archive.ipu.org/parline-e/reports/arc/2145_98.htm

The government had a good reason to push indirect tax reform. Both industry and consumers were facing the problem of multiple taxes. These also had a cascading effect. These taxes ultimately led to the evasion and revenue loss for the government. A number of countries in Asia and the world had already moved to the new system of tax, that is, VAT. India had also made a move in this direction through the introduction of MODVAT on selected commodities.

Yashwant Sinha called a meeting of chief ministers of all the states of the country in October 1999. He persuaded Jyoti Basu, the chief minister of West Bengal, to head the group of chief ministers on the proposed new tax which Basu accepted. Basu was the only chief minister in the country to have served for 23 years at a stretch. This committee's report laid the ground for states to converge towards a common meeting ground. It was a strategic political move of Yashwant Sinha. Basu was one of the biggest critics of the BJP-led NDA government. He was also the senior most and longest serving chief minister of the country. He also had a highly qualified finance minister, Asim K. Dasgupta who later became the convener/chairman of the EC.

The Standing Committee of Finance Ministers was later converted into Empowered Committee of Finance Ministers on VAT on 17 July 2000, so that the chief ministers do not have to be bothered every now and then. Empowerment meant that the state finance ministers came prepared to take decisions on behalf of their states. The EC really speeded up the process for the introduction of VAT. The EC was formed with the finance ministers of Delhi, Gujarat, Karnataka, Maharashtra, Madhya Pradesh, Meghalaya, Punjab, Uttar Pradesh and West Bengal as its members. Later, finance ministers of Assam, Jammu and Kashmir, Rajasthan, Jharkhand and Tamil Nadu were also notified as the members of EC.

Later, the GoI reconstituted the EC with state finance/taxation ministers of all states as its members on 12 August 2004.[2] The EC was later registered as a trust under the Societies Registration Act (XXI of 1860) on 17 August 2004. The EC had its office in Delhi Sachivalaya,

[2] Department of Revenue, 'Introduction (Empowered Committee of State Government)',

I. P. Estate, New Delhi. It was getting funds from central government and state governments to meet its administrative expenses and to undertake other activities.

The objective behind the formation of EC was to monitor the implementation of uniform floor rates of sales tax by states and union territories, to monitor the phasing out of the sales tax-based incentive schemes, to decide milestones and methods of states to switch over to VAT and to monitor reforms in the CST system existing in the country.[3] Yashwant Sinha, who is the chief architect of VAT, believed that more such joint mechanisms needed to be evolved. 'The implementation of VAT has been achieved only because we have had this device. Neither the Centre nor the states could have done it alone.'

The EC of State Finance Ministers was always headed by the finance minister of an opposition party ruled state. The first Chairman of EC, Asim K. Dasgupta, was a former professor of economics at Calcutta University, who brought credibility and respect to the EC. However, in 2010, Dasgupta, who had completed about 80 per cent of the work had to step down because he ceased to be the finance minister of West Bengal. Sushil Kumar Modi, deputy chief minister and finance minister of Bihar, succeeded him in July 2011. Sushil Kumar Modi demitted the office of Chairman on 17 June 2013. Abdul Rahim Rather, finance affairs minister of Jammu and Kashmir, succeeded Sushil Kumar Modi on 22 July 2013. He demitted office on 9 January 2015. K. M. Mani, finance minister of Kerala, succeeded Abdul Rahim on 20 March 2015. Amit Mitra, the finance minister of West Bengal, succeeded K. M. Mani on 19 February 2016 who resigned as finance minister on 10 November 2015. He is the present Chairman of EC. Mitra, an economist, was the secretary general of the industry association FICCI.

The EC conducted its meetings on a regular basis. The meetings of EC were attended by finance ministers of state governments, senior officials of ministry of finance of union government, finance

---

[3] EC of Finance Ministers, *Annual Report (2005–06)*.

secretaries and commissioners of commercial tax of states. During 2005–2006, EC met 11 times, 11 times during 2006–2007, 7 times during 2007–2008, 8 times during 2008–2009, 11 times during 2009–2010, 8 times during 2010–2011, 7 times during 2011–2012, 4 times during 2012–2013, 5 times during 2013–2014, 5 times during 2014–2015, and 5 times during 2015–2016.[4] EC also conducted its AGMs every year, and released its annual reports. Eleven annual reports have been published so far. All the reports are available on EC's official website.[5]

The EC submitted a White Paper on State-level VAT on 17 January 2005. The State VAT was introduced on 1 April 2005, but the EC was requested to continue and work on GST. It submitted the First Discussion Paper for GST on 10 November 2009. GST was finally introduced with effect from 1 July 2017.[6]

The EC of State Finance Ministers has lost its relevance with the formation of the GST Council and has not been assigned any new function. It called a meeting on 14 December 2017 to discuss the revenue resources of states and best practices in respect to administering resources outside GST. 'The Empowered Committee has neither been assigned new functions nor a fresh mandate has been given to it.'[7] Perhaps it could survive in future as a 'trade union' of state finance ministers.

[4] Ibid., 28; *Annual Report (2006–07)*, 23; *Annual Report (2007–08)*, 28; *Annual Report (2008–09)*, 23–24; *Annual Report (2009–10)*, 7; *Annual Report (2010–11)*, 7; *Annual Report (2011–12)*, 35; *Annual Report (2012–13)*, 6; *Annual Report (2013–14)*, 7; *Annual Report (2014–15)*, 7; *Annual Report (2015–16)*, 31.

[5] http://empcom.gov.in/index.aspx

[6] See the chapters on State VAT and GST for the task of EC.

[7] IANS, 'Sushil Modi Urges Amit Mitra'.

The New Regime of Goods and Services Tax

B

Background of Goods and Services Tax

Background

India is a 'union of states', but it has strong federal features too. There are two levels between which the Constitution divides the powers of governance: the union government at the centre and the state governments at state level. The Constitution empowered the union to levy excise duty on manufacturing of products and service tax. The Constitution further entitled states to levy sales tax/VAT on sale of goods. Moreover, union levied CST on inter-state trade/commerce, but the tax was collected and retained by the exporting state. States also levy an entry tax on the entry of goods in local areas. This was the tax structure that the British had left behind. It was indeed a very complicated system of taxation.

The division of fiscal power between union and states led to a multiplicity of indirect taxes. The multiplicity of indirect taxes at both union and states had an intricate tax structure with hidden costs for business. Every state had its own tax structure and rates. There was no uniformity in tax structure and tax rates across the states. This resulted in cascading effect of taxes as a result of tax on tax. There was no credit for the CED or service tax to traders in State VAT and vice versa. No credit of tax paid in one state was available in another state. The cascading of taxes affected the prices of goods and services as the prices were artificially inflated.

To remove the myriad taxes and eliminate the cascading effect of taxes, the government introduced MODVAT on manufacturing in 1986, CENVAT on excise in 2002 and State VAT in place of sales tax in 2005. But there were still some shortcomings. CENVAT did not include several union taxes, such as additional customs duty, surcharge, etc. Further, CENVAT did not apply to VAT chain in distribution trade. It was only limited to manufacturing.

The introduction of State VAT was a crucial improvement over CED at national level and sales tax at state level. But State VAT also suffered from certain infirmities. There were a number of state taxes of indirect nature. These taxes, like luxury tax, entertainment tax, etc., were not subsumed in State VAT.

The CST was also a cause of distortion because of its cascading nature. The government did a lot to harmonize the tax structure in the VAT regime. But there were too many barriers in the movement of goods in the national market. The main barrier was procedural requirement under VAT and CST.

The government was making efforts to overcome these shortcomings. The next logical step in the process was the introduction of GST. The new tax was rolled out in the historic central hall of the Parliament by the President and Prime Minister of India on 1 July 2017. It was a historic moment.

There is a misconception that GST is just VAT plus service tax. It is an improvement over the previous CENVAT, State VAT and service tax. It is the biggest tax reform of indirect taxes. GST is indeed as an important step towards achieving perfection in the reform of the indirect tax structure of the country.

Genesis of GST and Its Progress through Various Regimes

The reform process in indirect taxes was started with the constitution of the Matthai committee in 1953. It reached its desired goal with the formation of the Task Force in 2003 which suggested the introduction of GST. The process of reform and introduction of GST was continued by the United Progressive Alliance (UPA) I and UPA II governments. Finally, GST was introduced by the NDA II government. Let us discuss the progress of GST under different regimes.

NDA I Government

Keeping the importance of tax reforms in mind, the Vajpayee-led NDA I government took a number of steps during its tenure to clean up indirect tax regime at both the centre and state levels. In 2003, it formed Task Force on Fiscal Responsibility and Budget Management. The task force was chaired by the eminent economist and civil servant Vijay Kelkar. The task force submitted its report in 2005 along with a number of recommendations. It recommended the replacement of CENVAT, State VAT and all indirect taxes except customs duty by one GST. It also recommended the early roll out of GST. The Thirteenth Finance Commission headed also by Vijay Kelkar had earlier made the same recommendation, namely the introduction of GST.

UPA I Government

The election of fourteenth Lok Sabha was held in 2004 and led to a change of government. Manmohan Singh, the finance minister of P. V. Narasimha Rao government and an eminent economist, was sworn in as the thirteenth prime minister of India. P. Chidambaram became the finance minister.

Chidambaram took up the threads of state VAT from where the NDA government had left it. After the successful implementation of State VAT, he started working on GST. He announced in his budget speech for 2007–2008 the intention of his government to introduce GST with effect from 1 April 2010.

He requested the EC of State Finance Minister to prepare the structure of the new tax and a road map for its implementation. The EC constituted a joint working group on 10 May 2007 to study the international models of GST around the world. The group had representatives of the centre as well as the states. The group interacted and discussed the matter with experts and submitted its report to the EC on 19 November 2007.

The EC called a meeting on 28 November 2007. The report of the joint working group was discussed in detail in this meeting and certain modifications were suggested. The final version was a report titled *A Model and Roadmap for Goods and Services Tax in India* which was submitted to the government on 30 April 2008.

The government was happy with the report. Chidambaram in the budget speech for 2008–2009 said that he was happy with the progress for the preparation of the roadmap for the introduction of GST with effect from 1 April 2010. However, the introduction of GST missed its first deadline by over seven years.

The report submitted by EC contained the structure, design and the roadmap for the introduction of GST. The revenue department made some suggestion which the government sent to the EC on 12 December 2008. The EC called a meeting to discuss the suggestions made by the government on 16 December 2008.

The suggestions made by the revenue department were further discussed in the meeting of a committee of principal secretaries, secretaries of finance and taxation, and commissioners of trade taxes of states. The EC accepted the views of committee on 21 January 2009.

EC again formed a working group of the officials of state governments. The group in association with senior officials of the GoI submitted its recommendations on the structure of GST. The issue of revenue loss to the states due to the phasing out of CST was discussed between Finance Minister Pranab Mukherjee and the EC on 19 October 2009.

UPA II Government

The UPA was re-elected in the fifteenth general elections held in 2009. While Manmohan Singh continued as prime minister, P. Chidambaram was replaced by Pranab Mukherjee as the union finance minister. The finance minister in his budget for 2009–2010 rationalized the rates of service tax and excise duty to enable the final move to GST from 1 April 2010.

Meanwhile, the EC continued its discussion with officials of the working group. It also discussed the matter within itself and with the union government. Finally, the EC submitted its report on the structure of GST as 'First Discussion Paper for GST' on 10 November 2009. The objective of the paper was to generate a debate and get inputs from the stakeholders. The discussion paper was divided into four parts. Part I dealt with the process of introduction of the VAT. It also discussed how GST could subsume the existing VAT. Part II explained the process for the preparation of GST. Part III gave the comprehensive structure of GST, and Part IV was an annexure that gave a list of the frequently asked questions and their answers.

The government was trying to generate a wide consensus on the design of GST. The task force of the Thirteenth Finance Commission had also made a number of recommendations on GST. The finance minister announced a new date, 1 April 2011, for the introduction of GST in his budget speech for 2010–2011.[1] He laid emphasis on the need to revamp the internal work processes of the indirect tax administrations of the union and the states. The Automation of Central Excise and Service Tax project was introduced throughout the country in 2010. The government also approved a mission mode project for the computerization of commercial taxes in states.

Pranab Mukherjee informed Parliament in his budget speech for 2011–2012 that the dialogue with the states had made considerable progress during the last four years and the areas of divergence had been narrowed. He proposed to introduce Constitution (Amendment) Bill (CAB) in that session of the Parliament. The work to draft the model legislation for the centre and states of GST was already underway.

The amendment in the Constitution was necessary for implementing the dual GST. Accordingly, the government formed a joint working group. The additional secretary (revenue) of the GoI was the chairman, and the member secretary of the EC was the co-chairman of the working group. The senior officers of Department of Revenue, Ministry of Law, and state governments were the members of the group.

The government prepared a draft of CAB and shared it with the EC. Thereafter, the government drafted two more CABs and sent them to

---

[1] GoI, *Budget Speech, 2010–11*, Para 26.

the EC. The EC considered the three drafts of CAB in its meeting and sent them back to the government with its recommendations.

Finally, Finance Minister Pranab Mukherjee introduced the most awaited Constitution (115th Amendment) Bill, 2011 (hereafter, CAB 2011) in Lok Sabha on 22 March 2011 to facilitate the introduction of GST. The speaker of Lok Sabha referred the bill to the Parliamentary Standing Committee on Finance for examination and report.

Meanwhile, Pranab Mukherjee became the President of India on 25 July 2012. It must however be recorded that GST did make considerable progress during Mukherjee's tenure as finance minister.

P. Chidambaram returned as finance minister after Mukherjee and took the charge of GST. He discussed the progress of GST with the EC. He shared the contents of his discussion with the EC with the Parliament in his budget speech for 2013–2014. He said,

> The state governments—or, at least, the overwhelming majority—are agreed that there is need for a Constitutional amendment; there is need for state governments and the central government to pass a GST law that will be drafted by the state finance ministers and the GST Council; and there is need for the Centre to compensate the States for loss due to the reduction in the CST rate.[2]

The Parliamentary Standing Committee on Finance headed by Yashwant Sinha examined the bill and submitted its report on 7 August 2013.[3] The ministry of finance examined the recommendations of the Standing Committee and accepted most of them. The government revised the bill to accommodate the recommendations of the Standing Committee and prepared a new draft of CAB 2013. It discussed the revised CAB with the states. Thereafter, a revised draft was sent to the EC on 18 September 2013 for its comments. After the EC sent its comments to the government, it considered the recommendations of the EC and included them in the draft. The revised draft was again sent to the EC on 18 March 2014 for its consideration.[4]

[2] GoI, *Budget Speech, 2010–11*, Para 186.

[3] See Appendix C for detail.

[4] EC of State Finance Ministers, *Annual Report for 2015–16*, 41.

But the government could not take the bill back to Parliament for its consideration and passing before the dissolution of Lok Sabha and the proposed CAB 2011 lapsed.

NDA II Government

There was a change of government after the general elections of 2014. Narendra Modi was sworn in as the fourteenth prime minister of India, and Arun Jaitley became his finance minister.

Earlier, when Modi was the chief minister of Gujarat, he had opposed the introduction of GST. But, he dramatically changed his views when he became the prime minister. The government started discussions with the states, and the finance minister in his maiden budget speech for 2014–2015 told Parliament that the debate on the introduction of GST should come to an end.

The government decided to draft a fresh CAB. It decided to incorporate all the earlier recommendations, the pending demands of finance ministers of state governments and the recommendations of the Standing Committee. The revised draft of the Constitution (122nd Amendment) Bill, 2014 (hereafter, CAB 2014) was sent to the EC on 4 December 2014. But the revised bill did not meet all the recommendations of the EC.

Subsequently, a series of meetings were held among the union finance minister, the chairman of the EC and the finance ministers of state governments on 11, 15 and 16 December 2014. The government finalized the bill after making some minor amendments. CAB 2014 was introduced in Lok Sabha on 19 December 2014. The government fixed another deadline of 1 April 2016 to introduce GST in the budget speech for 2015–2016. Lok Sabha approved the bill on 6 May 2015. Thereafter, the Bill was tabled in Rajya Sabha on 12 May 2015.

The opposition parties led by the Congress and the Left Front members were demanding that the bill be referred to a Select Committee of Rajya Sabha. The members of the house did not agree to several provisions relating to taxation in the bill. The bill was referred to the Select Committee on 14 May 2015. The Select

Committee led by Bhupendra Yadav of the BJP submitted its report to Rajya Sabha on 22 July 2015.

Rajya Sabha passed the Bill by two-thirds majority on 3 August 2016 with some amendments, and thereafter it was passed by Lok Sabha on 8 August 2016. The union finance minister said while thanking the members of Rajya Sabha, 'There has been major consensus building that has taken place. I am extremely thankful to all opposition parties especially Ghulam Nabi Azad'.

The Congress also acknowledged the efforts of the finance minister. The former finance minister P. Chidambaram said, 'I'm glad FM acknowledged that it was UPA govt. that first officially announced the intention to bring GST'.

The amended bill was sent to all the states for ratification. Since CAB 2014 was passed unanimously by all parties, it took only 23 days to receive ratification from states with Assam being the first one to ratify the bill. The government sent the bill to the President after receiving ratification of the bill by 17 states. The Presidential assent was obtained on 8 September 2016.[5] CAB 2014 became the Constitution (101st Amendment) Act, 2016. The new act was enacted by a notification on 12 September 2016 and thus the GST Council came into existence. The remaining provisions of the Act were notified on 16 September 2016.

Finally, GST was rolled out on the midnight of 1 July 2017 at the Central Hall of the Parliament. The prime minster said, 'GST will put India on path of a system that will be transparent, simple and keeps tabs on corruption'. The government claimed that GST was the biggest taxation reform since Independence. 'The roll out of GST is the best example of cooperative federalism and success of Indian democracy.'[6] The foreign media also appreciated the introduction of GST. The *New York Times*[7] praised the GoI for spearheading taxation reform.

---

[5] *The Economic Times*, April 13, 2017

[6] https://zeenews.india.com/economy/india-launches-historic-indirect-tax-regime-gst-5-top-quotes-of-pm-narendra-modi-2020297.html

[7] Shaikh, 'GST Roll-out'.

Concept of GST

GST is based on the concept of 'one nation one tax'. Its virtues are that it applies to the whole country. The new tax unified 1.3 billion people and the $2 trillion economy of the country into one unified market. GST is a single tax that is levied on the supply of goods and services or both, right from the manufacturer/service provider to the consumer. It is a destination-based consumption tax.[8] ITC is paid at each stage and is available at subsequent stages of value addition. It is a tax that is charged only on value addition at each stage. Thus, the final consumer bears only the tax charged by the dealer in the supply chain along with set-off benefit at previous stages. The main objective of GST is to have one tax and for each assessee to have one assessing officer. It is completely based on IT which will help end inspector raj. It subsumed a number of taxes and cesses to create a uniform market.

In its first discussion paper on GST in India, the EC had explained how GST would work, using a hypothetical example. Suppose there are three parties in the manufacturing and trading process—one producer (P), one wholesaler (W) and one retailer (R). They are producing a product on which the GST rate is 18 per cent. The producer sells his goods to the wholesaler in the supply chain. The wholesaler sells the goods to retailer. The producer buys raw materials of ₹10,000 and pays tax of ₹1,800 (18% of ₹10,000). He adds value of ₹3,000 on his purchase of ₹10,000 in the production process. Then the producer will pay GST of ₹540 after setting off ₹1,800 as GST paid on his inputs (ITC) from a gross GST value of ₹2,340 when the producer sells the goods to the wholesaler.

When the wholesaler sells the same goods with a value addition of ₹2,000, he will pay net GST of ₹360 only because ITC of ₹2,340 will be set off from the gross GST of ₹2,700 to the producer. Similarly, the retailer will sell the same goods with value addition of ₹1,000. He will pay net GST of ₹180 only, as he will also set off ₹2,700 from the gross GST of ₹2,880 paid to wholesaler.

---

[8] Destination-based taxation: Tax accrues to the destination place where consumption of the goods or services takes place. The earlier State VAT regime was based on origin principle where CST was assigned to the state of origin where production or sale happened and not to the state where consumption happened.

Hence, the producer, wholesaler and retailer will pay only ₹1,080 (₹540 + ₹360 + ₹180) as GST in the entire production and supply chain after setting off GST paid at the earlier stages. The total burden of GST on a product will thus be much lower compared to taxes paid earlier. Table 7.1 illustrates the calculation of net GST.

VAT vs GST

VAT was a precursor of GST. While VAT was levied at different stages of production of an article, GST is being levied on the supply of goods and services. However, VAT was applicable only to the goods sold. It did not apply to services; services came under service tax. GST is applicable to both goods and services at a uniform rate. The difference between VAT and GST is explained in Table 7.2.

Taxes Subsumed under GST

EC examined all indirect levies of the centre, the states and the local bodies to identify the possibility of subsuming all indirect taxes under the new GST. Finally, the new tax subsumed 17 indirect taxes and 23 cesses into one tax.[9] The central and state taxes that have been subsumed under GST are mentioned in Table 7.3.

Taxes Outside GST

The new tax, that is, GST, has been introduced and applied on the supply of all goods and services or both except alcohol for human consumption. It is applicable to five specified petroleum products—crude oil, petrol, diesel, natural gas and aviation turbine fuel—from the date to be recommended by the GST Council. Let us see the taxes which are outside of GST ambit (Table 7.4).

Alcohol and Petroleum Product

Alcoholic beverages for human consumption and petroleum products have been major revenue contributor to states. State governments were unanimously asking to keep these products outside the ambit of GST.

[9] TNN, 'It Should Be Called 'RSS Tax', Says Chidambaram'.

Table 7.1 *Net GST*

Stages	Purchase Value of Input	Value Addition	Value at Which Supply of Goods and Services Made to Next Stage	GST Rate (%)	GST on Output	Input Tax Credit	Net GST = (GST on Output − ITC)
Producer	10,000	3,000	13,000	18	2,340	1,800	2,340 − 1,800 = 540
Wholesaler	13,000	2,000	15,000	18	2,700	2,340	2,700 − 2,340 = 360
Retailer	15,000	1,000	16,000	18	2,880	2,700	2,880 − 2,700 = 180
Total	6,000				1,800 + 1,080 = 2,880		1,080

Source: Authors.

Table 7.2 *VAT vs GST*

S. No.	Difference	Value Added Tax	Goods and Services Tax
1.	Structure of tax	The state-wise structure of VAT was not same. The rate of tax was not same.	The state-wise structure of GST is same. GST is a dual tax levied by both the centre and states at same rate.
2.	Cascading effect	CENVAT and VAT have not yet been extended to include the chain of value addition and thus the benefits of a comprehensive input tax and service tax set-off remains out of the reach of manufacturers/ dealers.	The introduction of GST will not only include more indirect central taxes and integrate goods and services taxes for set-off relief but will also capture value addition in distributive trade and a continuous chain of set-off from the original producer's and service provider's point up to the retailer's level. This would eliminate the burden of all cascading effects. Also, major central and state taxes will get subsumed into GST, reducing the multiplicity of taxes.
3.	Coverage	Relatively narrow base and separate service tax.	Wider base and applied on both goods and services. GST is a consumption-based tax which will be collected by the states where the goods or services are actually consumed.
4.	Procedures for collection of tax	It varies from state to state.	Likely to be uniform throughout the country.
5.	Tax administration	Complex due to number of taxes.	Intention is to make it simple, easy and taxpayer friendly
6.	Use of IT	Not much	Completely IT based. Its success to a great extent will depend on IT for which the GST Network (GSTN), a separate company has been formed.

Source: empcom.gov.in (website of EC of State Finance Minister).

Table 7.3 *Taxes Subsumed under GST*

S. No.	Central Level	State Level
1.	Central Excise Duty (except five Petroleum[10] and tobacco products)	State VAT/Sales Tax
2.	Duties of Excise (Medicinal and Toilet Preparations)	Central Sates Tax
3.	Additional Duties of Excise (Goods of Special Importance)	Purchase Tax
4.	Additional Duties of Excise (Textiles & Textile Products)	Luxury Tax
5.	Additional Duties of Customs (known as CVD)	Entry Tax (all forms)
6.	Special Additional Duty of Customs (SAD)	Taxes on advertisements
7.	Service Tax	Taxes on lotteries, betting and gambling
8.	Cesses and surcharge in so far as they relate to supply of goods and services.	Entertainment Tax and Amusement Tax (except those levied by the local bodies)
9.		State cesses and surcharges in so far as they related to supply of goods and services

Source: http://www.gstcouncil.gov.in/brief-history-gst

Table 7.4 *Taxes Outside GST Ambit*

S. No.	Tax	Who will tax
1.	Liquor for human consumption	Power to tax remains with the state
2.	Petroleum products: (a) crude oil, (b) petrol, (c) diesel, (d) natural gas and (e) Aviation Turbine Fuel	GST Council to decide the date from which GST will be applicable
3.	Tobacco	Part of GST but power to levy additional excise duty with central government
4.	Entertainment tax levied by local bodies	Power to tax remains with local bodies

Source: http://gstcouncil.gov.in/sites/default/files/01092018_GST_PPT_An_Update.pdf

[10] Petroleum crude, high speed diesel, motor spirit (commonly known as petrol), natural gas and aviation turbine fuel.

They were uncertain about the effect of the new tax on their exchequer. Indeed, they were afraid of fall in their revenue collection because of GST. Liquor for human consumption and five petroleum products (crude oil, petrol, diesel, natural gas, aviation turbine fuel) were therefore kept out of the purview of GST in CAB 2011. The Standing Committee on Finance recommended keeping petroleum products under GST's purview. Section 5 of CAB 2011 stated that the GST Council should recommend the date on which GST would be levied on petroleum crude, high-speed diesel, motor sprit, natural gas and aviation turbine fuel.

Accordingly, government kept alcohol for human consumption outside the ambit of GST. Section 12(5) of Constitution (101st Amendment) Act made a provision to the effect that the five petroleum products would be brought under GST from the date to be recommended by the GST Council.

Finally, GST was introduced and applied on the supply of all goods and services except alcohol for human consumption and the five petroleum products.

Tobacco and Tobacco Products

The union government has retained the power to tax tobacco and tobacco products, though these are under GST. In addition, central government would have the power to levy excise duty on these products.

The process of introduction of GST took one and a half decades. Pranab Mukherjee, the then President of India, said at the launch of GST, 'This historic moment is the culmination of a 14-year-long journey that began in December 2002'.[11] The work on VAT was begun by NDA I, but the credit for its implementation went to the UPA I, and the potentially much bigger game changer, GST went to NDA II because they happened to be in power when the final moment came. It should not be forgotten however that all governments contributed to it in a substantial measure when in office.

---

[11] Pranab Mukherjee the then President on the launch of GST.

The Constitution Amendment Bills

India's Constitution bestowed taxation powers to both the centre and the states according to separate lists given in the Constitution. To change the indirect tax structure, therefore, the government had to amend the Constitution and the same had to be ratified by at least 50 per cent of the state legislatures. The amendment process has been spelt out in Article 368 of Part XX of the Constitution of India. Amendment of Constitution means making changes in the supreme law of the country.

According to Article 368, Parliament can amend the Constitution by way of addition, variation or repeal of any provision. Amendment of the Constitution may be initiated only by the introduction of a bill for the purpose in either Houses of the Parliament. The bill must be passed in each House by a majority of the total membership of the House present and voting. If the amendment is related to the states, then, as per Article 368(2e), the amendment shall also require to be ratified by the state legislatures of not less than one half of the states, before the bill is presented to the President of India for his assent.

During the tenure of UPA I, the government decided to replace the existing tax structure with a new GST. The UPA II government introduced the GST CAB, but it could not be passed in the Parliament. In 2014, the NDA II government decided to reintroduce the bill with some amendments, which later became an act. In this chapter, we will discuss the GST CABs of the UPA government and the NDA government.

The Constitution (115th Amendment) Bill, 2011

The UPA II government introduced CAB 2011 in the Lower House on 22 March 2011.[1] The GST Bill, 2011, was the fourth draft of the central government and was the culmination of a series of discussions among the centre, the states and the EC. The government planned to roll out the new tax from 1 April 2010. But Pranab Mukherjee deferred GST to 1 April 2011.

CAB 2011 contained 19 sections. The bill proposed to amend the Constitution by inserting new Articles 246A, 269A, 279A and 279B with the intention of making special provisions for GST, levying and collecting GST in the case of inter-state trade or commerce and creating the GST Council, respectively. The GST Bill proposed to amend Articles 248, 249, 250, 268, 270, 271, 286, 366 and 368, and Entry 52, 54 and 84 of the Constitution. The bill also intended to amend the Sixth and the Seventh Schedules. There was a provision in the bill to omit Article 268A, Clause 29A of Article 366, Entry 92 and 92C of List I, and Entry 55 of List II in the Seventh Schedule.

As per procedure generally followed in the case of important bills, the Speaker of Lok Sabha referred the bill to the Standing Committee on Finance on 29 March 2011 for examination and report. The committee was headed by the former Finance Minister Yashwant Sinha. The committee started the examination of the bill in right earnest and was keen to submit its report to Parliament latest by the monsoon session of Parliament, 2012.

The committee has been blamed in some quarters that it delayed its report thus preventing the UPA government from finalizing the bill and making GST a reality. First, the finalization of the report of the committee was not easy and second, the delay was largely on the part of the government itself and not the committee. The issue has been dealt with in detail in the report of the committee. According to the report of the committee, it requested the Ministry of Finance to submit their reply to the queries raised by the members of the committee.

[1] Bill Number 22/2011.

But the ministry submitted its interim reply to these queries only in August 2012, which was the deadline fixed by the committee for the submission of its final report. The committee again requested the ministry for its final views on the queries as well as on the design of GST and CST compensation. The ministry informed the committee that it would be able to communicate its views only by January 2013. The ministry again told the committee in March 2013 that the government had constituted a committee to further study the amendments required in the GST Constitution Amendment Bill.

The ministry also informed the committee that the 'conclusive view on the changes to be made in the Bill would, however be taken only after taking into account the observations and recommendations of the Standing Committee on Finance'.[2] The committee was surprised at this response because government was keen to re-introduce the bill in Parliament. Anyway, the standing committee submitted its report on 7 August 2013 with a note of dissent of the Samajwadi Party member. But, CAB 2011 remained pending with the government. As it was the last year of UPA II government and had the bill not passed, it would have lapsed. Finally, when the President dissolved the fifteenth Lok Sabha, as expected, the bill lapsed. The only conclusion one can draw from the above narrative is that the UPA II government was not so keen to get the CAB passed during its tenure and deliberately delayed the implementation of GST by at least a couple of years.

The committee had taken the special permission of the Speaker of Lok Sabha to examine the representatives of some of the state governments. The representatives of the government of Gujarat led by Minister Saurabh Patel, among others, appeared before the committee. He made such a convincing case against GST before the committee that most members were strongly convinced that the whole concept was wrong and therefore should be rejected lock, stock and barrel. Vijay Kelkar was therefore requested to appear before the committee again in order to get a correct perspective of the whole issue. He was

---

[2] GoI, *Seventy Third Report*, 64.

able to again convince the members of the committee that GST should receive the support of the committee. It was thus that the committee finally gave its report in support of CAB, of course, with many worthwhile recommendations to improve the bill.

The Constitution (122nd Amendment) Bill, 2014

The NDA II came to power in 2014. The government took the initiative to introduce a new GST Bill. As the government had majority in the Lok Sabha, it was expected that the bill would get the nod of the Lower House without difficulty. The challenge was to get the approval of the Upper House where the government did not enjoy a majority. CAB 2014 was tabled in Lok Sabha on 19 December 2014. As expected, CAB 2014 was passed in the Lower House on 6 May 2015.

Subsequently, CAB 2014 was introduced in the Upper House on 12 May 2015. But due to the resistance of Congress-led opposition, the bill was referred to a Select Committee of Rajya Sabha for examination and report. The chairman of the committee was Bhupendra Yadav of the BJP. The committee submitted its report to Rajya Sabha on 22 July 2015 with three notes of dissent.

CAB 2014 contained 21 sections. The bill proposed to amend the Constitution by inserting new Articles—246A, 269A, and 279A—in order to make special provisions for GST,[3] levy and collection of GST in the case of inter-state trade or commerce, and creation of the GST Council, respectively.

CAB 2014 also proposed to amend Articles 248, 249, 250, 268, 269, 270, 271, 286, 366 and 368, and Entry 54, 62 and 84 of the Constitution. The bill also pretended to amend the Sixth and the Seventh Schedules as well. There was a provision in the bill to omit Article 268A, Clause 29A of Article 366, Entry 92 and 92C of List I, and Entry 52 and 55 of List II in the Seventh Schedule.

---

[3] GoI, *Report of the Select Committee*, 9.

CAB 2011 vs CAB 2014

CAB 2011 was introduced in Lok Sabha by the then Finance Minister Pranab Mukherjee on 22 March 2011. CAB 2014 was introduced by Finance Minister Arun Jaitley on 19 December 2014. The aim of both the bills was to introduce a new tax structure with the amendment in the Constitution of India. Where CAB 2011 contained 19 sections, CAB 2014 contained 21 sections. A comparative picture of both the bills may be seen in Appendix B at the end of the book.

CAB under UPA II and NDA II vis-à-vis Standing Committee

The purpose of CAB of UPA II and CAB of NDA II was to provide concurrent power to central government and state governments to introduce legislation on GST. Let us now compare the provisions of CAB 2011, the recommendations of the Standing Committee on Finance and the changes made by the NDA II government in CAB 2014 (Table 8.1). Later on, CAB 2014 became the Constitution (101th Amendment) Act, 2016.

Table 8.1 *CAB 2011 vs CAB 2014*

S. No.	Contents	CAB 2011 of UPA II	Recommendations of Standing Committee	CAB 2014 of NDA II	Comment
1.	Consensus	CAB 2011 made the provision that all decision of GST Council shall be taken on the basis of consensus of all the members present at the meeting.	The Standing Committee of Finance recommended that the decision in any meeting shall be taken either on the basis of consensus or with the votes of more than three-fourths votes of members present in the meeting.	CAB 2014 accepted the recommendation of the Standing Committee and made the provision that all decisions of the council shall be taken by a majority not less than three-fourths of the votes of the members present.	Standing Committee of Finance recommendations: Incorporated.
2.	Proportion of voting	There was no provision of the weight of the votes of the centre and the states.	The committee recommended that one-third of the weightage was to stay with the centre while the states would have two-thirds weightage. A decision could be taken with three-fourths majority.	CAB 2014 implemented the recommendation and made the provision that the vote proportion of central government shall be a weightage of one-third of total votes cast, and vote proportion of states shall be weightage of two-thirds of total votes cast, in the meeting.	Standing Committee of Finance recommendations: Incorporated.

		The bill proposed	The committee	The bill implemented the	Standing Committee
3.	Quorum	The bill proposed that one-third of total number of members of GST Council shall constitute the quorum of GST Council meetings.	The committee recommended that the number be increased from one-third to half for the Quorum of meeting.	The bill implemented the recommendations and made the provision that half of the total number of members of GST Council shall constitute the quorum of GST Council meetings.	Standing Committee of Finance recommendations: Incorporated.
4.	Exclusions	The bill proposed to exclude taxes on the supply of crude petroleum, high-speed diesel, motor spirit (known as petrol), liquor for human consumption, natural gas and aviation turbine fuel from the preview of GST.	The committee recommended that the exclusion provision of CAB 2011 may be omitted from the bill. There is no need to make provision of exclusion in the Constitution and to make GST very rigid.	CAB 2014 implemented the recommendations and omitted the provision of exclusion of CAB 2011. But the bill excluded liquor for human consumption from GST. The bill referred other items to GST Council to decide when it may be taxed.	Standing Committee of Finance recommendations: Incorporated.

(continued)

(continued)

S. No.	Contents	CAB 2011 of UPA II	Recommendations of Standing Committee	CAB 2014 of NDA II	Comment
5.	Special rate(s) for a specified period	There was no provision in CAB 2011 for special rate or rates for a specified period.	The committee recommended that CAB should insert a new sub-clause under Clause 4 of Article 279A to give requisite flexibility to both centre and states to raise additional revenue during period of natural calamities or disasters.	The bill implemented the recommendations and made a provision of special rate/rates for a specified period under Clause 4F in Article 279A to raise additional revenue during any natural calamity or disaster.	Standing Committee of Finance recommendations: Incorporated.
6.	Special provision	There was no provision in this regard in CAB 2011.	The committee recommended that the proposed Clause 4 of Article 279A of CAB 2011 may also be amended to provide special schemes for north-eastern states, J&K, and other special category states. The committee further recommended that union government should have the flexibility to levy cess/surcharge whenever it requires/during extra ordinary circumstances.	The bill implemented the recommendations and made a special provision under Clause 4G in Article 279A for the states of Assam, Arunachal Pradesh, Himachal Pradesh, Uttarakhand, J&K, Meghalaya, Manipur, Mizoram, Nagaland, Sikkim and Tripura.	Standing Committee of Finance recommendations: Incorporated.

7.	Harmonized tax Standing Committee of Finance recommendations: Structure	The bill inserted new Article 279A. As per Clause 5 of proposed Article 279A, GST Council shall harmonize the structure of GST and for the development of harmonized national market for goods and services.	The committee recommended that such ambiguity should not be in the bill. The word 'harmonized structure' may be clearly defined. The provision should be like a guiding principle for GST Council not mandatory/obligatory in nature.	The provision of CAB 2011 retained in CAB 2014.	Standing Committee of Finance recommendations: Not incorporated.
8.	Compensation to states for revenue loss	There was no provision in CAB 2011 for compensation revenue loss to states.	The committee recommended that a well-defined automatic compensation mechanism should be built in. For the purpose, a GST compensation fund may be created under GST Council.	Clause 19 of the Bill made provision for a law to be enacted to compensate states on the recommendation of the GST Council for revenue loss to states arising due to implementation of GST for the period of five years.	Standing Committee of Finance recommendations: Incorporated.

(continued)

(continued)

S. No.	Contents	CAB 2011 of UPA II	Recommendations of Standing Committee	CAB 2014 of NDA II	Comment
9.	GST Dispute Settlement Authority	The Bill inserted new Article 279B that made the provision the establishment of GST Dispute Settlement Authority to resolve any dispute/ complaint referred to the authority by state/central governments.	The committee recommended that the GST Council be empowered to settle such disputes. The establishment of GST Dispute Settlement Authority would affect the power of the Parliament and legislatures of states. The committee recommended that such provisions should be omitted.	There was no provision for constituting GST Dispute Settlement Authority. GST Council would decide the mechanism to resolve disputes.	Standing Committee of Finance recommendations: Incorporated.
10.	Entry Tax	The Bill made provision to substitute Entry 52 of the Seventh Schedule, i.e., entry tax. As per provision of the Bill, entry tax would be levied and collected by a panchayat/ municipality.	The committee did not agree with the formulation. The committee asked that entry tax should be subsumed in proposed GST.	The Bill dropped the provision allowing states to levy entry tax on goods entering local area. The remaining provisions of the Bill of 2011 were retained unchanged.	Standing Committee of Finance recommendations: Incorporated.

| 11. | Levy and collection of GST in course of Inter-state trade/ commerce | CAB 2011 inserted new Article 269A in the Constitution that stated that GST on supply in the case of inter-state trade/commerce shall be levied and collected by central government. Such tax shall be distributed between centre and states in a mechanism prescribed by the Parliament. | The committee recommended that central government should act as a clearing agent for IGST. The committee said that modified bank model shall be used for the settlement of proceeds arising out of inter-state trade. They further suggested that the model suggested by Task Force on GST of the Thirteenth Finance Commission can be considered for the same. | The Bill stated that such tax shall be distributed between centre and states in a mechanism prescribed by the Parliament by law on the recommendations of GST Council. | Standing Committee of Finance recommendations: Incorporated. |

Source: Computed from Constitution Amendment Bill 2011 and 2014.

The Constitution Amendment Acts and Legislations

The government changed the indirect tax structure of the country by introducing GST. For this, the Constitution of India was amended as a first step. The second step was for the centre and the states to pass new laws to levy the new tax. The third stage of the legislative process in India is to frame rules under the act in order to get the new law notified for implementation. In this chapter, we shall discuss the constitutional amendments and the different legislations of GST.

The Constitution (101st Amendment) Act, 2016

That government amended the Constitution of India in order to introduce GST in 2016. The Constitution Amendment Bill (CAB) was introduced soon after the government assumed office in 2014. The bill got the approval from both Houses of Parliament and the same was then sent for ratification by the state legislatures. After getting the assent of the President of India on 8 September 2016, the GST Bill became the Constitution (101st Amendment) Act, 2016. The amendment in the Constitution was notified by the central government as per Section 1(2) of the Constitution on 16 September 2016. The amendment in the Constitution introduced a new tax in the country, GST, with effect from 1 July 2017. Let us look at the amendments in the Constitution in Table 9.1.

Table 9.1 *The Constitution (101st Amendment) Act, 2016 at a Glance*

S. No.	Sections	Heads	Change(s)
1.	Section 1	Short title and commencement	Section 1 is related to title and commencement of Constitution (101st Amendment) Act, 2016. Section 1(2) tells that the amendments will come into force from the date of notification by the central government in the Gazette. The government notified the amendment on 16 September 2016.
2.	Section 2	Introduction of new Article 246A w.r.t. GST	A new Article 246A has been inserted that enables provisions for the union and the states w.r.t. to GST legislation. As per the provision, the Parliament has exclusive power to make law w.r.t. GST on supply of goods/services for inter-state trade or commerce. Accordingly, the central government has made CGST and IGST and states have made SGST.
3.	Section 3	Amendment in Article 248	The Article 248 has been amended to make the provision of Section 2 of the GST Bill, i.e., Article 246A.
4.	Section 4	Amendment in Article 249	The Article 249 has been amended to make the provision of Section 2 of the GST Bill. This provision enabled the Parliament to make law in national interest as per the procedure given in the act.
5.	Section 5	Amendment in Article 250	The Article 250 has been amended to make the provision of Section 2 of the Act. The amendment gives power to the Parliament to legislate in the case of any emergency.

(continued)

(continued)

S. No.	Sections	Heads	Change(s)
6.	Section 6	Amendment in Article 268	Section 6 seeks to amend Article 268 and omit excise duty on medical and toilet preparations because it has come under the new tax.
7.	Section 7	Article 268A omitted	Section 7 omitted Article 268A. This article was inserted by Constitution (88th) Amendment Act, 2003 to levy tax on services. As service tax has come under GST, Article 268A was no longer required.
8.	Section 8	Amendment in Article 269	Section 8 amended Article 269. The provision of this article was for the taxes levied and collected by union but assigned to states. For this, the Parliament has inserted Article 269A.
9.	Section 9	Introduction of amendment in Article 269A w.r.t. levy and collection of GST for inter-state trade and commerce	Section 9 inserted Article 269A for levy and collection of GST on inter-state trade and commerce. As per the Article, GST on supply of goods and services in the case of inter-state trade or commerce shall be levied and collected by union government and such tax be apportioned between centre and states. The Parliament may formulate the principles for determining the place of supply and when a supply of goods/services or both will take place in the case of inter-state trade or commerce.
10.	Section 10	Amendment in Article 270	Section 10 amended Article 270 for the distribution of GST, which is collected by union, between centre and states.

S. No.	Sections	Heads	Change(s)
11.	Section 11	Amendment in Article 271	The amendment in Article 271 restricts the power of the Parliament to levy surcharge under GST. As per the provision, the surcharge cannot be levied on goods and services which are subject to tax under Article 246A.
12.	Section 12	Introduction of new Article 279A w.r.t. GST Council	Section 12 introduced a new Article 279A for GST Council. This section also discusses what recommendations GST Council can make to the union and states. The same can be seen in Chapter 10 of the book.
13.	Section 13	Amendment in Article 286	The amendment in Article 286 includes supply of goods or services or both under the preview of GST than just sale/purchase of goods.
14.	Section 14	Amendment in Article 366	Section 14 was amended in Article 366 to exclude liquor for human consumption from the preview of GST. All other alcoholic products for medical/toilet preparations and industrial use comes under GST.
15.	Section 15	Amendment in Article 368	Section 15 is related to amendment in Article 368. The amendment provides a procedure to ratify the bill by the legislators with not less than one-half of states besides voting method for amendment under the Constitution. Hence, any change in GST council also requires ratification by legislators of not less than one-half of states.

(continued)

(continued)

S. No.	Sections	Heads	Change(s)
16.	Section 16	Amendment in Sixth Schedule	Section 16 is related to amendment in Sixth Schedule of the Constitution. The amended schedule empowers district council to levy and collect taxes on entertainment and amusements.
17.	Section 17	Amendment in Seventh Schedule	Section 17 is related to amendment in Seventh Schedule of the Constitution. This section made changes in Union List and State List. Both List I and List II have been omitted or substituted to restrict the power to levy tax on goods and services mentioned these lists. The amendment also takes away the powers to tax goods and services or both.
18.	Section 18	Compensation to states	Section 18 is related to the provision for compensation to states during transition period. The union will compensate revenue loss of states due to introduction of GST for a period of five years. The amendment also deleted the provision of 1 per cent additional tax on inter-state transaction.
19.	Section 19	Provisions-related transition period	Section 19 is related to the provision for transition period. The amendment is given a time frame of one year; during the period, different indirect taxes subsume into GST. It enables the legislature to amend/repeal their existing legislation to pave the way for imposition of SGST in states.

S. No.	Sections	Heads	Change(s)
20.	Section 20	Power of the President	Section 20 discusses the power of the President of India to remove difficulties related to GST within three years. The President may make such provisions, any adaption/modification of any provision as amended by this act/law, as appear to President to be necessary/expedient for the purpose of removing the difficulty.

Legislations for GST

A law is enacted by local, state or national legislatures under the powers conferred on it by the Constitution. The review and amendment of existing legislation and formulation of new legislation are the main tasks of legislatures. After Parliament amended the Constitution and made a new legislation for the introduction of GST, it took the GST Council a number of meetings to finalize the draft of GST laws for the Central GST (CGST), Integrated GST (IGST), State GST (SGST) and Union Territory GST (UTGST). The government approved the four bills in March 2017:

*   The Central Goods and Services Tax Bill
*   The Integrated Goods and Services Tax Bill
*   The Union Territory Goods and Services Tax Bill
*   The Goods and Services Tax (Compensation to States) Bill

The above four key bills were passed by Lok Sabha on 29 March 2017 and by Rajya Sabha on 6 April 2017. The 'Congress withdrew all the amendments it had moved against the Bill'.[1] Members of AIADMK were opposing the bill and were absent from voting.[2] After getting approval from both the Houses, and the required number of state

[1] *Business Line*, 'GST Bills Passed in Rajya Sabha'.
[2] *Dawn*, August 3, 2016.

legislatures, the bills were sent to the President for his assent. The President gave his assent to the four key bills on 12 April 2017.[3] 'These Bills were enacted on April 12, (2017).'[4] Now, we have following four legislations for GST.

The Central Goods and Services Tax Act, 2017 (hereafter, CGST Act, 2017): The CGST Act, 2017 came into existence on 12 April 2017. It extends to the whole of India except Jammu and Kashmir to which it was extended later. The act makes provisions for the levy and collection of tax on intra-state supply of goods and services or both within the boundary of a state by the central government. There are 21 chapters in the Act along with 174 sections and three schedules.

Integrated Goods and Services Tax Act, 2017 (hereafter, IGST Act, 2017): The IGST Act, 2017 came into existence on 12 April 2017. It extends to the whole of India except the state of Jammu and Kashmir to which it was extended later. The act makes provision for the levy and collection of tax on inter-state supply of goods and services or both by central and state governments. There are 9 chapters in the act along with 25 sections.

The Union Territory Goods and Services Tax Act, 2017 (hereafter UTGST Act, 2017): This Act came into existence on 12 April 2017. It extends to the Union Territories of Andaman and Nicobar Islands, Dadra and Nagar Haveli, Lakshadweep, Daman and Diu, Chandigarh and other union territories. The act makes provision for the levy and collection of tax on intra-state supply of goods and services or both within the union territories. There are 9 chapters in the act along with 26 sections.

The Goods and Services Tax (Compensation to States) Act, 2017: The Goods and Services Tax (Compensation to States) Act too came into existence on 12 April 2017. It extends to the whole of India. The act makes provisions to provide compensation to states for the loss of

[3] PTI, 'President Pranab Mukherjee Gives Assent'.

[4] CBIC, *The Economic Times*, April 13, 2017.

revenue incurred on account of implementation of GST. There are 14 sections along with one schedule in the act.

State Goods and Services Tax

Subsequently, all the other states and union territories with legislatures have also enacted their SGST Acts (except Jammu and Kashmir). The State of Jammu and Kashmir passed the SGST Act on 8 July 2017 and subsequently GoI extended the CGST Act, 2017 to Jammu and Kashmir. SGST Acts of respective states were also notified to make provisions for the levy and collections of tax on intra-state supply of goods or services or both by respective states. There are 21 chapters in each SGST act along with 174 sections and three schedules. Let us see the implementation of SGST.

The Andhra Pradesh GST, 2017: The Andhra Pradesh GST Act received the assent of the governor on 5 June 2017. The said act came into existence on 7 June 2017. It extends to the whole of the state of Andhra Pradesh. The act makes provisions for the levy and collection of tax on intra-state supply of goods and services or both within the boundary of the state of Andhra Pradesh.

The Arunachal Pradesh GST, 2017: The Arunachal Pradesh GST Act received the assent of the governor on 15 June 2017. The said act came into existence on 24 June 2017. It extends to the whole of the state of Arunachal Pradesh. The act makes provisions for the levy and collection of tax on intra-state supply of goods and services or both within the boundary of the state of Arunachal Pradesh.

The Assam GST, 2017: The Assam GST Act received the assent of the governor on 24 May 2017. The said act came into existence on 1 June 2017. It extends to the whole of the state of Assam. The act makes provisions for the levy and collection of tax on intra-state supply of goods and services or both within the boundary of the state of Assam.

The Bihar GST, 2017: The Bihar GST Act received the assent of the governor on 8 May 2017. The said act came into existence on the same day. It extends to the whole of the state of Bihar. The act makes provisions for the levy and collection of tax on intra-state supply of goods and services or both within the boundary of the state of Bihar.

The Chhattisgarh GST, 2017: The Chhattisgarh GST Act received the assent of the governor on 14 June 2017. The said act came into existence on the same day. It extends to the whole of the state of Chhattisgarh. The act makes provisions for the levy and collection of tax on intra-state supply of goods and services or both within the boundary of the state of Chhattisgarh.

The Delhi GST, 2017: The Delhi GST Act received the assent of the Lt. governor on 8 June 2017. The said act came into existence on 14 June 2017. It extends to the whole of the state of Delhi. The act makes provisions for the levy and collection of tax on intra-state supply of goods and services or both within the boundary of the state of Delhi.

The Goa GST, 2017: The Goa GST Act received the assent of the governor on 23 May 2017. The said act came into existence on 26 May 2017. It extends to the whole of the state of Goa. The act makes provisions for the levy and collection of tax on intra-state supply of goods and services or both within the boundary of the state of Goa.

The Gujarat GST, 2017: The Gujarat GST Act received the assent of the governor on 9 June 2017. The said act came into existence on the same day. It extends to the whole of the state of Gujarat. The act makes provisions for the levy and collection of tax on intra-state supply of goods and services or both within the boundary of the state of Gujarat.

The Haryana GST, 2017: The Haryana GST Act received the assent of the governor on 7 June 2017. The said act came into existence on 8 June 2017. It extends to the whole of the state of Haryana. The act makes provisions for the levy and collection of tax on intra-state supply of goods and services or both within the boundary of the state of Haryana.

The Himachal Pradesh GST, 2017: The Himachal Pradesh GST Act received the assent of the governor on 22 June 2017. The said act came into existence on 23 June 2017. It extends to the whole of the state of Himachal Pradesh. The act makes provisions for the levy and collection of tax on intra-state supply of goods and services or both within the boundary of the state of Himachal Pradesh.

The Jharkhand GST, 2017: The Jharkhand GST Act received the assent of the governor on 15 June 2017. The said act came into existence on 19 June 2017. It extends to the whole of the state of Jharkhand. The act makes provisions for the levy and collection of tax on intra-state supply of goods and services or both within the boundary of the state of Jharkhand.

The Karnataka GST, 2017: The Karnataka GST Act received the assent of the governor on 27 June 2017. The said act came into existence on on the same day. It extends to the whole of the state of Karnataka. The act makes provisions for the levy and collection of tax on intra-state supply of goods and services or both within the boundary of the state of Karnataka.

The Kerala GST, 2017: The Kerala GST Act received the assent of the governor on 22 June 2017. The said act came into existence on the same day. It extends to the whole of the state of Kerala. The act makes provisions for the levy and collection of tax on intra-state supply of goods and services or both within the boundary of the state of Kerala.

The Madhya Pradesh GST, 2017: The Madhya Pradesh GST Act received the assent of the Governor on 9 June 2017. The said act came into existence on 12 June 2017. It extends to the whole of the state of Madhya Pradesh. The act makes provisions for the levy and collection of tax on intra-state supply of goods and services or both within the boundary of the state of Madhya Pradesh.

The Maharashtra GST, 2017: The Maharashtra GST Act received the assent of the governor on 15 June 2017. The said act came into existence on 15 June 2017. It extends to the whole of the state of Maharashtra. The act makes provisions for the levy and collection of tax on intra-state supply of goods and services or both within the boundary of the state of Maharashtra.

The Manipur GST, 2017: The Manipur GST Act received the assent of the governor on 14 June 2017. The said act came into existence on the same day. It extends to the whole of the state of Manipur. The act makes provisions for the levy and collection of tax on intra-state supply of goods and services or both within the boundary of the state of Manipur.

The Meghalaya GST, 2017: The Meghalaya GST Act received the assent of the governor on 15 June 2017. The said act came into existence on 19 June 2017. It extends to the whole of the state of Meghalaya. The act makes provisions for the levy and collection of tax on intra-state supply of goods and services or both within the boundary of the state of Meghalaya.

The Mizoram GST, 2017: The Mizoram GST Act received the assent of the governor on 26 May 2017. The said act came into existence on the same day. It extends the whole of the state of Mizoram. The act makes provisions for the levy and collection of tax on intra-state supply of goods and services or both within the boundary of the state of Mizoram.

The Nagaland GST, 2017: The Nagaland GST Act received the assent of the governor and came into existence in 2017. It extends to the whole of the state of Nagaland. The act makes provisions for the levy and collection of tax on intra-state supply of goods and services or both within the boundary of the state of Nagaland.

The Odisha GST, 2017: The Odisha GST Act received the assent of the governor on 20 June 2017. The said act came into existence on 21 June 2017. It extends to the whole of the state of Odisha. The act makes provisions for the levy and collection of tax on intra-state supply of goods and services or both within the boundary of the state of Odisha.

The Puducherry GST, 2017: The Puducherry GST Act received the assent of the Lt. governor and came into existence on 1 June 2017. It extends to the whole of the state of Puducherry. The act makes provisions for the levy and collection of tax on intra-state supply of goods and services or both within the boundary of the state of Puducherry.

The Punjab GST, 2017: The Punjab GST Act received the assent of the governor on 22 June 2017 and came into existence on 23 June 2017. It extends to the whole of the state of Punjab. The act makes provisions for the levy and collection of tax on intra-state supply of goods and services or both within the boundary of the state of Punjab.

The Rajasthan GST, 2017: The Rajasthan GST Act received the assent of the governor and came into existence on 28 April 2017. It extends to the whole of the state of Rajasthan. The act makes provisions for the levy and collection of tax on intra-state supply of goods and services or both within the boundary of the state of Rajasthan.

The Sikkim GST, 2017: The Sikkim GST Act received the assent of the governor and came into existence in 2017. It extends to the whole of the state of Sikkim. The act makes provisions for the levy and collection of tax on intra-state supply of goods and services or both within the boundary of the state of Sikkim.

The Tamil Nadu GST, 2017: The Tamil Nadu GST Act received the assent of the governor on 22 June 2017. The said act came into existence on 23 June 2017. It extends the whole of the state of Tamil Nadu. The act makes provisions for the levy and collection of tax intra-state supply of goods and services or both within the boundary of the state of Tamil Nadu.

The Telangana GST, 2017: The Telangana GST Act received the assent of the governor and act came into existence in 2017. It extends to the whole of the state of Telangana. The act makes provisions for the levy and collection of tax on intra-state supply of goods and services or both within the boundary of the state of Telangana.

The Tripura GST, 2017: The Tripura GST Act received the assent of the governor on 13 June 2017 and came into existence on 16 June 2017. It extends to the whole of the state of Tripura. The act makes provisions for the levy and collection of tax on intra-state supply of goods and services or both within the boundary of the state of Tripura.

The Uttarakhand GST, 2017: The Uttarakhand GST Act received the assent of the governor on 25 May 2017 and came into existence on 26 May 2017. It extends to the whole of the state of Uttarakhand. The act makes provisions for the levy and collection of tax on intra-state supply of goods and services or both within the boundary of the state of Uttarakhand.

The Uttar Pradesh GST, 2017: The Uttar Pradesh GST Act received the assent of the governor on 18 May 2017 and came into existence on 19 May 2017. It extends to the whole of the state of Uttar Pradesh. The act makes provisions for the levy and collection of tax on intra-state supply of goods and services or both within the boundary of the state of Uttar Pradesh.

The West Bengal GST, 2017: The West Bengal GST Act received the assent of the governor on 21 June 2017 and came into existence the very next day. It extends to the whole of the state of West Bengal. The act makes provisions for the levy and collection of tax on intra-state supply of goods and services or both within the boundary of the state of West Bengal.

Amendment in Act

GST Council conducts its meetings on a regular basis to resolve the glitches which have arisen during the implementation of GST. In a meeting held on 21 July 2018 at New Delhi, the council recommended to the centre and states to amend the CGST Act, 2017; the IGST Act, 2017; the UTGST Act, 2017, and the GST (Compensation to States) Act, 2017. Parliament has also given its nod and the amendment has been enacted after receiving the assent of President on 29 August 2018. All the above Acts were notified on 29 August 2018 and were made effective from 1 February 2019. The said Acts will be known as the following:

- The Central Goods and Services Tax (Amendment) Act, 2018
- Integrated Goods and Services Tax (Amendment) Act, 2018

- Union Territory Goods and Services Tax (Amendment) Act, 2018
- The Goods and Services Tax (Compensation to State) (Amendment) Act, 2018

Accordingly, state governments are also amending their SGST. Few states have already amended and a few are in the process to amend their Acts.

Notification of Changes

The government is issuing notifications related to rates, amendment of rules and waiver of penalty on a regular basis. The first notification came on 22 June 2017. Since then, 607 notifications have been issued so far. There are 226 notifications under CGST which have been issued to notify sections, rules and waiver of penalty, etc. Notifications 20, 34 and 3 have been issued under IGST, UTGST and GST (Compensation to States) Act, respectively. Besides that, Notifications 103, 106, 103 and 12 related to rates have also been issued under CGST, IGST, UTGST and GST (Compensation to States) Act, respectively (see Table 9.2). States are also issuing the same notifications under their SGST Acts.

Table 9.2 *Notifications at a Glance*

S. No.	Year	CGST Act		IGST Act		UTGST Act		GST (Compensation to State) Act	
		Rules & Waiver of Penalty	Rate	Rules & Waiver of Penalty	Rate	Rules & Waiver of Penalty	Rate	Rules & Waiver of Penalty	Rate
1.	2017	75	47	12	50	17	47	01	07
2.	2018	79	30	04	31	15	30	01	02
3.	2019	72	26	04	25	02	26	01	03
Total		226	103	20	106	34	103	03	12

Source: Computed from CBIC website.

Apart from notifications, 132 circulars and 18 orders have also been issued on various subjects such as proper officers, ease of exports and extension of last dates to file various forms (see Tables 9.3 and 9.4).[5]

Table 9.3 *Circulars at a Glance*

S. No.	Year	CGST Act	IGST Act	UTGST Act	GST (Compensation to State) Act
1.	2017	26	02	00	01
2.	2018	55	01	00	00
3.	2019	46	01	00	00
Total		127	04	00	01

Source: CBIC.

Table 9.4 *Orders at a Glance*

S. No.	Year	CGST Act	UTGST Act
1.	2017	11	01
2.	2018	04	00
3.	2019	02	00
Total		17	01

Source: CBIC.

[5] CBIC, 'Goods and Services Tax (GST)'.

Administration of GST

The Central Board of Excise and Customs was responsible for administering the indirect tax regime in the country. GST is an indirect tax. Its implementation called for the constitution of a new CBIC, the GST Council, and the Appellate Tribunal (AT) and Advance Ruling Authority (ARA) for the smooth functioning of the new tax regime. Besides, the GST Network (GSTN) is also playing a crucial role in this entire operation. In this chapter, we shall discuss the role and responsibility of these authorities.

GST Council

The seed for the formation of the GST Council was actually sown by Yashwant Sinha when he encouraged the setting up of the Empowered Committee of State Finance Ministers during his tenure as finance minister. The same EC was later asked to prepare the structure of GST. There was no doubt whether the EC should continue to administer the GST or a new authority should be constituted for it. Finally, the government decided to give it a constitutional status by making a provision for the GST Council under Article 279A of the Constitution (101st Amendment) Act of India. The presidential order dated 15 September 2016 put the final seal of approval for the formation of the GST Council. The members of the Council are both from the union and the state governments. The Council is empowered to determine its own procedure for its functioning. The head office of the council is situated in New Delhi. The Secretary (Revenue) is the ex-officio secretary of the council. The central government provides funds for all the expenses of the Council.

Members

GST Council is a joint forum of the centre and the states. The representatives of the union in the council command one-third of the votes and the states command two-thirds. The composition of the council is as follows:

1. Union finance minister—chairperson
2. Union minister of state in charge revenue or finance—member
3. Minister in charge of finance or taxation

   a. Or any other minister nominated by state governments—member

As per Section 12(3) of the Constitution, GST Council members can choose a vice-chairman from among themselves for such period as the members may decide. The chairperson of CBIC is a permanent invitee (non-voting) to all the meetings of the council. The GST Council can make recommendations on the following:

1. Taxes, surcharges and cesses levied via centre, states and local bodies that can be subsumed under GST
2. Threshold limit of turnover below which goods and services may be exempted from tax
3. Model goods and services law, principles of levy, distribution of IGST and principles that govern the place of supply
4. Exemption of goods and services from GST
5. GST rates, including floor rate along with band
6. Special rate(s) for a specific time to raise additional revenue during any disaster or natural calamity
7. Special provisions related to Himachal Pradesh, Jammu and Kashmir, the North-Eastern States and Uttarakhand
8. Any other matter as the Council decides

Functions

The functions of the GST Council are given in Section 12(6) of the Constitution. As per this section, the Council shall work for the harmonization of the structure of GST and for the harmonization of the national market.

Quorum and Decision of Meeting

As per Section 12(7) of the Constitution, the quorum of meeting shall be one half of the total number of the Council. The decisions of the Council shall be taken by a majority of not less than three-fourths of the weighted votes of the members present and voting. Thus, the centre and a minimum 20 states would be required for majority of three-fourths. As per Section 12(10) of the Constitution, the act or proceedings of the Council cannot be declared invalid because of the following:

1. Any vacancy in the Council
2. Any defect in the appointment of a person as a member of the Council
3. Any procedural irregularity of the Council

Dispute Settlement

In case a dispute arises, the Council can establish a mechanism to adjudicate it. As per Section 12(11) of the Constitution, the Council shall set such a mechanism for resolving disputes which may arise:

1. Between central government and state or states
2. Between central government and any state or states on one side and state or states on other
3. Between two or more states

Meeting(s)

The GST Council is meeting regularly to resolve the glitches in the new tax regime. Total of 38 meetings of the council have been held so far. The first meeting was held on 22–23 September 2016 and the 38th meeting was held on 19 December 2019. The date of the meetings and places can be seen in Table 10.1.

Table 10.1 *GST Council Meetings*

S. No.	Number	Date	Place
1.	1st GST Council Meeting	22–23 September 2016	Vigyan Bhawan, New Delhi
2.	2nd GST Council Meeting	30 September 2016	New Delhi
3.	3rd GST Council Meeting	18–19 October 2016	New Delhi
4.	4th GST Council Meeting	3–4 November 2016	New Delhi
5.	5th GST Council Meeting	2–3 December 2016	New Delhi
6.	6th GST Council Meeting	11 December 2016	New Delhi
7.	7th GST Council Meeting	22–23 December 2016	New Delhi
8.	8th GST Council Meeting	3–4 January 2017	New Delhi
9.	9th GST Council Meeting	16 January 2017	New Delhi
10.	10th GST Council Meeting	18 February 2017	Udaipur, Rajasthan
11.	11th GST Council Meeting	4 March 2017	New Delhi
12.	12th GST Council Meeting	16 March 2017	New Delhi
13.	13th GST Council Meeting	31 March 2017	New Delhi
14.	14th GST Council Meeting	18–19 May 2017	Srinagar, Jammu and Kashmir
15.	15th GST Council Meeting	3 June 2017	New Delhi
16.	16th GST Council Meeting	11 June 2017	Vigyan Bhawan, New Delhi
17.	17th GST Council Meeting	18 June 2017	Vigyan Bhawan, New Delhi
18.	18th GST Council Meeting	30 June 2017	Vigyan Bhawan, New Delhi

S. No.	Number	Date	Place
19.	19th GST Council Meeting	17 July 2017	Prime Minister Office, New Delhi
20.	20th GST Council Meeting	05 August 2017	Vigyan Bhawan, New Delhi
21.	21st GST Council Meeting	09 September 2017	Hyderabad
22.	22nd GST Council Meeting	06 October 2017	Vigyan Bhavan, New Delhi
23.	23rd GST Council Meeting	10 November 2017	Guwahati, Assam
24.	24th GST Council Meeting	16 December 2017	New Delhi
25.	25th GST Council Meeting	18 January 2018	Vigyan Bhavan, New Delhi
26.	26th GST Council Meeting	10 March 2018	New Delhi
27.	27th GST Council Meeting	4 May 2018	Video Conferencing, New Delhi
28.	28th GST Council Meeting	21 July 2018	New Delhi
29.	29th GST Council Meeting	4 August 2018	New Delhi
30.	30th GST Council Meeting	28 September 2018	Video Conferencing, New Delhi
31.	31st GST Council Meeting	22 December 2018	New Delhi
32.	32nd GST Council Meeting	10 January 2019	New Delhi
33.	33rd GST Council Meeting	24 February 2019	New Delhi
34.	34th GST Council Meeting	19 March 2019	New Delhi
35.	35th GST Council Meeting	21 June 2019	New Delhi
36.	36th GST Council Meeting	27 July 2019	New Delhi
37.	37th GST Council Meeting	20 September	Goa
38.	38th GST Council Meeting	19 December 2019	New Delhi

Source: Authors.

Goods and Services Tax Network

The structure of GSTN was prepared by the EC of State Finance Ministers.[1] The government selected NSDL as the technology partner for incubating the national information utility.[2] The government incorporated GSTN as a private limited company on March 2013 as per Section 25 of the Companies Act, 1956.

The paid-up capital of GSTN is ₹10 crore. The government holds 49 per cent stake that is equally divided between central government and the state governments. The balance 51 per cent is held by non-government financial institutions.[3] However, the GST Council has changed the shareholding pattern of GSTN in its 27th meeting. The Council has approved the acquisition of 51 per cent holding by private/non-governmental institutions in the GSTN, amounting to ₹5.1 crore which will be equally shared by the centre and the states.

GSTN is providing three front-end services: registration, tax payment and return of taxes. The aim of GSTN is to provide a uniform interface to taxpayers and share infrastructure with the centre and the states. The centre and states are registering the taxpayers at GSTN. Over 1.22 crore businesses have been registered under GSTN so far.

Central Board of Indirect Tax and Customs

The government introduced the Central Board of Revenue Act in 1924 to administer direct and indirect taxes. After that, the government segregated the board into the CBDT and CBEC in 1963. The CBEC was further renamed as Central Board of Indirect Taxes and Customs (CBIC) in 2018. It is supposed to play a crucial role in the implementation of GST. It is a part of the revenue department under the Ministry of Finance of the GoI. The main task of CBIC is the formulation of policy related to levy and collection of all indirect taxes.

[1] GoI, *Union Budget, 2012–13*, Para 28.

[2] GoI, *Budget Speech, 2011–12*, Para 24.

[3] ICICI Bank (10%), NSE SI (10%), HDFC and HSFC Bank (20%), LIC HF (10%).

Appellate Tribunal

Appellate Tribunal (AT) is a quasi-judicial body. It is the second forum and will mediate in indirect tax disputes between the states and the centre. The tribunal will hear appeals against the order passed by the AT/Revision Tribunal. Provision for AT is given in Sections 109–116 of the CGST Act, 2017. It will be located in Delhi. 'A person can knock at the doors of the First Appellate Authority to appeal against the decision of the Adjudicating Authority'.[4] States have also adopted this provision in the SGST Act. The government has approved the creation of GST AT on 23 January 2019, to be known as the Goods and Services Tax Appellate Tribunal. The AT would consist of a president and two technical members[5]—one for the centre and one for the state GST—and one judicial member in every bench of the tribunal.

Advance Ruling Authority

Since the introduction of GST, trade and industry has faced multiple issues relating to uploading of returns, confusion regarding the generation of e-way bills, availing of legacy CENVAT credit under TRAN-1 form and many more other issues. To solve these issues, there is a provision for an Advance Ruling Authority (ARA) under the GST law. States have created ARAs to solve the taxation problems in their respective states. But, we have seen that a number of contradictory verdicts on the same issue have been given by the ARAs of various states. It is defeating the purpose of creating such authorities. The Telangana ARA and the West Bengal ARA gave contradictory verdicts with regard to the methodology on how to conclude a case. To solve this problem, the GST Council has approved the creation of a Centralized Appellate Authority for Advance Ruling in its 31st meeting held on 22 December 2018. The formation of a National ARA will remove conflicting rulings given by the state ARAs. The purpose of ARA is making the taxpayers aware of the treatment of transactions in advance.

---

[4] https://www.hrblock.in/earlygst/appeal-first-appellate-authority-gst/
[5] According to Section 109 of Chapter XVIII of the CGST Act, 2017.

The Structure of the New Tax System

The introduction of GST is a crucial step in the history of reform of indirect taxes. It has subsumed a number of union and state taxes and converted them into a single tax. The new tax is being levied simultaneously by the union and states on the supply of goods and services except on exempted goods and services, goods that are outside the ambit of GST and transactions which are less than the threshold limits. Earlier, it was levied on the manufacture of goods, on sale of goods and on provision of services. GST was introduced with the expectation that it will give relief to trade, industry and consumers through a more comprehensive and wider coverage of input credit. Prime Minister Modi tweeted with the hash tag 'GST for new India'. He wrote, 'The GST had brought growth, simplicity, and transparency. It had boosted formalization, enhanced productivity, and furthered ease of doing business'.[1] As GST is a new taxation system, we must understand the structure of the new tax regime. Let us look at the structure of GST.

GST Model

We have opted for a dual GST model because of the federal structure of our Constitution. The GST levied by the union is known as CGST and that which is being levied by the state governments is known as SGST. SGST is also known as UTGST in union territories without legislature. The inter-state supply of goods and services is the subject of IGST. IGST is being levied on inter-state supply of goods and services including stock transfers from one state to another. Import of goods and services

[1] *Business Standard*, July 2, 2018, p. 1.

are treated as inter-state supplies and are subject to IGST in addition to applicable custom duties. As per Clause (1) of Article 269A of the Constitution, IGST will be levied on all imports in the territory of India.

IGST is equal to CGST and SGST on all inter-state supply of goods and services. IGST is being levied and collected by the union government, and such tax is apportioned between the union and states in the manner provided by Parliament by law on the recommendation of the GST Council.

Figures 11.1 and 11.2 depict the working of the GST model. Table 11.1 tells us what payment has to be made under GST.

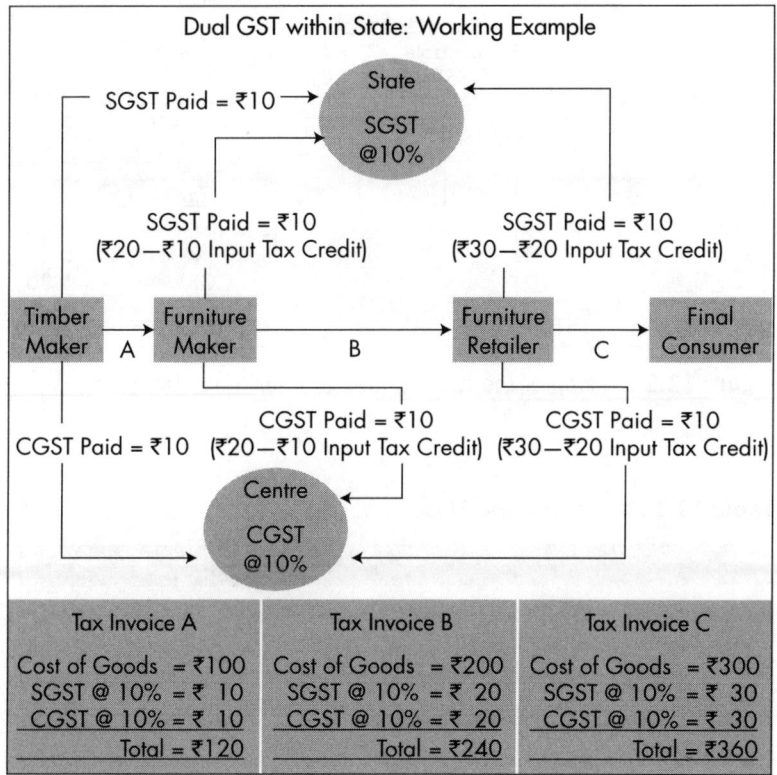

Figure 11.1 *Working of the Dual GST Model within a State*

Source: pib.nic.in

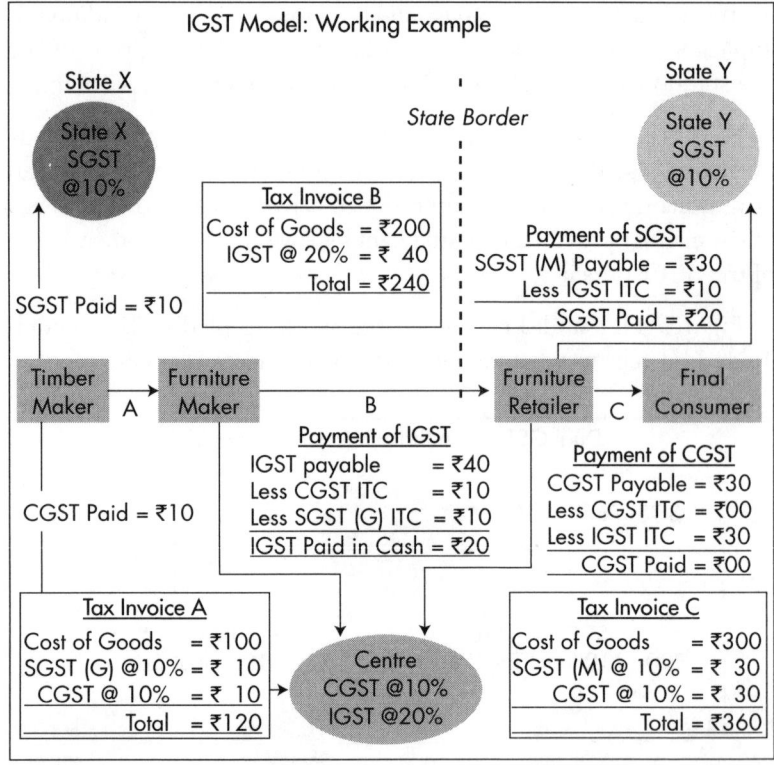

Figure 11.2 *Working of the IGST Model for Inter-State Transactions*

Source: pib.nic.in

Table 11.1 *Payments to Be Made under GST*

S. No.	Transactions	CGST	SGST	IGST
1.	Goods/services sold from Delhi to Allahabad	X	X	✓
2.	Goods/services sold within Delhi	✓	✓	X
3.	Goods/services sold from Allahabad to Kanpur	✓	✓	X

Source: Authors.

Threshold Limit

The tax threshold is a limit of turnover at which taxpayers start to pay tax. A common threshold limit is applied to both CGST and SGST. Under GST, the taxpayer whose annual turnover does not exceed ₹20 lakh is not liable to pay tax. The limit is set at ₹10 lakhs for the special category North-Eastern and hilly states. These states are Assam, Arunachal Pradesh, Himachal Pradesh, Uttarakhand, Manipur, Jammu and Kashmir, Mizoram, Meghalaya, Sikkim, Nagaland and Tripura. But GST is applicable on inter–state supply of goods and services irrespective of threshold.[2]

Registration

Business concerns registered under the GST legislation are supposed to pay GST. They are also supposed to register themselves under GST whose turnover exceeds ₹20 lakhs [3] and ₹10 lakhs[4] in the case of the North-Eastern states. The registration under GST is state specific and PAN based. Business concerns should complete their registration online on the GSTN portal. The suppliers of goods or services in different states must register themselves in each of such states or UTs from where it effects the supply. A scanned copy of all documents required for registration must be submitted along with an application for registration. After the review of the application and scanned documents, respective authorities grant a GST registration certificate. They also allot a 15-digit GST identification number to the applicant. The business concerns having their business in multiple states from where they make taxable supply of goods or services must take separate state-wise registrations.

But if an entity has different branches within a state, it may have only one registration. It must declare the principal place of business and the other paces as branches. As per Section 2(18) of CGST Act, 2017,

[2] *Live Mint,* June 30, 2017.

[3] GST Council increased exemption limit to ₹40 lakh from the earlier cap of ₹20 lakh during its 32nd meeting.

[4] GST Council increased exemption limit to ₹20 lakh from the earlier cap of ₹10 lakh during its 32nd meeting.

the business concern which has separate business in one state can get separate registration for their different business verticals. In the earlier tax regime, there were 66 lakh registrations, and, in GST, it has increased to 1.2 crore. This is a 40 per cent increase in the number of taxpayers.

Revenue Neutral Rate

RNR is a single rate of tax that ensures that the revenue collected by the new tax regime is the same as that collected under the previous tax regime. RNR neutralizes the adverse effect on the revenue of central government and the state governments due to the change in the tax rate. So, the tax rates have been designed on the basis of RNR.

The GoI formed a committee under the chairmanship of the then Chief Economic Advisor of the Ministry of Finance, Arvind Subramanian, to recommend RNR. The committee led by Subramanian suggested an RNR of 15–15.5 per cent for the centre and states combined. It recommended a lower rate of 12 per cent for certain goods consumed by the poor and a sin or demerit rate of 40 per cent to be applicable on pan masala, tobacco, aerated beverages and luxury cars. The Thirteenth Finance Commission also worked on RNR. The commission estimated and fixed RNR at 11 per cent. They further bifurcated the 11 per cent RNR into two rates, 5 per cent for CGST and 12 per cent for SGST.

In its report, the task force led by Kelkar had suggested 20 per cent tax rate for centre and states combined. In the 20 per cent, 12 per cent would be for the centre and 8 per cent for the states. A study of Satya Poddar and Amaresh Bagchi suggested that RNR for the centre and the states should not be more than 12 per cent.[5] The rate should apply on all goods and services except fuels.

Tax Rates

The government adopted a five-slab rate structure of 0, 5, 12, 18, and 28 per cent for GST (Table 11.2). Along with the five slabs, a

---

[5] Poddar and Bagchi, 'Revenue-Neutral Rate for GST'.

Table 11.2 *Tax Rate of GST*

| S. No. | IGST (%) | | | Number of Items | | |
| | CGST (%) | SGST (%) | Total (%) | Goods | | Services |
				01.07.2017	15.11.2017	
1.	1.5	1.5	03	18	–	–
2.	0.125	0.125	0.25	03	03	–
3.	0	0	0	149	149	87
4.	2.5	2.5	05	263	262	12
5.	06	06	12	242	242	07
6.	09	09	18	453	453	09
7.	14	14	28	228	228	04

Source: GST Council, as on 24 September 2018.

3 per cent and a 0.25 per cent rates were also fixed. The 3 per cent tax rate is applicable on precious metals. The government also decided to levy a rate of 0.25 per cent on precious stones and diamonds. Besides, a compensation cess is also being levied over the peak rate of 28 per cent on demerit goods. The purpose of levying the cess was to compensate the states for revenue loss due to the change in the tax regime. The government has categorized all items under various tax slabs. Thus, the government has actually adopted a seven-slab rate structure for goods and a five-slab rate structure for services.

Account Settlement

Settlement of account means the distribution of revenue between the centre and the states. The government is doing this on a periodic basis. The purpose is to settle the account to ensure that the credit of SGST used for the payment of IGST is transferred to the centre by the exporting state. Likewise, the credit for IGST is used for the payment of SGST by transferring it to the importing state by the centre. Subsequently, the amount of SGST share in IGST collected on the supply of B2C is transferred to the respective states by the centre. All the transfers are executed on the basis of the information contained in the returns filed by the taxpayers.

Composition Scheme

There is an optional and simpler tax provision for small taxpayers under GST. This scheme is not available for the service provider. The composition scheme can be opted for by those traders whose aggregate turnover is below ₹1 crore in an FY.[6] The limit for the traders of Himachal Pradesh and the North-Eastern states is ₹75 lakh. Under this scheme, a trader can pay tax as a fixed percentage of his turnover without ITC benefit during the year. PAN is taken into consideration for the calculation of turnover. The tax rate under composition scheme may be seen in Table 11.3.

---

[6] Turnover limit recommended to be raised to ₹1.5 Cr in 23rd GST Council meeting: Necessary amendment in the Act has been carried out.

Table 11.3 *Composition Threshold Limit*

S. No.	Categories	CGST (%)	SGST (%)	Total (%)
1.	Traders	0.5	0.5	1
2.	Manufacturers	0.5	0.5	1
3.	Restaurants (not serving alcohol)	2.5	2.5	5

Source: Borpuzari. 'GST: Composition Scheme for Small Taxpayers Extended to ₹1.5 Crore'.

Administrative Control

The issue of administrative and dual control over assesses was discussed in the 21st meeting of the GST Council on 9 September 2017. In this meeting, the GST Council defined the parameters for administrative control over taxpayers. Accordingly, the council divided taxpayers' base between the centre and the states and issued a notification on 20 September 2017.[7] The division is to be done in each state using computers on the basis of stratified random sampling at the state level. The notification stated that geographical location and types of taxpayers could be considered for the division of control. The control power under IGST would be cross empowered on the same as in CGST and SGST, with few exceptions. States have the power to collect GST in territorial waters. The single interface administrative controls can be seen in Table 11.4.

The administrative control is to be divided on the basis of the turnover of the assesses. For this purpose, the GST Council has

Table 11.4 *Administrative Control*

		Tax Administration	
S. No.	Turnover	State Control	Central Control
1.	Below ₹1.5 cr	90% of taxpayers	10% of taxpayers
2.	Above ₹1.5 cr	50% of taxpayers	50% of taxpayers

Source: Authors.

[7] 01/2017 F. No. 166/Cross Empowerment/GSTC/2017

Table 11.5 *Computation of Turnover*

S. No.	Taxpayer	Basis for Division
1.	Registered only under central excise or service tax	Total annual turnover declared in their returns
2.	Registered only under value added tax	Total annual turnover of state under VAT (along with exports, inter-state sales, and exempt goods)
3.	Registered under central excise and VAT both	Annual turnover of state under VAT
4.	Registered under service tax and VAT both	Total non-overlapping turnover (service tax + VAT – any turnover which is included in both)

Source: 'Centre or States? GST Council Lists Norms on Administrative Control of Taxpayers', *Business Line*, September 21, 2017.

extended the definition of turnover. The computation of turnover will be as shown in Table 11.5.

Compensation to States

There is a provision of compensation to the states in the GST (Compensation to States) Act. The act gives guidelines for compensation to states for revenue loss due to the introduction of GST. The centre is to compensate the states for a period of five years. The FY 2015–2016 is the base year for calculating compensation during the transition period. The projected revenue growth rate subsumed for a state shall be 14 per cent. The centre has levied a GST compensation cess to finance the compensation to states.[8] It must be noted however that even this has now run into problems with the centre withholding the compensation due to the states.

Input Tax Credit

ITC means that a businessman who is paying tax on the output of goods or services can reduce the amount of tax which has been paid

[8] CBIC, 'Goods and Service Tax (GST)', 29–30.

Table 11.6 *Input Tax Credit Uses*

S. No.	Credit	For First Payment of	For Further Payment of
1.	CGST	SGST	IGST
2.	SGST/UTGST	SGST /UTGST	IGST
3.	IGST	IGST	CGST then SGST/UTGST

Source: Authors.

already on inputs. They are required to pay only the balance amount. It is a mechanism to avoid the cascading effect of taxes. Cascading means tax on tax. Businesses that are registered under GST can avail of ITC of the tax paid on the inward movement of goods or services or both. ITC can be used as per Table 11.6. Tax credit of CGST paid on inputs can be used only for the payment of CGST, and the credit of SGST/UTGST paid on inputs can be used only for the payment of SGST/UTGST. Tax credit of CGST cannot be used for the payment of SGST/UTGST and vice versa.

ITC Accumulation

Accumulation of ITC arises when the tax paid on inputs is more than the tax liability. It can be carried forward to the next FYs until it is fully used up by the taxpayer for the payment of outward tax liability. The legislation allows refund of unused ITC to business concerns under only two conditions: if the accumulated credit is (a) because of zero-rated supplies and (b) because of inverted duty structure with some exceptions. A registered concern can claim refund of unused ITC at the end of any tax period.

E-Way Bill

It is an e-document which is issued by a transporter with details and instructions related to the shipment of consignment of goods. The document includes name of consignee and consignor, origin point of consignment, destination and route. It was introduced for all inter-state movement of goods with effect from 1 April 2018 with an option to states to select a date for intra-states supplies on/or before 3 June 2018. All the states have notified it for intra-state supplies. The last state that introduced it from 16 June 2018 was NCT Delhi. It is an electronically generated number to track the movement of goods on trucks. All the consignments of ₹50,000 or more requires an e-way bill for their inter-state movement. It is not required for those transporters where the value of a consignment is below ₹50,000.

E-way bill is valid for fixed number of days depending upon the distance the goods have to be transported. It is valid for one day if goods are to be transported up to 100km. The validity increases by one day for every 100 km thereafter. A transporter can increase the validity of e-way bill online on their own system without approaching tax authorities.

Dipak Dash, a journalist of *The Times of India* travelled with a truck driver, Raju, and shared his experience.[9] The Haryana-registered container truck moved from Manesar at 2200 hours and headed for Hyderabad. It was a smooth journey.

This is what he wrote about his experience. The driver said that the checks had been reduced since the introduction of the e-way bill. He said, prior to GST, it used to take at least three hours at every state border. There were a number of hassles to clear the documents. But now 'you don't need to worry if you have all the necessary papers. Last time while returning from Mumbai, the sales tax officials from Maharashtra wanted to see the e-way bill. They checked the documents and keyed in some details into their mobile phones and we were done within five minutes'.

This is not the story of Raju alone, other truckers have shared the same experience. This is the reason why more than 10 crore e-way bills have been issued so far since its inception. Most of the e-way bills, about 76 per cent, were generated via the website. The system has the capacity to generate 7.5 million e-way bills daily and can handle more than 40,000 concurrent users.

[9] Dash, 'A Year of GST', 21–22.

Evaluation of GST after Two-and-a-Half Years

12

GST was introduced as a landmark legislation for indirect tax reforms in India. Its launch at the midnight of 30 June–1 July in the central hall of Parliament was meant to raise it to the level of the other midnight saga, namely the announcement of India's independence from British yoke on 14–15 August 1947. But sadly, it failed miserably to live up to people's expectations. The speeches delivered by the finance minister, the prime minister and the President of India on the occasion were pedestrian compared to the stirring 'Tryst with Destiny' speech delivered by Pandit Jawaharlal Nehru on that occasion. But that was not the only disappointment. The GST design unfolded that day was itself macabre, to say the least. It was riddled with multiple flaws which increased the burden on businesses instead of lowering them. GST was still a work in progress when it was thrust upon an unsuspecting nation. A day before its launch, the GST Council met in Delhi and made its first amendment in the rate of tax fixed by reducing GST on fertiliser to 5 per cent from the earlier 12 per cent. Why did it not occur to the worthies constituting the Council, specially the union finance minister, that the rate fixed earlier would not be acceptable to the suffering farmers of India? No rocket science was needed to understand this simple fact. But it was only the beginning. The Council, under the leadership of the union finance minister, has gone on merrily making changes in tax rates, procedures, exemption limits and other changes as if it was their right to make a new budget every day. By now, these changes run into hundreds and we are not done with them yet. God alone knows what happened to the famous RNR rate which is obviously in a shambles today and nobody talks of it anymore.

It was not that the ministers did not have a guide to go by. After all, Yashwant Sinha had earlier fixed three rates of CENVAT in 2002: a mean rate of 16 per cent, a merit rate of 8 per cent and demerit rate of 24 per cent. Despite the tinkering done by subsequent finance ministers, these three rates had survived by and large. Everyone had agreed that a single rate GST would really qualify as a good and simple tax. But if that was not possible to achieve immediately, what prevented the ministers from adopting the three-slab formula? The union finance minister should have provided the necessary leadership in this matter. He failed woefully to do so. Was it ignorance? Was it incompetence? Was it just a cavalier attitude and lack of application of mind? We leave the judgement to the reader.

The main objective of GST was to bring all indirect taxes and services under the umbrella of one tax. But a few items such as diesel, petrol and liquor are not included in GST. The discontinuation of local taxes is also not clear. We have seen cases in Tamil Nadu and Maharashtra. The state government imposed an entertainment tax over and above a 28 per cent GST. Maharashtra has also increased Motor Vehicles Tax to compensate the losses due to the introduction of GST and to preserve revenue collections.

The government is calling it as a 'Good and Simple Tax' which has increased the number of indirect taxpayers, registered number of enterprises.

In just one year after the introduction of GST, the number of new enterprises registered is 48 lakh. Around 350 crore invoices were produced and 11 crore returns were filed.... The implementation of the GST, which is bringing more businesses into the tax net, will further push formalization of the economy.[1]

On the other hand, opposition led by congress has called it a 'grossly scary tax'. 'The GST was implemented without adequate preparation and this reflected in various ways – ranging from technical glitches to

[1] *Live Mint*, July 2, 2018

lack of clarity about the rates, to the general confusion about filing of returns and approval of refunds'.[2]

Rahul Gandhi, the then President of Indian National Congress and the main opponent of ruling party, said, 'This GST is a way of removing money from the pockets of the poor'. During the campaigning of the Gujarat assembly elections, he further added, 'This is not GST, this is Gabbar Singh Tax'.[3]

The business concerns are suffering with a number of hurdles along with high compliance cost. Tilak Raj Bathla is a business man. He has a tiny weaving factory in Panipat. He said,

> His neighbours, most of them unschooled, could not comply with monthly online filings required under the GST regime. Some of his customers and suppliers could not afford to hire accountants to navigate a system which has been amended more than 200 times already, while others struggled to cope with delays in tax returns caused by glitches in the centralised software.[4]

It is not the problem of only Tilak Raj Bathla. It is the problem of all business concerns.

'A poorly-executed Goods and Services Tax (GST) has increased the compliance burden on Indian businesses, now facing more-complex-than-ever paperwork and long delays in refunds and export credits that are key elements of a well-functioning GST'.[5] 'This did create initial problems, triggering litigations. In most cases, the government has come out with clarifications. But harnessing full benefits of the biggest tax reform since Independence could be delayed if the complexities faced by the industry keep increasing'.[6]

---

[2] Seth, 'Compliance Still a Challenge', 9.

[3] The villain in one of most popular movies of India.

[4] Reuters, 'GST Effect'.

[5] Subramanya, 'A Missed Opportunity', 66.

[6] Mahanta and Dave, 'EU Countries Looking at India's GST'.

BBC says, 'Businesses have been asking for more time to implement changes as they are worried of being not ready for a switch to the new system'.[7] A journalist of *ET Retail* writes that 'If there's one word that sums up the response of India's businesses and consumers to the country's new national sales tax, it's confused'.[8] It is expected that GST will mitigate ill effects of cascading or double taxation in a major way. 'The government is hoping not just to streamline the myriad levies on businesses but to quiet the critics who say Mr Modi has failed to deliver on his policy promises'.[9]

Prime Minister Narendra Modi had also asked Finance Minister Jaitley on 5 October 2017 to 'ensure that GST rules were amended such as to make doing business easier in India'.[10] The government set up 13 committees to address specific issues regarding GST.[11] The government has made as yet 385 changes in goods and services tax since its inception by issuing circulars and coming out with clarification about refund, exemption and rates.

Amarjit Kaur, National Secretary of the All India Trade Union Congress (AITUC), states that 'about 230,000 small businesses have closed down due to compliance and cash flow problems, leading to large-scale job losses'.[12]

AITUC conducted a survey in July 2018. The survey found that 'a fifth of India's 63 million small businesses—contributing 32% to the economy and employing 111 million people—faced a 20% fall in profits since the GST rollout, and had to sack hundreds of thousands of workers'.[13] Manoj Kumar further quotes in his article of the survey of the Centre for Monitoring Indian Economy, 'Nearly five million workers lost their jobs over the past year'.[14]

---

[7] Expert Web Desk, 'India ushers in GST'.

[8] Bloomberg, 'Good, Bad and Ugly'.

[9] Anand, 'After Killing Currency'.

[10] Dutta, '98 Days of GST'.

[11] Seth, 'Compliance Still a Challenge', 13.

[12] Reuters, 'GST Effect'.

[13] Kumar, 'India's Tax Effect'.

[14] Ibid.

Arvind P. Datar and K. Vaitheeswaran, the senior advocates of Madras High Court, evaluated GST in their article in the *Indian Express*. They write,

> Even the most ardent supporter of the GST cannot deny that the new system has not been as beneficial as expected. The present GST system, like socialism, sounds wonderful in theory but is completely unworkable in practice. It is dangerous to proceed with the hope that things will eventually settle down. Immediate steps are necessary to ensure that India's second tryst with destiny does not become a tryst with disaster.[15]

The Bureau of Outreach and Communication under the ministry, in its RTI response to a query on the sum spent by the centre on advertising and awareness campaigns on GST, confirmed that the government spent ₹1.32 billion on advertisements for GST. The expenditure on print media stood at ₹1.26 billion. They spent ₹54 million for advertisement in outdoor media.[16]

We shall analyse the major glitches that have arisen just because of the introduction of GST in the next sections.

GDP vis-à-vis GST

GST was introduced with the expectation that it would simplify the tax structure, eliminate the cascading effect of taxes and increase government's revenue. This would lead to increase in the GDP of the country. The National Council of Applied Economic Research conducted a study and submitted a report to GoI in which it said that the introduction of GST would increase the economic growth of the country by 0.9 per cent to 1.7 per cent. Finance Minister Arun Jaitley had also anticipated that 'the uniform tax system would help generate revenue and strengthen the Gross Domestic Product (GDP)'.[17] Prakash Chawla, a senior journalist, also asserted that GST would increase the GDP. He wrote an article for the *Press Information Bureau* in which he said that 'GST should lead to a tax buoyancy and push to the Gross Domestic Product between 1–1.5% with clearance of the cob web of

---

[15] Datar and Vaitheeswaran, 'A GST Good and Simple'.

[16] PTI. 'Govt Spent ₹1.32 bn on GST Advertisements'.

[17] *The Asian Age*, 'India will Set Example'.

taxes'.[18] The British lender HSBC also expected that GST would push the economy of India. HSBC said, 'GST impact will help push the Indian GDP growth to 7% in FY19'.[19] But there is no evidence so far to suggest that these predictions have come true. In fact, India's GDP appears to have declined after the introduction of GST (at 5% in 2019) or at best remained static (see Table 12.1).

However, the GDP growth of 8.2 per cent during the first quarter of 2018–2019 led some of the supporters of the government, including the CII, to claim that this was on account of the introduction of GST. It said in a statement, 'The 8.2% economic growth in the first quarter of 2018–19 is an outcome of key reforms like GST and liberalisation of FDI norms initiated by the government'.[20] Adi Godrej, a supporter of reform in tax, also gave credit to GST for growth in GDP.

Table 12.1 *GDP Growth*

Year	Quarter	GDP (%)	IMF Projection
2015–2016	Q1	7.9	
	Q2	7.4	
	Q3	7.3	
	Q4	7.9	
	Annual	7.6	
2016–2017	Q1	7.1	
	Q2	7.3	
	Q3	7.0	
	Q4	6.1	
	Annual	6.9	
2017–2018	Q1	5.7	
	Q2	6.3	
	Q3	7.2	
	Q4	7.7	
	Annual	6.7	

[18] Chawla, 'GST: A Game-Changer for India'.

[19] PTI. 'GDP may Grow to 7% in FY19'.

[20] PTI. '8.2% GDP Growth an Outcome of Modi'.

Year	Quarter	GDP (%)	IMF Projection
2018–2019	Q1	8.1	
	Q2	7.1	
	Q3	6.6	
	Q4	5.8	
	Annual	6.8	7.3
2019–2020	Q1	5.0	7.4
	Q2	4.5	

Source: Authors.

He said, 'GST has done very well. It has added to India's GDP growth quite considerably'.[21] These predictions were made on too thin an evidence and subsequent quarterly growth figures of the GDP belied these claims. But the protagonists of GST are now quiet. According to many analysts, a botched up GST has mainly been responsible for the decline in GDP.

HSN Code Problem

The coding of goods under various Harmonized System Nomenclature (HSN) brackets has been always a key challenge. The businesses and government continue a delicate balancing act over the HSN. The business concerns had also faced the same problems at the start of GST. Let us look at the problem with two cases of plastic and quilts.[22] The furniture sellers were struggling with the classification of plastic to calculate GST. They wanted to know how plastic chairs would be classified. Plastic goods were attracting multiple tax rates. At that time, plastic items were being taxed at 12 per cent or 18 per cent, while plastic furniture items were taxed at 28 per cent. These problems had created a confusion: Should the item be treated as a plastic item and get bracketed under 12 per cent or 18 per cent or treated as furniture and clubbed in the 28 per cent tax bracket.

The same problem arose with the rate of tax on quilts. Quilts were also attracting multiple tax rates. The sellers of quilts in Rajasthan

[21] Kelkar, 'GST Gave Big Boost to India's GDP Growth'.
[22] Aanchal Magazine and Verma, 'Goods and Services Tax: Businesses Struggle', 22.

were confused about the HSN code. There were three rates for quilts: 12 per cent tax rate for wholly made quilted textile materials, 18 per cent for cotton pillows, mattress and quilts, and 28 per cent for quilts in the category of mattress supports. They were confused as in what rate should apply to the quilts.

We can also see the bracket problem in another case of wood. 'In its various manifestations, wood finds its way into every tax bracket. There is a five per cent tax on wood chips and particles, for example, while the rate is 18% on sawed lumber'.[23] It is not the problem of only plastic and quilts; there were a number of items that HSN code was confusing.

One Nation, One Tax, One Market

The government claimed that GST created 'one nation, one tax, and one market'. The government also claimed that GST subsumed all earlier taxes into one tax. But we have three GSTs: CGST, SGST/UTGST and IGST. Businesses with presence in more than one state are supposed to have multiple GST numbers. They also have to file multiple returns with multiple GST logins.

The government also claimed that GST led to the creation of one nation and one market. But the prices of a few products appear to vary according to location. According to a study of E-retail, the price of Baleno Sigma gasoline model of Maruti Suzuki is ₹635,000 in Navi Mumbai while the same model is priced at ₹664,952 in Bengaluru. 'Movie tickets in Tamil Nadu and Maharashtra became costlier as the states imposed additional taxes, defeating the purpose of a unified tax'.[24]

One Registration

The government's claim is that GST has led to 'one nation one registration'. In other words, only one registration is required for the

---

[23] Anand, 'After Killing Currency'.

[24] Bloomberg, 'Good, Bad and Ugly'.

payment of tax. It is a crucial component of the GST structure. GST has been implemented in 29 states and 2 union territories under CGST SGST/UGST and IGST. Therefore, a national business concern is required to register at 31 different places to collect and pay SGST. The renowned economist and indeed the father of GST in India, Vijay Kelkar, wrote an article in *Live Mint* in which he criticized the number of registrations required for GST. He said that the registration process was time consuming for manufacturers. He wrote, 'Modalities could be put in place for central registration under GSTN, with state governments having the liberty to cancel the registration in their states if the mandatory physical inspection of the dealer's premises within a specified period reveals irregularities'.[25] The ET Bureau also wrote an article on the success and failure of GST. It also criticized the cumbersome registration system under GST. It said, 'Multiple registration requirements have complicated things for industry, which was expecting simplicity. In many cases, registration is required in all states. Companies fear that multiple audits and assessments due to multiple registrations could make life more difficult for them going forward'.[26]

Multiplicity of Rates

GST was introduced with five rates, namely 0 per cent, 5 per cent, 12 per cent, 18 per cent and 28 per cent, along with two small tax rates of 0.25 per cent on rough diamonds and precious stones and 3 per cent on gold and silver. Demerit and luxury goods, which come under the bracket of 28 per cent tax slab, are subject to an additional cess of 1–15 per cent. Hence, we have multiple rates for GST.

The World Bank conducted a survey and compared the rate of GST/ VAT of 115 countries. They found that GST of India is 'one of the most complex with the second highest tax rate in the world among a sample of 115 countries which have a similar indirect tax system'.[27] 'The

[25] Kelkar, 'GST: Make Haste Slowly'.

[26] ET Bureau, 'One Year of GST'.

[27] World Bank, *India Development Update*.

multiple rate structure and other features could give rise to high compliance and administrative costs'.[28] 'The many rates complicate life, especially for retail grocery stores hosting a wide range of products, but aside from making them groan, it is not really making them scale down their operations'.[29]

> Businesses are confused by a complicated structure, which includes four tax slabs ranging from 5% to 28% and numerous exemptions. It's also not clear what sort of damage the nationwide rollout will inflict on the country's fast-growing, $2 trillion economy before the long-term benefits kick in.[30]

There are 49 countries around the world which have single-slab GST. All countries with GST have either one or two rates, not multiplicity of rates. A total of 28 countries have two slabs, and only 5 countries including India have four non-zero slabs for GST. Luxembourg, Ghana, Pakistan and Italy are using four or more slabs of GST. Hence, India has the highest number of GST slabs in the world.

'World over, GST is one rate. You can't say, I am introducing GST but will have multiple rates, call it by some other name, call the RSS tax', said Congress leader Kapil Sibal and urged the centre to reduce the slabs of the GST.[31] 'What we have got today is not a one-market one-rate GST, but we have four market rates, a five per cent rate, a 12% rate, an 18% rate and a 28% rate'.

The opposition led by Congress asked the government to reduce the number of rates under GST. P. Chidambaram said, 'The multiple GST rates must be reduced immediately to five and then to three in short time frame and finally to a single rate with exemption from tax for the truly merit goods and services. The single rate must not exceed 18%'.[32] The former economic advisor to finance minister, Arvind

---

[28] PTI, '"Milestone" GST Reforms'.

[29] Rajaraman, 'GST Features Contributing to GDP'.

[30] Marlow et al., 'Businesses Brace for Chaos'.

[31] Chidambaram, 9.

[32] Rajagopalan, 'Unsung Heroes', 6.

Subramanian, in an interview pointed out that the '28% tax slab has to go. The cesses may have to remain, but there should be just one rate on cesses'.[33]

However, the then finance minister 'dismissed the idea of a single GST'.[34] Prime minister ruled out a single GST rate. 'It would have been very simple to have just one slab but it would have meant we could not have food items at 0% tax rate. Can we have milk and Mercedes at the same rate?'[35]

The government chose a multiplicity of tax rates and missed out on the opportunity to really simplify the indirect tax regime in the country. Multiplicity of tax rates brings its own evils. Multiplicity of rates in indirect taxes is the enemy of simplicity.

Tax Rate Flaws

There were many defects in the tax rates fixed. Tax rates also depended on the price of the product even if it was the same product. For example, 'the kurta shirts at Rizwan Siddique's air-conditioned store in Crawford Market in Mumbai which are to be taxed at 5% if their price is under 1,000 rupees, or US $16, and 12% if they are priced higher'.[36] Sanitary napkins were taxed at 12 per cent. When it was criticized by women's groups, the GST Council exempted it from tax in its 28th meeting.

The same confusion prevailed in the case of footwear. 'Footwear below ₹500 will be taxed at 5% while the rest would be in the 18% bracket.[37] The tax levied on Gold is 3 per cent while biscuits were taxed at 18 per cent. Is it justifiable?

---

[33] Arvind Subramanian in an interview with *The Indian Express*, July 1, 2018, p. 10.

[34] PTI, 'Rahul Gandhi's idea of single rate for GST "flawed", says Arun Jaitley'.

[35] TNN, 'Milk and Mercedes Can't Be Taxed at Same Rate, Says PM'.

[36] Anand, 'After Killing Currency'.

[37] PTI, 'GST to be 5% on Footwear'.

Bracket Changes

The government is bringing changes in GST tax brackets of various items almost on a regular basis. It is not correct and one is completely dismayed at the approach of the GST Council. No one seems to be there to tell the people what the financial implications of all the changes are? In the first meeting of the GST Council, the tax on fertilizer was brought down from 18 per cent to 5 per cent. Fertilizer is used in agriculture. Why was the GST rate fixed at 18 per cent for fertilizer and then reduced? The rate for air-conditioned restaurants was hiked to 18 per cent from the pre-GST rate of 6 per cent. After widespread concern from industry and consumers, it was reduced to 5 per cent. 'When the rate was 18%, customers blamed us although the money was going to the government'.[38] According to PTI,

> The GST Council has pruned the 28% slab by cutting tax rates on 191 goods over the last one year, leaving just 35 items, including AC, digital camera, video recorders, dishwashing machines and automobiles, in the highest tax bracket. There were around 226 goods in the 28% category when Goods and Services Tax (GST) was implemented on July 1, 2017.... The rate cuts would lead to a revenue loss of about ₹6,000 crore.[39]

The GST Council in its 23rd meeting on 10 November 2017 recommended big ticket changes in GST. The Council decided to keep the highest 28 per cent tax on luxury and sinful goods only. As a result, 178 items were shifted to the 18 per cent bracket and two items to the 12 per cent bracket. GST on many items has also been reduced. A total of 13 items shifted from 18 per cent to 12 per cent and 6 items from 18 per cent to 5 per cent; 8 items shifted from 12 per cent to 5 per cent and 6 items from 5 per cent to 0 per cent bracket. Both AC and non-AC restaurants now attract 5 per cent GST unlike the previous 12 per cent.

[38] Mani, 'GST Impact on Household'.
[39] PTI, 'Now, Only 35 Goods in Highest Tax'.

In the meeting held on 18 January 2018, GST Council changed the rates for 21 more items, and 40 services were also exempted from tax. The GST Council has approved more than 200 amendments since the law came into force. Too many changes in rules and rates are damaging particularly for small businesses. The changes could also widen country's fiscal deficit.

Lobbying

The real bane of multiplicity of tax rates and frequent shifting of items from one tax bracket to another is that it leads to lobbying, litigation and use of discretion. Somebody at 28 per cent tax rate would always try to come down to 18 per cent tax rate and someone who is at 18 per cent will try to go to 12 per cent. This process will continue further. And then there are classification problems as we have shown above: 'Textile traders have been protesting demanding that fabrics be exempted from tax'.[40] 'Sweet shop owners in West Bengal had also protested against the imposition of five per cent GST on their products'.[41]

Return File Problem

GST was introduced with the requirement to file Goods and Services Tax Return (GSTR) 1, GSTR 2 and GSTR 3; every taxpayer had to file three returns per month and one annual return which made a total of 37 returns to be filed annually (Table 12.2). 'It is not hard to see why some businesses are complaining'.[42] The filing of three returns along with one annual return was found extremely daunting and should be brought down to one return a month and one annual return.

'The introduction of three monthly returns and matching of inward supplies of the buyer with outward supplies of supplier on a monthly

[40] Bloomberg, 'Good, Bad and Ugly'.

[41] *The Indian Express*, 'One Year of GST'.

[42] Anand, 'After Killing Currency'.

Table 12.2 *Number and Frequency of Returns before and after GST*

S. No.	Tax	Frequency of Returns			Total Number of Returns
		Monthly	Biannual	Annual	
1.	State VAT	1	–	1	13
2.	Service Tax	0	2	0	02
3.	Central Excise	1	–	1	13
4.	GST	3	–	1	37
5.	GST (revised)	1	–	1	13

Source: Authors.

basis was criticized by industry'.[43] P. Chidambaram observed that under the present system, 'all-India business is required to file over 1,000 returns a year'. He further said, 'Only one return must be required to be filed once in a quarter'.[44]

This process increased the workload of businesses. The tax return filing procedure under GST has become a major cause of headache for small businesses. No one seemed to be sure about the appropriate process for filing GSTR. Later, it was amended and government asked concerned businesses to file only one return every month and an annual tax return. Late fee for delayed filing of return in form GSTR 3B for the months of July 2017 to September 2017 was waived.[45] The amount of late fee already paid but subsequently waived off was to be re-credited to the Electronic Cash Ledger of the registered person under 'Tax' head instead of 'Fee' head.

[43] ET Contributors, 'One year of GST'.

[44] Express News Service, 'GST has Become Bad Word', 7.

[45] From October 2017 onwards, the amount of late fee for late filing of GSTR 3B payable by a registered person is as follows: whose tax liability for that month was 'NIL' will be ₹20 per day instead of ₹200 per day; whose tax liability for that month was not 'NIL' will be ₹50 per day instead of ₹200 per day.

Matching of Invoices

The next hurdle after filing GSTR was matching of invoices. Invoices can be uploaded continuously by the supplier and continuously viewed and locked by the buyer for availing ITC. For filing the return, the process had to match the sales invoices submitted by a supplier with the corresponding purchase invoice submitted by a buyer.

> The invoice that is uploaded has to be cross verified by the 15 digit number on it and each of the 15 digits has to be matched with the buyer claiming a credit, but issues may arise when the matching is done line by line, with almost ten different tax rates and each line requiring a separate HSN code.[46]

The matching of invoices does not exist anywhere in the world. But it was introduced in India. It placed a huge burden on the electronic infrastructure and entailed huge compliance costs for the small and medium enterprises.

GSTN Problem

For months since the introduction of GST, taxpayers struggled with the problem of filing their returns due to the problems encountered with the GSTN server. The agency was not adequately prepared. There were a number of glitches in the GSTN portal that resulted in huge losses for business concerns missing deadlines.

'The biggest dampener was the compliance process, as information technology glitches took more than the anticipated time to be resolved'.[47] Due to technical glitches in the GSTN portal (e.g., affixing of digital signatures, delay in making cash payments, etc.), many taxpayers were unable to file returns in the first month.

The e-way bill was planned to be rolled out from February 2018, but, due to overload, GSTN failed. Because of this, the introduction of e-way bill was postponed to April 2018.

---

[46] Aanchal Magazine and Verma, 'Goods and Services Tax: Businesses Struggle' 22.
[47] ET Bureau, 'One Year of GST'.

'The GSTR 2 buyer return form and GSTR 3 input–output return form had been suspended after a hue and cry and the collapse of the GSTN system'.[48]

The government extended the due dates several times owing to the inability of GSTN to carry the load of the information fed by business concerns as part of periodic compliances. 'The government rushed into GST although it knew that the GSTN was not ready to cope with the challenges of handling complexities of the laws and massive amount of data'.[49]

E-way Bill

The e-way bill system has been introduced nationwide for all inter-state movement of goods with effect from 1 April 2018. The e-way bill provisions for interstate movement of goods are uniform. But the same cannot be said about intrastate movement of goods.

Refund and ITC

In the new tax regime, business concerns can claim several types of refunds on GST deposited. The maximum number of claims of refunds arises from exports. The settlement of refund, especially export-linked refund also came under fire. Exporters claimed that over 60 per cent of their refunds were stuck with the government.

> The refund mechanism for exporters, including data matching law, besides procedures governing them, have irked the sector, particularly smaller entities that saw their working capital requirements rise. Though several efforts have been made to address the issue, it may require more intervention.[50]

The refunds were flowing on a monthly basis, but, since February 2018, the government has decided to use cumulative figures. It also creates a glitch. Experts say, 'Having an error in any month is enough

[48] Seth, 'Compliance Still a Challenge', 13.

[49] Rajagopalan, 'Unsung Heroes', 6.

[50] ET Bureau, 'One Year of GST'.

to disrupt the entire process and as a result, many refunds have got stuck'.[51]

Under the earlier system, exporters were allowed duty free imports of goods used for making products for export. In the GST regime, they have to first pay the duty and after that apply for a refund. To get the refund, the export firm has to first file an online application and after that their cash ledger will be debited. Afterwards, the firm has to get a printout of the same and file it with the tax authorities. But tax authorities are not ready to accept it quickly. Hence, many refunds are left waiting to be filed. There are a number of reports to suggest that this has increased administrative tax compliance burden on export firms. The increased administrative tax compliance burden is locking up the working capital of exporters. Because of this, the cost has increased by up to 1.25 per cent since 1 July 2017.

The government has promised to refund 90 per cent of the amount due within seven days of a refund application by exporters. But it still takes at least a month. Even exporters have been unable to file applications for refund of ITC because of GSTN problems, resulting in serious working capital pressure on exporters. 'The carpet industry says ₹400 crore is stuck in GST refunds.... For the textile sector 5–10% of working capital being blocked alongside banks' skepticism about lending to it is bad news'.[52]

Litigation Problem

The new GST is far different from the original GST which was initiated by the earlier government. In the beginning, it encountered various glitches—multiple tax slabs, exemptions, cumbersome returns and compliance procedures. These led to avoidable litigation as it had enough room for them. Hence, a number of petitions were filed in various High Courts on different issues against the new tax regime. 'The Allahabad and Kerala High Courts have been flooded with writ

[51] Chakrborty, 'Exporters Face a Long Wait', 13.
[52] Suneja, 'Refund Mechanism Still a Pain'.

petition challenging its provisions. The judiciary's response reveals a culpable revenue administration overzealously guarding evasion, with taxpayers sharing the blame for failure to comply with appropriate documentation under the new law'.[53]

E-Wallet Scheme

In the beginning of the introduction of GST, exporters were facing the problems of refund. Their working capital requirement and consequently shipments were hit due to delays in refunds which in some cases were delayed for over eight months. *The Business Line* wrote on behalf of the exporters that refund of about ₹20,000 crore was stuck due to delays in refunds.[54] The *Indian Express* wrote that the Federation of Indian Export Organizations had estimated that nearly $2 billion tax credits of small exporters was not refunded because of the software glitches and difficulties in matching the hundreds of thousands of invoices.[55]

The e-wallet scheme is a creation of electronic e-wallets. Government has introduced the scheme from 1 October 2018 as a relief for the exporters who encountered working capital problems due to delayed GST refunds. In the new e-wallet mechanism, exporters would get a notional credit in their account based on their past record.[56] The notional credit can be used to pay taxes on inputs. The exporters can use this currency for the payment of GST or IGST on goods imported or procured by them.

[53] Bhutani and Jain, 'GST: A Year of Learning', 9.
[54] Prabhu, 'E-Wallet will Address GST Refund'.
[55] Kumar, 'GST Effect: Hundreds of Thousands'.
[56] Prabhu, 'E-Wallet will Address GST Refund Issue'.

GST Revenue, Settlement of IGST and Compensation to the States

Pre-GST Indirect Tax Collection

India has a federal structure where the union and the states both have the constitutional power to levy taxes. As we have already discussed in Chapter 1 of the book, prior to the introduction of GST, while the union was levying Customs Duties, Union Excise Duties, CENVAT, Service Tax, and CST, the states were levying State Excise Duty, Stamp and Registration Fees, General Sales Tax, Taxes on Vehicles, Entertainment Tax, Tax on Goods and Passengers, Taxes and Duty on Electricity, and Taxes on Purchase of Sugarcane. As per the Department of Economic Affairs of GoI, the total budgeted indirect tax collection in 2015–2016 was ₹1,605,732 crore. Tax collection was growing since 2007–2008 at the rate of 14.6 per cent, and the growth rate of 2015–2016 was 16.2 per cent (Table 13.1).

Revenue from Taxes Subsumed under GST

The Task Force on GST constituted by the Thirteenth Finance Commission calculated RNR for GST. For this purpose, they calculated revenue from those taxes which were to be subsumed under GST. The group had used the FY 2007–2008 as the base year for the calculation of RNR. The breakup of the collections for central government is given in Table 13.2. The sin goods are still subject to dual levy comprising CGST and central excise. The total collection from these central taxes (including collection from petroleum and tobacco products) was ₹233,435 crores in 2007–2008. The collection from non-sin

Table 13.1 Combined Revenue Receipts of the Centre and States *(in Rupees Crore)*

Year	1990–1991	2000–2001	2007–2008	2008–2009	2009–2010	2010–2011	2011–2012	2012–2013	2013–2014	2014–2015 RE	2015–2016 BE
Customs	20,644	47,542	104,119	99,879	83,324	135,813	149,328	165,346	172,085	188,713	208,336
Union Excise Duties	24,514	68,526	123,611	108,613	102,991	137,701	144,901	175,845	169,455	184,731	229,054
Service Tax	–	2,613	51,302	60,941	58,422	71,016	97,509	132,601	154,780	168,132	209,774
State Excise Duty	4,992	15,929	35,738	42,688	50,391	61,698	75,125	86,442	85,557	98,835	114,639
Stamp & Registration Fees	2,128	9,365	36,662	35,108	40,607	54,239	66,826	78,889	80,528	92,272	105,171
General Sales Tax	18,228	72,874	167,731	190,817	231,461	293,256	361,332	422,578	475,131	544,256	622,855
Taxes on Vehicle	1,593	6,528	14,296	15,362	19,532	25,095	29,988	35,445	37,471	42,866	48,531
Entertainment Tax	422	1,204	866	1,086	1,160	1,244	1,920	2,030	2,198	2,245	2,530
Tax on Goods & Passengers	1,100	2,045	6,596	8,313	9,810	11,309	11,681	15,316	19,578	20,537	23,200
Taxes & Duty on Electricity	1,190	4,402	7,233	7,166	12,235	17,422	17,300	22,201	22,485	26,625	28,428
Taxes on Purchase on Sugarcane	88	190	548	729	329	192	269	329	163	167	188
Others	564	2,339	2,787	16,767	13,586	11,858	10,317	10,378	10,745	12,022	13,026
Total Indirect Tax Revenue	75,463	233,557	551,489	587,469	623,849	820,843	966,496	1,147,400	1,230,177	1,381,401	1,605,732

Source: Computed from GoI, *Indian Public Finance Statistics 2015–2016*, p. 4 (https://dea.gov.in/sites/default/files/IPFS%20English%202015-16.pdf)

Table 13.2 *Revenue from Central Taxes Subsumed under GST for 2007–2008*

S. No.	Nature of tax	Non-Sin Goods	POL	Tobacco	Total
1.	CVD	53,510	5199	0	58,709
2.	Union Excise Duties	52,922	60,231	10,272	123,425
3.	Service tax	51,301	0	0	51,301
4.	Total	157,733	65,430	10,272	233,435

Source: Computed from the *Report of Task Force on Goods and Services.*

goods and services was ₹157,733 crores only. Since excise duty is still applicable on sin goods, the Task Force included only non-sin goods and services for the calculation of RNR, and the amount was calculated at ₹157,733 crore.

The breakup of the collection by the state governments is given in Table 13.3. The total collection from EC taxes was ₹118,356 crore in 2007–2008. The amount did not include the collection from petroleum, alcohol and tobacco products. The total collection from TF taxes was ₹188,285 during the same period. The TF taxes also did not include collection from petroleum, alcohol and tobacco products. The group was of the view that all the TF taxes should be subsumed under SGST. Thus, they used ₹188,285 crore for the calculation of RNR.

Table 13.3 *Revenue from State Taxes Subsumed under GST for 2007–2008*

S. No.	Nature of Tax	Non–sin Goods	POL	Tobacco	Alcohol	Total
1.	Stamp Duty	38,473	–	–	–	38,473
2.	Taxes on Vehicles	15,549	–	–	–	15,549
3.	Taxes on Goods and passengers	6,719	–	–	–	6,719
4.	Taxes and Duties on Electricity	9,188	–	–	–	9,188

(continued)

(*continued*)

S. No.	Nature of Tax	Non–sin Goods	POL	Tobacco	Alcohol	Total
5.	Sales Tax/VAT (including CST and Purchase Tax)	110,826	56,442	3000	11,450	181,718
6.	Entertainment Tax	1,062	–	–	–	1,062
7.	Entry Taxes not in lieu of Octroi	3,914	–	–	–	3,914
8.	Other Taxes and Duties	2,554	–	–	–	2,554
9.	Total (Sum of 1–8)	188,285	56,442	3,000	11,450	259,177
10.	TF Taxes (Sum of 1–8)	188,285	–	–	–	–
11.	EC Taxes (Sum of 5–8)	118,356	–	–	–	–

Source: Computed from *Report of Task Force on Goods and Services.*

Projected Tax Revenue

The Task Force calculated the total collection of central and state governments from the taxes which were subsumed under GST as ₹346,018 crore (₹157,733 crore of the central government and ₹188,285 crore of the state governments) for 2007–2008. The central government-projected nominal growth rate of revenue subsumed during the transition period was to be 14 per cent per annum.[1] We have calculated the revenue for 2017–2018, 2018–2019 and 2019–2020 (see Table 13.4) from the taxes which were subsumed under GST on the basis of ₹346,018 crore for 2007–2008.

Post-GST Indirect Tax Collections

GST was introduced from 1 July 2017. The finance minister in his budget speech for 2017–2018 talked about the benefits of GST for the

[1] Press Information Bureau, 'GST Compensation to States'.

Table 13.4 *Projected Total Revenue from Central and States Taxes Subsumed under GST*

S. No.	Year	Taxes Subsumed under GST (in Rupees Crore)		Total Revenue (in Rupees Crore)
		Central	States	
1.	2007–2008	157,733	188,285	346,018
2.	2017–2018	584,751	698,014	1,282,765
3.	2018–2019	666,616	795,736	1,462,352
4.	2019–2020	759,943	907,139	1,667,082

economy such as spurring growth, competitiveness, indirect tax simplification and greater transparency.[2] There is a one-month lag in the collection of GST, for example, the revenue of GST for the month of January would be received in the month of February but, IGST and the cesses on imports are collected in the same month.[3]

The target to collect revenue through GST should have been at least ₹1,282,765 crore or ₹106,897 crore per month for 2017–2018, ₹1,462,352 crore (₹121,863 crore per month) for 2018–2019, and ₹1,667,082 crore (₹138,924 crore per month) for 2019–2020. However, the central government has set a budgetary target of ₹100,000 crore per month as average collection of revenue under GST. Even this reduced target has been achieved only eight times so far.

We may now look at the month-wise GST revenue collection of CGST, SGST, IGST and the cesses since 1 July 2017 in the following sub-headings which may be seen in Tables 13.5, 13.6, 13.7 and 13.8.

GST Revenue for 2017–2018

As GST was introduced with effect from 1 July 2017, the total tax mop-up pertains only for a nine-month period from July 2017 to

[2] GoI, *Budget Speech, 2017–18*, Para 10.

[3] Press Information Bureau, 'GST Revenue Collections'.

Table 13.5 *GST Collection for 2017–2018 (in Rupees Crore)*

		Revenue	
S. No.	*Months*	*Amount*	*Growth (%)*
1.	August	95,633	–
2.	September	94,064	–1.6
3.	October	93,333	–0.8
4.	November	83,780	–10.2
5.	December	84,314	0.6
6.	January	89,825	6.5
7.	February	85,962	–4.3
8.	March	92,167	7.2
Average Collection		89,885	–0.4
Total Collection		719,078	–

Source: Press Information Bureau. 'Revenue from Goods and Services Tax (GST) Touched ₹7.19 Crore', August 3, 2018.

March 2018 for FY 2017–2018. The government did not fix any target for the collection of GST in FY 2017–2018 in the budget for 2017–2018. However, the central government revised the estimates and fixed the amount of ₹444,631 crore for the collection of GST for FY 2017–2018 in the budget of 2018–2019. As per the mid-term budget estimates for 2019–2020, GST collection was ₹442,561 crore in FY 2017–2018.

The total revenue collection was ₹7.19 lakh crore under GST in the first eight months of FY 2017–2018.[4] This comprises of ₹1.19 lakh crore of CGST, ₹1.72 lakh crore of SGST, ₹3.66 lakh crore of IGST including ₹1.73 lakh crore on imports, and ₹62,021 crore of cess including ₹5,702 crore on imports. The average monthly collection of GST was ₹89,885 crore and average growth rate was –0.4 per cent in

[4] August 2017 to March 2018

2017–2018. The average collection was much less than the projected target of ₹121,863 crore.

GST Revenue for 2018–2019

The central government had made a budget provision of ₹743,900 crore for FY 2018–2019.[5] However, GST collections of central government have fallen short of the budget target by ₹100,000 crore. Therefore, the target was revised downward to ₹643,900 crore in the midterm budget review for 2019–2020.

The total collection of GST for 2018–2019 was ₹1,177,369 crore. This comprises ₹2.02 lakh crore of CGST, ₹2.78 lakh crore of SGST, ₹5.98 lakh crore of IGST including collection from imports, and ₹97,369 crore of cesses. The average monthly collection of GST in 2018–2019 has been ₹98,114 crores. The average collection was much less than the projected target of ₹138,924 crore. The government has set a budgetary target of over ₹100,000 crore monthly average collections in FY 2019.[6] Let us see the month-wise revenue collection of CGST, SGST, IGST and cess for 2018–2019 (Table 13.6).

Let us further discuss the month-wise revenue collection of CGST, SGST, IGST and cess in the following sub-headings.

The revenue collection for April 2018 was a landmark, when for the first time the government collected a revenue of ₹100,000 crore. GST collection crossed ₹100,000 crore four times in FY 2018–2019. Finance minister tweeted, 'With the improved economic climate, introduction of e-way bill and improved GST compliance, GST collections would continue to show a positive trend'.[7]

The gross GST revenue collection under different heads was, for the month of: April 2018, ₹103,458[8] crore; May 2018, ₹94,016[9] crore;

[5] Budget for 2018–2019.

[6] ET Online, 'GST Collections Cross ₹1 Lakh'.

[7] ET Online, 'GST Revenue Collection Exceeds ₹1 Lakh Crore'.

[8] Press Information Bureau, 'GST Revenue Collection for April 2018'.

[9] Press Information Bureau, 'GST Revenue Collection for May 2018'.

Table 13.6 GST Collection for 2018–2019 *(in Rupees Crore)*

S. No.	Months	Revenue		CGST		SGST*		IGST*		Cess	
		Amount	Growth	Amount	Growth	Amount	Growth	Amount	Growth	Amount	Growth
1.	April	103,458	12.3	18,652	–	25,704	–	50,548	–	8,554	–
2.	May	94,016	–9.1	15,866	–14.9	21,691	–15.6	49,120	–2.8	7,339	–14.2
3.	Jun	95,610	1.7	15,968	0.6	22,021	1.5	49,498	0.8	8,122	10.7
4.	Jul	96,483	0.9	15,877	–0.6	22,293	1.2	49,951	0.9	8,362	3.0
5.	Aug	93,960	–2.6	15,303	–3.6	21,154	–5.1	49,876	–0.2	7,628	–8.8
6.	Sept	94,442	0.5	15,318	0.1	21,061	–0.4	50,070	0.4	7,993	4.8
7.	Oct	100,710	6.6	16,464	7.5	22,826	8.4	53,419	6.7	8,000	0.1
8.	Nov	97,637	–3.1	16,812	2.1	23,070	1.1	49,726	–6.9	8,031	0.4
9.	Dec	94,726	–3.0	16,442	–2.2	22,459	–2.6	47,936	–3.6	7,888	–1.8
10.	Jan	102,503	8.2	17,763	8.0	24,826	10.5	51,225	6.9	8,690	10.2
11.	Feb	97,247	–5.1	17,626	–0.8	24,192	–2.6	46,953	–8.3	8,476	–2.5
12.	Mar	106,577	9.6	20,353	15.5	27,520	13.8	50,418	7.4	8,286	–2.2
	Average	98,114	1.4	16,870	1.1	23,235	0.9	49,895	0.1	8,114	0.0
	Total	1,177,369	–	202,444	–	278,817	–	598,740	–	97,369	–

Source: Press Information Bureau. 'Revenue from Goods and Services Tax', August 3, 2018.
Note: *Including collection on import

June 2018, ₹95,610[10] crore; July 2018, ₹96,483[11] crore; August 2018, ₹93,960[12] crore; September 2018, ₹94,442[13] crore; October 2018, ₹100,710[14] crore; November 2018, ₹97,636[15] crore; December 2018, ₹94,726[16] crore; January 2019, ₹102,503[17]; February 2019, ₹97,247 crore; and March 2019, ₹106,577 crore.

The CGST collection was: ₹18,652 crore in April 2018; ₹15,866 crore in May; ₹15,968 crore in June; ₹15,877 crore in July; ₹15,303 crore in August; ₹15,318 crore in September; ₹16,464 crore in October; ₹16,812 crore in November; ₹16,442 crore in December 2018; ₹17,763 crore in January 2019; ₹17,626 crore in February 2019; and ₹20,353 crore in March 2019.

The total SGST collection was: ₹25,704 crore in April 2018; ₹21,651 crore in May; ₹22.021 crore in June; ₹22,293 crore in July; ₹21,154 crore in August; ₹21,061 crore in September; ₹22,826 crore in October; ₹23,070 crore in November; ₹22,459 crore in December 2018; ₹24,826 crore in January 2019; ₹24,192 crore in February 2019; and ₹27,520 crore in March 2019.

The total IGST collection was: ₹50,548 crore (including ₹21,246 crore collected from imports) in April 2018; ₹49,120 crore (including ₹24,447 crore from imports) in May; ₹49,498 crore (including ₹24,493 crore collected from imports) in June; ₹49,951 crore (including ₹24,852 crore collected on imports) in July; ₹49,876 crore

---

[10] Press Information Bureau Press Release, dated 1 July 2018

[11] Press Information Bureau, 'GST Revenue Collection for July 2018'.

[12] Press Information Bureau, 'GST Revenue Collection for August 2018'.

[13] Press Information Bureau, 'GST Revenue Collection for September 2018'.

[14] Press Information Bureau, 'GST Revenue Collection for the Month of October 2018'.

[15] Press Information Bureau, 'GST Revenue Collection for the Month of November 2018'.

[16] Press Information Bureau, 'GST Revenue Collection for the Month of December 2018'.

[17] Press Information Bureau, 'GST Revenue Collection for the Month of January 2019'.

(including ₹26,512 crore collected on imports) in August; ₹50,070 crore (including ₹25,308 crore collected on imports) in September; ₹53,419 crore (including ₹26,908 crore collected on imports) in October; ₹49,726 crore (including ₹24,133 crore collected on imports) in November; ₹47,936 crore (including ₹23,635 crore collected on imports) in December 2018; ₹51,225 crore (including ₹24,065 crore collected on imports) in January 2019; ₹46,953 crore (including ₹21,384 crore collected on imports) in February 2019; and ₹50,418 crore (including ₹23,521 crore collected on imports) in March 2019.

The total compensation cess was: ₹8,554 crore (including ₹702 crore from imports) in April 2018; ₹7,339 crore (including ₹854 crore from imports) in May 2018; ₹8,122 crore (including ₹773 crore from imports) in June 2018; ₹8,362 crore (including ₹794 crore collected on imports) in July 2018; ₹7,628 crore (including ₹849 crore collected on imports) in August 2018; ₹7,993 crore (including ₹769 crore collected on imports) in September 2018; ₹8,000 crore (including ₹955 crore collected on imports) in October 2018; ₹8,031 crore (including ₹842 crore collected on imports) in November 2018; ₹7,888 crore (including ₹838 crore from imports) in December 2018; ₹8,690 crore (including ₹902 crore from imports) in January 2019; ₹8,476 crore (including ₹910 crore from imports) in February 2019; and ₹8,286 crore (including ₹891 crore from imports) in March 2019.

The extraordinary growth achiever states in total tax collection in October 2018 were Kerala with 44 per cent, Jharkhand with 20 per cent, Rajasthan with 14 per cent, Uttarakhand with 13 per cent and Maharashtra with 11 per cent.

The total revenue collection was ₹11.77 lakh crore under GST in FY 2018–2019. This comprises ₹2.02 lakh crore of CGST, ₹2.78 lakh crore of SGST, ₹5.98 lakh crore of IGST, including ₹2.90 lakh crore on imports, and ₹55,998 crore of cess including ₹10,079 crore on imports. The average monthly collection of GST was ₹98,114 crore and average growth rate was –0.3%. The average revenue collection was much less than the projected target of ₹121,863 crore.

GST Revenue for 2019–2020

The government announced in Parliament that the country had undertaken path-breaking reforms by introducing GST.[18] The government has budgeted estimate of ₹761,200 crore for the collection of GST in the budget for 2019–2020 for the FY 2019–2020. It is about 18.2 per cent higher than the revised estimate of ₹643,900 crore for 2018–2019.[19] However, the new finance minister, Nirmala Sitharaman, revised budget estimates to ₹663,343 crores in her maiden budget speech for 2019–2020. In FY 2019–2020 also GST collection crossed ₹100,000 crore four times. Let us see the month-wise revenue collection of CGST, SGST, IGST and cess for 2019–2020 in Table 13.7.

Let us discuss the month-wise revenue collection of CGST, SGST, IGST and cess in the following sub-headings.

The gross GST revenue collection under different heads was, for the month of: April 2019, ₹113,865[20] crore; May 2019, ₹100,289[21] crore, June 2019, ₹99,939[22] crore; July 2019, ₹102,083[23] crore; August 2019, ₹98,202[24] crore; September 2019, ₹91,916[25] crore; October 2019, ₹95,380[26] crore; and November 2019, ₹103,492[27] crore.

[18] GoI, *Budget Speech, 2019–20*, Para 10.

[19] https://www.ndtv.com/business/gst-collection-jan-2019-gst-collection-amount-at-1-02-lakh-crore-rupees-in-january-gst-igst-sgst-1987596

[20] Press Information Bureau, 'GST Revenue collection for April, 2019 recorded highest collection since GST implementation', May 1, 2019.

[21] Press Information Bureau, GST Revenue collection for May, 2019, June 1, 2019.

[22] Press Information Bureau, GST Revenue collection for the month of June, 2019 stands at ₹99,939 crore, July 1, 2019.

[23] Press Information Bureau, GST Revenue collection for July, 2019? 1,02,083 crore total gross GST revenue collected in July, August 1, 2019.

[24] Press Information Bureau, GST Revenue collection for August, 2019, September 1, 2019.

[25] Press Information Bureau, GST Revenue collection for September, 2019, 2019, October 1, 2019.

[26] Press Information Bureau, ₹95,380 crore gross GST Revenue collected in October, November 1, 2019.

[27] Press Information Bureau, GST Revenue collection for November, 2019, December 1, 2019.

Table 13.7 GST Collection for 2019–2020 (in Rupees Crore)

S. No.	Months	Revenue		CGST		SGST*		IGST*		Cess	
		Amount	Growth	Amount	Growth	Amount	Growth	Amount	Growth	Amount	Growth
1.	April	113,865	6.8	21,163	4.0	28,801	4.7	54,733	8.6	9,168	10.6
2.	May	100,289	−11.9	17,811	−15.8	24,462	−15.1	49,891	−8.8	8,125	−11.4
3.	June	99,939	−0.3	18,366	3.1	25,343	3.6	47,772	−4.2	8,457	4.1
4.	July	102,083	2.1	17,912	−2.5	25,008	−1.3	50,612	5.9	8,551	1.1
5.	August	98,202	−3.8	17,733	−1.0	24,239	−3.1	48,958	−3.3	7,273	−14.9
6.	September	91,916	−6.4	16,630	−6.2	22,598	−6.8	45,069	−7.9	7,620	4.8
7.	October	95,380	3.8	17,582	5.7	23,674	4.8	46,517	3.2	7,607	−0.2
8.	November	103,492	8.5	19,592	11.4	27,144	14.7	49,028	5.4	7,727	1.6
	Average	100,645.8	−1.4	18,171.0	−1.8	24,875.0	−1.9	49,078.9	−0.9	8,114.4	−0.8
	Total	805,166	–	146,789	–	201,269	–	392,580	–	56,801	–

Source: Press Information Bureau. 'Revenue from Goods and Services Tax', August 3, 2018.
Note: *Including collection on import

The CGST collection was: ₹21,163 crore in April 2019; ₹17,811 crore in May 2019; ₹18366 crore in June 2019; ₹17,912 crore in July 2019; ₹98,202 crore in August 2019; ₹16,630 crore in September 2019; ₹17,582 crore in October 2019; and ₹19,592 crore in November 2019.

The total SGST collection was: ₹28,801 crore in April 2019; ₹24,462 crore in May 2019; ₹25,343 crore in June 2019; ₹25,008 crore in July 2019; ₹24,239 crore in August 2019; ₹22,598 crore in September 2019; ₹23,674 crore in October 2019; and ₹27,144 crore in November 2019.

The total IGST collection was: ₹54,733 crore (including IGST from imports in September 2017 of ₹23,289 crore) in April 2019; ₹49,891 crore (including ₹24,875 crore from imports) in May 2019; ₹47,772 crore (including IGST from imports in September 2017 of ₹21,980 crore); ₹50,612 crore (including ₹24,246 crore collected on imports) in July 2019; ₹48,958 crore (including ₹24,818 crore collected on imports) in August 2019; ₹45,069 crore (including ₹22,097 crore collected on imports) in September 2019; ₹46,517 crore (including ₹21,446 crore collected on imports) in October 2019; and ₹49,028 crore (including ₹20,948 crore collected on imports) in November 2019.

The total compensation cess was: ₹9,168 crore (including ₹1,053 crore from imports) in April 2019; ₹8,125 crore (including ₹953 crore from imports) in May 2019; ₹8,457 crore (including ₹876 crore from imports) in June 2019; ₹8,551 crore (including ₹797 crore collected on imports) in July 2019; ₹7,273 crore (including ₹841 crore collected on imports) in August 2019; ₹7,620 crore (including ₹728 crore collected on imports) in September 2019; ₹7,607 crore (including ₹774 crore collected on imports) in October 2019; and ₹7,727 crore (including ₹869 crore collected on imports) in November 2019.

The total revenue collection is ₹8.05 lakh crore under GST in FY 2019–2020 up to November 2019. This comprises ₹1.46 lakh crore of CGST, ₹2.01 lakh crore of SGST, ₹3.92 lakh crore of IGST and ₹56,801 crore of cess. The average monthly collection of GST was ₹100,645 crore and average growth rate was –1.4 per cent.

Budget Estimate versus Revised Estimate versus Actual Revenue

Let us see the budget estimate, revised estimate and actual GST revenue in Table 13.8.

Table 13.8 clearly depicts that the CGST revenue was short of the revised estimates in 2018–2019. It was also short of the budget estimates for 2018–2019. The CGST revenue did not meet the target even of RE and fell short by ₹100,000 as compared to the original BE of CGST.

Settlement of IGST Funds

IGST is being levied on inter-state supplies of goods and services. It is applicable in both the cases of import into India and export from India. The exports would be zero rated under IGST. IGST shall be collected and levied by GoI and such tax shall be apportioned between union and states. The government maintains the data of IGST collected and apportioned. The collection of IGST is being transferred to CGST and SGST. Table 13.8 reflects the data of the settlement of IGST between centre and states. The revenue earned by the central government and the state governments after settlement may be seen in Table 13.9.

Settlement of IGST Funds for 2017–2018

Revenue earned from IGST is being apportioned among union and states by Parliament on the basis of the recommendation of GST Council. The government settled ₹10,348 crore to CGST and ₹14,488 crore to SGST from IGST during the month of December 2017. The government further settled ₹11,327 crore to CGST and ₹13,479 crore to SGST from IGST during the month of January 2018 (see Table 13.10).

Settlement of IGST Funds for 2018–2019

The total revenue earned by union and state governments after settlement in the month of April 2018 was ₹32,493 crore for CGST and ₹40,257 for SGST.[28]

[28] Press Information Bureau, 'GST Revenue Collection for April 2018'.

Table 13.8 GST: Budget Estimate, Revised Estimates and Actual Receipts (in Rupees Crore)

Year	Budget Estimates (BE)			Revised Estimates (RE)			Actual GST		
	CGST	IGST	Cess	CGST	IGST	Cess	CGST	IGST	Cess
2017–2018		No BE		221,400	161,900	61,331	203,261	176,688*	62,612
2018-19	603,900	50,000	90,000	503,900	50,000	90,000	457,535#	28,947#	95,081#
2019-20	526,000	28,000	109,343	–	–	–	–	–	–

Source: GoI, CAG Report No. 11 of 2019 (Indirect Taxes—Goods and Services Tax), 26.

Notes: *₹67,998 crore assigned to the States and balance ₹108,690 crore retained by the centre.

#March 2019 provisional figures as available on CGA website.

Table 13.9 *Transfer of Funds (in Rupees Crore)*

S. No.	Months	Total	IGST CGST	SGST
		2017–2018		
1.	December	24,836	10,348	14,488
2.	January	24,806	11,327	13,479
		2018–2019		
3.	October	32,597	17,490	15,107
4.	November	33,966	18,262	15,704
5.	December	33,202	18,409	14,793
6.	January	33,011	18,344	14,667
7.	February	35,217	19,470	15,747
8.	March	30,950	17,261	13,689
		2019–2020		
9.	April	36,345	20,370	15,975
10.	May	32,536	18,098	14,438
11.	June	31,782	18,169	13,613
12..	July	NA	NA	NA
13.	August	39,788	23,165	16,623
14.	September	36,252	21,131	15,121
15.	October	34,613	20,642	13,971
16.	November	42,581	25,150	17,431

Source: Authors.

Table 13.10 *Total Revenue of Central and State Governments after Transfer of Funds (in Rupees Crore)*

S. No.	Months	Total Earnings	Central Government	State Governments
		2018–2019		
1.	April	72,750	32,493	40,257
2.	May	62,817	28,797	34,020
3.	June	68,328	31,645	36,683
4.	July	–	–	–

S. No.	Months	Total Earnings	Central Government	State Governments
5.	August	78,099	36,963	41,136
6.	September	65,589	30,574	35,015
7.	October	101,888	48,954	52,934
8.	November	73,847	35,073	38,774
9.	December	90,103	43,851	46,252
10.	January	75,610	36,107	39,503
11.	February	77,034	37,095	39,939
12.	March	98,823	47,614	51,209
		2019–2020		
1.	April	98,309	47,533	50,776
2.	May	74,809	35,909	38,900
3.	June	75,491	36,535	38,956
4.	July	NA	NA	NA
5.	August	81,760	40,898	40,862
6.	September	75,480	37,761	37,719
7.	October	75,869	38,224	37,645
8.	November	89,318	44,742	44,576

Source: Government of India, Press Information Bureau, Ministry of Finance.

The total revenue earned by the union and state governments after regular settlement in the month of May 2018 was ₹28,797 crore for CGST and ₹34,020 for SGST.

The total revenue earned by union and state governments after regular settlement in the month of June 2018 was ₹31,645 crore for CGST and ₹36,683 for SGST. The government had done an additional provisional settlement of ₹50,000 crore between the union and states. This settlement was in addition to the earlier provisional settlement of ₹35,000 crore in February 2018.

The total revenue earned by the union and state governments after the settlement including provisional settlement of ₹12,000 crore in the month of August 2018 was ₹36,963 crore for CGST and ₹41,163 for SGST.

The total revenue earned by the union and state governments after the settlement in the month of September 2018 was ₹30,574 crore for CGST and ₹35,015 for SGST.

The government also settled ₹17,490 crore to CGST and ₹15,107 crore to SGST from IGST during the month of October 2018. Further, a sum of ₹30,000 crore had been settled from the balance of IGST on provisional basis in the ratio of 50:50 between union and states. Therefore, the total revenue earned by union and state governments after regular settlement in the month of October 2018 is ₹48,954 crore for CGST and ₹52,934 for SGST.

The government settled ₹18,262 crore to CGST and ₹15,704 crore to SGST from IGST during the month of November 2018. Therefore, the total revenue earned by the union and state governments after regular settlement in the month of November 2018 was ₹35,073 crore for CGST and ₹38,774 for SGST.

The government settled ₹18,409 crore to CGST and ₹14,793 crore to SGST from IGST during the month of December 2018. Further, a sum of ₹18,000 crore had been settled from the balance of IGST on provisional basis in the ratio of 50:50 between union and states. Therefore, the total revenue earned by the union and state governments after regular settlement in the month of December 2018 is ₹43,851 crore for CGST and ₹46,252 for SGST.

The government also settled ₹18,344 crore to CGST and ₹14,677 crore to SGST from IGST during the month of January 2019. Therefore, the total revenue earned by the union and state governments after regular settlement in the month of January 2019 was ₹36,107 crore for CGST and ₹39,503 for SGST.

The government also settled ₹19,470 crore to CGST and ₹15,747 crore to SGST from IGST during the month of February 2019. Therefore, the total revenue earned by union and state governments after regular settlement in the month of February 2019 was ₹37,095 crore for CGST and ₹39,939 for SGST.

The government also settled ₹17,261 crore to CGST and ₹13,689 crore to SGST from IGST during the month of March 2019. Further, a sum of ₹20,000 crore had been settled from the balance of IGST on provisional basis in the ratio of 50:50 between union and states. Therefore, the total revenue earned by union and state governments after regular settlement in the month of March 2019 was ₹47,614 crore for CGST and ₹51,209 crore for SGST.

Settlement of IGST Funds for 2019–2020

The total revenue earned by the union and state governments after a settlement in the month of April 2019 was ₹20,370 crore for CGST and ₹15,975 for SGST. Further, a sum of ₹12,000 crore had been settled from the balance of IGST on provisional basis in the ratio of 50:50 between union and states. Therefore, the total revenue earned by the union and state governments after regular settlement in the month of April 2019 was ₹47,533 crore for CGST and ₹50,776 crore for SGST.

The total revenue earned by the union and state governments after regular settlement in the month of May 2019 was ₹18,098 crore for CGST and ₹14,438 for SGST. Therefore, the total revenue earned by the union and state governments after regular settlement in the month of May 2019 was ₹35,909 crore for CGST and ₹38,900 crore for SGST.

The government had settled ₹18,169 crore to CGST and ₹13,613 crore to SGST from IGST as regular settlement. The total revenue earned by the union and state governments after regular settlement in the month of June 2019 was ₹36,535 crore for CGST and ₹38,956 crore for SGST.

The government had settled ₹23,165 crore to CGST and ₹16,623 crore to SGST from IGST as regular settlement. The total revenue earned by the union and state governments after regular settlement in the month of August 2019 was ₹40,898 crore for CGST and ₹40,862 crore for SGST.

The government has settled ₹21,131 crore to CGST and ₹15,121 crore to SGST from IGST as regular settlement. The total revenue earned by the union and the state governments after regular settlement in the month of September 2019 was ₹37,761 crore for CGST and ₹37,719 crore for SGST.

The government had settled ₹20,642 crore to CGST and ₹13,971 crore to SGST from IGST as regular settlement. The total revenue earned by the union and state governments after regular settlement in the month of October 2019 was ₹38,224 crore for CGST and ₹37,645 crore for SGST.

The government has settled ₹25,150 crore to CGST and ₹17,431 crore to SGST from IGST as regular settlement. The total revenue earned by the union and state governments after regular settlement in the month of November 2019 was ₹44,742 crore for CGST and ₹44,576 crore for SGST.

Compensation to State

There is a provision of compensation to states in Section 7 of GST (Compensation to States) Act, 2017. The provision says that the loss of revenue arising on account of implementation of GST regime and compensation for the loss of revenue to states shall be provisionally calculated and released at the end of every two months for five years. The provision of compensation to states is to ensure that the revenue of states is protected at the level of 14 per cent over the base year, that is, tax collection in 2015–2016. Under GST, a cess is being levied on luxury demerit and sin goods to compensate revenue loss of states due to implementation of GST. The aim of GST compensation is to ensure that states do not face sudden fiscal problem due to the introduction of GST. The central government releases compensation to state governments on bimonthly basis. The amount of the release of compensation for the period of July 2017 to March 2018 and April 2018 to March 2019 may be seen in Tables 13.10 and 13.11.

GST Compensation for 2017–2018

The revenue gap of the states moved downward in the last eight months of FY 2017–2018. The average revenue gap of all states for last year was 17 per cent. To bridge the gap, central government released ₹48,178 crores as total GST compensation to the states for the FY 2017–2018. State-wise compensation of the months of July–August, September–October, November–December, January–February, and

March for 2017–2018 may be seen in Table 13.9. As per Table 13.11, Karnataka got maximum compensation from the centre at ₹7,535 crore, followed by Punjab at ₹4,618 crore, Gujarat at ₹4,277 crore, Bihar ₹3,140 crore, and Maharashtra ₹3,077 crore.

The central government released a total of ₹10,805 crore as compensation to the states for the month of July–August 2017, ₹13,694 crore for September–October 2017, ₹3,898 crore for November–December 2017, ₹13,085 crore for the month of January–February 2018 and ₹6,696 crore for compensation to the states for the month of March 2018 on 29 May 2018 (Table 13.10).

Table 13.11 Details of GST Compensation Released to States/UTs for FY 2017–2018 (in Rupees Crore)

S. No.	State/UT	GST Compensation					
		July–Aug 2017	Sep–Oct 2017	Nov–Dec 2017	Jan–Feb 2018	March 2018	Total
1.	Andhra Pradesh	116	266	0	0	0	382
2.	Arunachal Pradesh	15	0	0	0	0	15
3.	Assam	338	331	15	202	94	980
4.	Bihar	692	1,054	373	922	99	3,140
5.	Chhattisgarh	253	562	219	449	106	1,589
6.	Delhi	115	42	0	0	169	326
7.	Goa	68	35	99	50	29	281
8.	Gujarat	1,402	880	252	1,153	590	4,277
9.	Haryana	476	325	0	398	262	1,461
10.	Himachal Pradesh	0	0	539	336	184	1,059
11.	Jammu and Kashmir	367	314	127	329	23	1,160
12.	Jharkhand	313	489	94	369	103	1,368
13.	Karnataka	1,189	2,082	859	2,116	1,289	7,535
14.	Kerala	810	395	0	567	330	2,102
15.	Madhya Pradesh	433	908	0	1170	157	2,668
16.	Maharashtra	0	834	0	654	1,589	3,077
17.	Manipur	24	0	0	0	0	24
18.	Meghalaya	52	38	20	14	16	140

(continued)

(continued)

S. No.	State/UT	GST Compensation					
		July–Aug 2017	Sep–Oct 2017	Nov–Dec 2017	Jan–Feb 2018	March 2018	Total
19.	Mizoram	0	0	0	0	0	0
20.	Nagaland	0	0	0	0	0	0
21.	Odisha	333	687	306	693	245	2,264
22.	Puducherry	44	122	58	109	52	385
23.	Punjab	1,138	960	740	1,199	581	4,618
24.	Rajasthan	1,205	706	0	687	301	2,899
25.	Sikkim	0	0	0	6	0	6
26.	Tamil Nadu	530	102	0	0	0	632
27.	Telangana	7	162	0	0	0	169
28.	Tripura	31	43	14	41	20	149
29.	Uttar Pradesh	190	1,330	0	604	308	2,432
30.	Uttarakhand	223	460	183	417	149	1,432
31.	West Bengal	441	567	0	600	0	1,608
Total		**10,805**	**13,694**	**3,898**	**13,085**	**6,696**	**48,178**

Source: Government of India, Press Information Bureau, 'GST Compensation to States', 10 August 2018.

GST Compensation for 2018–2019

The central government released ₹48,202 crores until November 2018 for GST compensation to the states for the FY 2018–2019. The state-wise compensation from 1 April 2018 to 31 March 2019 may be seen in Table 13.12.

The central government released a total of ₹3,899 crore for compensation to the states in July 2018 for April–May 2018 (Table 13.12), ₹14,930 crore in August 2018 for June–July 2018, ₹11,922 crore in November 2018 for August–September 2018, ₹17,451 crore for October–November 2018 and ₹18,934 crore for February–March 2019.

Table 13.12 *GST Compensation to States/UTs for FY 2018–2019 (in Rupees Crore)*

S. No.	Name of State/UT	Compensation for April–May
1.	Andhra Pradesh	0
2.	Arunachal Pradesh	0
3.	Assam	0
4.	Bihar	325
5.	Chhattisgarh	257
6.	Delhi	0
7.	Goa	28
8.	Gujarat	174
9.	Haryana	0
10.	Himachal Pradesh	225
11.	Jammu and Kashmir	147
12.	Jharkhand	76
13.	Karnataka	792
14.	Kerala	67
15.	Madhya Pradesh	130
16.	Maharashtra	0
17.	Manipur	0
18.	Meghalaya	0
19.	Mizoram	0
20.	Nagaland	0
21.	Odisha	282
22.	Puducherry	79
23.	Punjab	944
24.	Rajasthan	106
25.	Sikkim	0
26.	Tamil Nadu	0
27.	Telangana	0
28.	Tripura	2
29.	Uttar Pradesh	0
30.	Uttarakhand	265
31.	West Bengal	0
Total		**3,899**

Source: Government of India, Press Information Bureau, 'GST Compensation to States', 10 August 2018.

GST Compensation for 2019–2020

The central government has released ₹17,789 crores[29] to the states as GST compensation for the months of April–May 2019, ₹27,955 crore for the months of June–July 2019 and ₹35,298[30] crore for the months of August–September 2019.

Almost two years have passed since the GST regime came into existence. An analysis of GST collections published in the *Economic Times* would show that as yet only three states—Mizoram, Manipur and Arunachal Pradesh—have collected surplus GST against the average monthly revenue they should have earned.[31] Thus they have ensured that the centre does not have to compensate them for any loss. On the other hand, six states—Bihar, Punjab, Himachal Pradesh, Jammu and Kashmir, Uttarakhand and Puducherry—have a deficit of up to 43 per cent. The average GST revenue of the country during August 2017–June 2018 had shown a shortfall of 13 per cent.

[29] Press Information Bureau, GST Revenue collection for July, 2019 ₹1,02,083 crore total gross GST revenue collected in July, August 1, 2019.

[30] FE Bureau, Under Fire, Centre releases ₹35298 crore to States, Financial Express, December 17, 2019, 2.

[31] Sidhartha, 'State, Union Territories have up to 43%'.

Table 13A.1 *Net GST Collection for FY 2017–2018*

Month	CGST				IGST				Comp. Cess			Total Net
	Gross	Refund	Settlement (+)	Net	Gross	Refund	Settlement (−)	Net	Gross	Refund	Net	
July	10	–	–	10	20,958	–	–	20,958	593	–	593	21,561
August	15,252	–	3,297	18,549	49,968	–	10,978	38,990	7,156	–	7,156	64,695
September	15,131	–	5,081	20,212	48,930	–	15,933	32,997	8,024	–	8,024	61,233
October	14,962	–	7,855	22,817	47,995	76	21,144	26,775	8,032	–	8,032	57,624
November	13,690	–	10,145	23,836	42,694	48	24,027	18,619	7,103	–	7,103	49,557
December	13,928	86	10,348	24,190	42,765	805	24,835	17,125	7,922	23	7,898	49,213
January	14,874	287	8,583	23,170	45,338	2,247	23,651	19,441	8,070	21	8,049	50,660
February	14,763	511	28,827	43,079	42,382	2,325	59,806	−19,749	8,196	23	8,172	31,502
March	16,266	1,015	12,140	27,390	46,326	7,294	25,564	13,468	7,520	42	7,478	48,336
Total	118,876	1,899	86,275	203,253	387,356	12,794	205,938	168,623	62,614	109	62,505	–

Source: http://pib.nic.in/PressReleseDetail.aspx?PRID=1541584

Table 13A.2 *Net GST Collection for FY 2018–2019*

Month	CGST				IGST				Comp. Cess			Total Net
	Gross	Refund	Settlement (+)	Net	Gross	Refund	Settlement (−)	Net	Gross	Refund	Net	
April	18,653	392	13,841	32,102	50,548	1,852	28,395	20,301	8,554	16	8538	60,942
May	15,866	681	12,931	28,116	49,120	5,800	25,261	18,060	7339	75	7265	53,440
June (FF)	15,968	593	15,676	31,052	49,498	9,223	30,338	9,937	8,122	105	8,017	49,005
Total	50,487	1,666	42,448	91,270	149,166	16,875	83,993	48,298	24,015	195	23,820	163,388

Source: http://pib.nic.in/PressReleseDetail.aspx?PRID=1541584

Return Filing in the GST Era

Return is a document that contains details of income of a taxpayer. The taxpayers file return with the tax administration authorities. The return includes purchase, sales, output GST (on sales) and ITC (GST paid on purchases). It permits taxpayers to calculate tax liability, schedule the payment of tax, ITC and refund request for over payment of taxes. It may be monthly, quarterly and/or annual. GST compliant sales and purchase invoices are required to file GSTR. The provisions regarding returns are given under Section 37–48 in the Chapter 9 of the CGST Act, 2017.

The taxpayers registered under GST and having aggregate turnover up to ₹1.5 crore in preceding FY will file GSTR 1 on a quarterly basis. The registered taxpayers who have aggregate turnover of more than ₹1.5 crore will file GSTR 1 on a monthly basis. The filing of GSTR 2 and GSTR 3 has been suspended for all normal taxpayers irrespective of turnover until further order in this regard.

The small businesses were struggling with process of filing return in the initial stage of the introduction of GST. The GST Council approved a new return format and associated changes in legislation for small businesses in the 28th meeting of Council held on 21 July 2018 at New Delhi. As per the approval, taxpayers having turnover up to ₹5 crore in the previous FY would have the facility to file quarterly return with monthly tax payment on self-deceleration basis. The Council has designed a simplified returns process—Sahaj and Sugam—for such taxpayers. Those taxpayers who have no purchases, no output tax liability and no ITC to avail in any quarter of the FY shall file one nil return for the entire quarter.[1]

[1] Press Information Bureau, Filings of GST Returns, August 10, 2018.

How to File Return

There is a common tax return for both taxes. All the taxpayers are required to file returns online. The return process under GST includes e-filing of returns, uploading of invoice information, auto-population of information of ITC from the returns of supplier to the recipient, matching of invoice information and auto-reversal of ITC, if it mismatches. The copy of return would be given to central authority and relevant state authority. The following three methods are available for filing return under GST.

GSTN Portal

GSTN portal is first method available to taxpayers to file return under GST. This method is useful for those taxpayers who have limited number of entries. They can directly enter the details on the GSTN portal. The taxpayers shall login to the GSTN portal using their user ID and password. The login will navigate to the return dashboard page where they can click on prepare online tab available on GSTR 1 tile to prepare their return. See the following box to know the process to file GSTR 3B step by step.

Process to file GSTR 3B

- Go to the GSTN portal
- Click on Services, select Returns from drop down and click on Returns Dashboard
- Then, select the FY and the filing period (which is September in this case)
- Click on prepare online button
- Enter values, including late fees and interest
- Click on 'Save GSTR 3B' button on the bottom of the page
- Click 'Submit'
- Scroll down and click 'Payment of Tax' button
- After checking details, click on 'Check Balance' button

- Click 'Ok' and provide details of available credit to offset liabilities
- After that, select 'GSTR 3B with DSC' or 'File GSTR 3B with EVC'
- Click Proceed
- Click OK filing success message

Source: The Financial Express, 24 October 2018.

Offline Utilities Provided by GSTN

An offline tool is also available for return file. The taxpayer can download the tool from the website of GST Council and install it in their computer. The return can be filed through installed tool in offline mode using excel without any Internet connection. The main features of offline tool are as follows:

1. The taxpayer can fill in invoices up to 19,000 line items
2. The taxpayer can upload their invoices in form GSTR 1, more than once, at any time during the day, week or month
3. The invoices uploaded by taxpayers in form GSTR 1 will be auto populated in GSTR 2A of the receiver and also will be available for view to the receiver
4. If invoices are more than 500, it will not be available for viewing online to taxpayers. But, taxpayers can download it and later on upload after edit.

GST Suvidha Providers (GSPs)

Taxpayers having very large number of invoices can directly furnish details of Form GSTR 1 to GST system using their accounting applications if they use the services of the GSPs to connect to the GST system through a secured MPLS network connectivity. If any taxpayer is already taking the services of ERP (e.g., SAP, tally and oracle), there will be a high likelihood that these ERP service providers would provide inbuilt services in the existing ERP system.

Types of Return

There are 14 types of tax returns, ranging from GSTR 1 to GSTR 11. But a taxpayer is not required to file all types of returns (see Table 14.1). The taxpayers are supposed to file return form GSTR 3B and pay tax on monthly basis. The registered business concerns are required to file GSTR based on the activities they undertake. A regular taxpayer is required to file monthly returns and one annual return. A separate return is required to be filed for non-resident taxpayers, the taxpayer registered under composition scheme, registered as an input service distributor, a person granted unique identification number, and a person liable to deduction/collection of the tax (Tax Deducted at Source [TDS]/TCS).

However, government has issued various notifications from time to time to solve the problems of return file (if any) under GST. On account of that, the date of filing returns may vary from the standard dates as given in Table 14.1. Table 14.2 depicts the calendar return as per the notifications issued by the government up to 29 December 2017.

Interlinkages between GSTR 1, GSTR 2 and GSTR 3

The beauty of return filing system under GST is that taxpayer has to file GSTR 1 via GSTN Easy upload tools provided by GSTN GSPs. GSTR 2 auto-populates from GSTR 1 filed by a taxpayer's suppliers. Taxpayer's GSTR 3 is auto populated from GSTR 1 to GSTR 2.

Revision of Returns: The process of filing revised return for any correction of errors or omission has been done away with. The taxpayers can rectify the errors or omissions in their return for subsequent months. However, taxpayers are not allowed to make any rectification after furnishing the return for the month of September following the end of FY to which such details pertain or furnishing of the relevant annual return, whichever is earlier.

Penalty for Non-Filing of Return: The taxpayers who do not file return within the due dates shall have to pay a late fee of ₹200 (₹100 for CGST and ₹100 for SGST) per day up to a maximum of ₹5,000 from the due date to the date when the returns are actually filed.

Table 14.1 *Returns in GST*

S. No.	Return	Description	Who Files	Interval	Due Date
1.	GSTR 1	It is a statement of outward supplies of goods and services.	Normal registered person	Monthly	10th of next month
2.	GSTR 2	It is a statement of inward supplies of goods and services.	Normal registered person	Monthly	15th of next month
3.	GSTR 3	It is a return for normal taxpayers	Normal registered person	Monthly	20th of next month
4.	GSTR 3B	Simple Monthly Return for the period Jul 2017–March 2018	Normal registered person	Monthly	20th of next month
5.	GSTR 4	It is a quarterly return	Taxable person opting for composition levy	Quarterly	18th of the month succeeding the quarter
6.	GSTR 5	It is a monthly return for a non-resident taxpayer	Non-resident taxpayer	Monthly	20th of the month succeeding tax period and within seven days after expiry of registration
7.	GSTR 5A	It is a monthly return for a person supplying OIDAR services from a place outside India to a non–taxable online recent.	Supplier of OIDAR services	Monthly	20th of next month
8.	GSTR 6	It is a monthly return for an input service distributor (ISD)	ISD	Monthly	13th of next month

(continued)

(continued)

S. No.	Return	Description	Who Files	Interval	Due Date
9.	GSTR 7	It is a monthly return for authorities deducting tax at source (TDS)	Tax dedicators	Monthly	10th of next month
10.	GSTR 8	It is a monthly return for e-commerce operators depicting supplies effecting through it	E-commerce operators	Monthly	10th of next month
11.	GSTR 9	It is an annual return	Normal registered person	Annually	31st December of next FY
12.	GSTR 9A	It is a simplified annual return under composition scheme	Taxpayers opting composition scheme	Annually	31st December of next FY
13.	GSTR 10	It is a final return	Those taxable persons whose registration has been either cancelled or surrendered	–	Within three months of the cancellation date or order cancellation date whichever is later
14.	GSTR 11	It is for a person having UIN to furnish details of inward supplies.	Taxpayers opting composition scheme	–	31st December of next FY

Source: Computed by authors from GST Council website.

Table 14.2 *Calendar of Return Filing*

S. No.	Return	Description	Interval	Due date
1.	GSTR 3B	It is for all taxpayers to file along with payment of tax	Every month until March 2018	20th of the succeeding month
2.	GSTR 1	It is for those taxpayers whose annual aggregate turnover is up to ₹1.5 crore to file return on quarterly basis.	July–Sep 2017	10 January 2018
			October–Dec 2017	15 February 2018
			Jan–Mar 2018	30 April 2018
		It is for those taxpayers whose annual aggregate turnover is more than ₹1.5 crore to file return on monthly basis.	July–October 2017	10 January 2018
			November 2017	10 January 2018
			Dec 2017	10 January 2018
			Jan 2018	10 January 2018
			Feb 2018	10 January 2018
			March 2018	10 January 2018
3.	GSTR 4	It is for those taxpayers who have opted for composition scheme to file every quarter.	Jul–Sep 2017	24 December 2017
4.	GSTR 5	It is for non–resident taxable persons to file return every month.	July–Dec 2017	31 January 2018
5.	GSTR 5A	It is for those taxpayers who supply OIDAR services from a place outside India to a non–taxable online recipient.	July–Dec 2017	31 January 2018
6.	GSTR 6	It is for input service provider.	July 2017	31 January 2018

Source: Computed by the authors from GST Council website.

Registration: The total number of taxpayers under GST is 13,883,971 and 176,077 taxpayers have opted for composition scheme.[2] In the FY 2017–2018 and 2018–2019, there was a progressive improvement in the compliance level.

Return Filing Experience

Table 14:3 depicts the percentage of returns that took place on due dates and the cumulative level of compliance for 2017–2018.

As per Table 14.3, the compliance level until due date has steadily increased. It has increased from around 57.69 per cent to 62.63 per cent. It is an average of 57.94 per cent. Table 14.4 depicts that the cumulative compliance levels for initial months has reached about 90 per cent. However, state-wise compliance level is varying until due date.

Table 14.3 *Monthly Return Filing during 2017–2018*

S. No.	Return Period	Required to File	Till Due Date		Cumulative (until now)	
			Returns	Percentage	Returns	Percentage
1.	July	6,647,581	3,834,877	57.69	6,388,549	96.10
2.	August	7,370,102	2,725,183	36.98	6,851,732	92.97
3.	September	7,823,806	3,934,256	50.29	7,109,143	90.87
4.	October	7,721,075	4,368,711	56.58	6,777,440	87.78
5.	November	7,957,204	4,913,065	61.74	6,765,603	85.02
6.	December	8,122,425	5,426,278	66.81	6,747,887	83.08
7.	January	8,322,611	5,394,018	64.81	6,694,387	80.44
8.	February	8,527,127	5,451,004	63.93	6,562,362	76.96
9.	March	8,715,163	5,458,728	62.63	5,630,683	64.61

Source: Press Information Bureau. 'GST Revenue Collections for the FY 2017–18', 27 April 2018.

[2] CBIC, Goods and Service Tax (GST) Concept and Status, as on August 1, 2019, 51. As on 30 June 2019, number of transited (migrated) taxpayers 6,625,077 + number of applications approved under GST 7,258,894 = 13,883,971. Total number of new applications received for registration were 8,570,881 and number of applications rejected were 1,260,462.

Table 14.4 *All Types of Return Filing During 2017–2018*

S. No.	Return Period	GSTR 3B	GSTR 1	GSTR 4	GSTR 2
1.	July	6,591,592	6,122,716	1,015,580	2,572,552
2.	August	7,181,706	2,577,170		
3.	September	7,531,709	6,959,392		
4.	October	7,290,864	2,662,397	1,525,609	
5.	November	7,386,672	2,708,655		
6.	December	7,473,816	7,075,096		
7.	January	7,594,141	2,721,864	1,583,499	
8.	February	7,721,477	2,736,103		
9.	March	7,834,743	7,310,507		
Total					**2,572,552**

Source: CBIC. 'Goods and Service Tax (GST) Concept and Status'.

GSTR 3B for 2018–2019

The total number of GSTR 3B filed for the month of April until 31 May was 62.47 lakh. The total number of GSTR 3B filed for the month of May until 30 June was 64.69 lakh. The total number of GSTR 3B filed for the month of July until 31 July was 66 lakh. The total number of GSTR 3B filed for the month of July until 31 August 2018 was 67 lakh. The number was slightly higher than that of June 2018. The last date to file return was extended for Kerala until 5 October 2018.

The total number of GSTR 3B filed for the month of August until 30 September was 67 lakh. The total number of GSTR 3B filed for the month of September until 31 October 2018 was 67.45 lakh. The total number of GSTR 3B filed for the month of October until 30 November 2018 was 69.6 lakh. The total number of GSTR 3B filed for the month of November until 31 December 2018 was 72.44 lakh.

The total number of GSTR 3B filed for the month of December until 31 January 2019 was 73.3 lakh. The total number of GSTR 3B filed for the month of January until 28 February 2019 was 73.48 lakh.

Table 14.5 *Return Filing during 2018–2019*

S. No.	Return Period	GSTR 3B	GSTR 1	GSTR 4	GSTR 2
1.	April	7,913,649	2,874,669	1,558,692	–
2.	May	8,059,421	2,904,310		–
3.	June	8,166,076	7,534,721		–
4.	July	8,263,212	2,941,650	1,520,285	–
5.	August	8,359,366	2,946,818		–
6.	September	8,435,694	7,690,704		–
7.	October	8,489,963	2,951,630	1,467,106	–
8.	November	8,407,516	2,934,152		–
9.	December	8,459,155	7,620,357		–
10.	January	8,471,583	2,899,216		–
11.	February	8,480,221	2,847,353		–
12.	March	8,390,708	7,019,590	1,378,433	–

Source: CBIC. 'Goods and Service Tax (GST) Concept and Status'.

However, the cumulative level of compliance of GSTR 3B, GSTR 1, GSTR 4 and GSTR 2 for 2018–2019 may be seen in Table 14.5 and for 2018–2019 may be seen in Table 14.6.

The filing of GSTR 3B is increasing month by month. There were only 6,512,178 GSTR 3B filed in July 2017 that increased to 7,402,151 in March 2018. In 2017–2018, on average 700,000 GSTR 3B were filed per month. On the other hand, the number of return filing of GSTR 1 is fluctuating. It was 2,517,163 in July 2017 that decreased to 2,183,680 by January 2019. It further increased to 2,572,552 in July 2019.

Table 14.6 *Return Filing during 2019–2020*

S. No.	Return Period	GSTR 3B	GSTR 1	GSTR 4	GSTR 2
1.	April	8,140,641	2,669,680		–
2.	May	8,013,501	2,530,548		–
3.	June	7,579,038	5,079,328		–
4.	July	–	2,572,552		–

Source: CBIC. 'Goods and Service Tax (GST) Concept and Status', as on August 1, 2019, 51–55.

Impact and Experience of the New Tax around the Country

Taxes have been with us since ancient times, from king Manu and great political economist Chanakya. VAT is only 64-year old and 8 year younger than the independent India. The credit for the concept of VAT goes to the German businessman Wilhelm Von Siemens. He came up with the idea of a VAT in the 1920s. But the idea of VAT was implemented in France by joint director of the French tax authorities Maurice Lauré in 1954. He is known as so-called father of VAT. It was followed by former French West Africa in the 1960s, Brazil in 1965, Denmark in 1967, Germany in 1968 and the United Kingdom in 1973. VAT was introduced in the European Countries back in the 1970s–80s.[1]

VAT was limited to 10 countries in the late 1960s.[2] By the end of 1980s, about 48 countries, primarily located in Western Europe and Latin America, had adopted VAT.[3] Today, out of 195 countries in the world, 165 have opted VAT or GST. 'The increasing importance of VAT as a source of government revenue is likely to continue as countries deal with fiscal consolidation pressures in the wake of the economic crisis while seeking to restore growth'.[4]

---

[1] There is a condition: for those who want to become member of EC must adopt VAT. Due to this, all European countries adopted VAT.

[2] Buydens, *Consumption Tax Trends 2008*, 23.

[3] Norregaard and Khan, 'Tax Policy: Recent Trends', 37.

[4] Owens, 'Improving Performance of VAT System', 8.

As per Organisation for Economic Co-operation and Development (OECD)[5] 165 countries in the world levied a VAT/GST. As per Malaysia government, 160 countries have opted for VAT/GST (Table 15.1).[6] All OECD countries have adopted the VAT except United States of America that has not implemented VAT/GST as yet. The total number of UN Member States is 193, and, out of them, only 41 members have not implemented VAT/GST.[7] VAT was adopted in Asia by Pakistan in 1990s, Bangladesh in 1991, China in 1994, Nepal in 1997 and India in 2005 (and GST in 2017). We can say that about 85 per cent of the world's population is living in countries that have opted VAT/GST. The revenue of these countries 'accounts on average for as much as a fifth of the total tax revenue'.[8] 'A growing number of countries that operate a VAT are considering fundamental reform to increase their revenue raising capacity and to address inefficiencies of the current system'.[9]

The latest countries to adopt GST are Seychelles, Congo, Gambia and Malaysia. There are 13 countries whose indirect tax system is known as goods and service tax. These countries are Australia, Belize, European Union, Jersey, Jordan, Malaysia, Maldives, New Zealand, Papua New Guinea, Sierra Leone, Singapore, India and Canada. 'In some countries, VAT is the substitute for GST, but conceptually, it is a destination based tax on consumption of goods and services'.[10]

---

[5] OECD, *International VAT/GST Guidelines*. https://www.oecd.org/ctp/international-vat-gst-guidelines-9789264271401-en.htm (accessed 21 December 2019).

[6] https://www.treasury.gov.my/pdf/gst/list_of_countries.pdf (accessed 21 November 2019).

[7] ASEAN 3 (Malaysia, Brunei, and Myanmar); Asia 14 (Afghanistan, Bahrain, Bhutan, Iraq, Kuwait, Maldives, North Korea, Oman, Qatar, Saudi Arabia, Syria, Timor-Leste, United Arab Emirates, Yemen), Europe 2 (Andorra, San Marino), Oceania 7 (Kiribati, Marshall Islands, Micronesia, Nauru, Palau, Solomon Islands, Tuvalu), Africa 10 (Angola, Comoros, Djibouti, Eritrea, Liberia, Libya, Sao Tome and Principe, Somalia, South Sudan, and Swaziland), Caribbean, South, Central and North America 5 (Bahamas, Cuba, Saint Lucia, Suriname, United States of America).

[8] Owens and Battiau, 'VAT's Next Half Century'.

[9] Owens, Improving Performance of VAT Systems', 10.

[10] Mail Today Bureau, 'India's GST Highest in the World'.

Table 15.1 *Countries Implemented GST/VAT*

S. No.	Region	Malaysia
1.	ASEAN	07
2.	Asia	19
3.	Europe	53
4.	Oceania	07
5.	Africa	44
6.	South America	11
7.	Caribbean, Central and North America	19
Total		**160**

Source: https://www.treasury.gov.my/pdf/gst/list_of_countries.pdf

The share of general consumption taxes of OECD countries as a percentage of GDP is increasing year by year. The 2016 figure is the highest recorded for OECD countries' average tax to GDP ratio since recording began in 1965. It has recorded 9.2 per cent increase during 1965–2016 (24.8% in 1965 compared with 34.3% in 2016). The average tax to GDP ratio in OECD countries' was 34.3 per cent in 2016 compared with 34.0 per cent in 2015 and 33.9 per cent in 2014. Denmark had the highest tax to GDP ratio in 2016 (45.9%) and Mexico the lowest (17.2%). Of the 33 countries for which data for 2016 are available, the ratio of tax revenues to GDP compared to 2015 rose in 20 and fell in 13.[11]

Tax Bracket

There are different slabs for tax rates in different countries. They are using single slab, dual slab, three slabs, four slabs and five slabs (see Appendix E). The World Bank conducted a study of 115 countries about their tax structure. It found that most of the countries around

---

[11] OECD, *Revenue Statistics 2017*, 2.

the world were using a single rate of GST. The conclusion of the study showed that 49 countries were using a single rate, 28 countries were using two rates and only 5 countries including India were using four or more rates. Italy, Pakistan, Ghana and Luxembourg are included in the countries that are using four or more rates of GST. Thus, 'India has among the highest number of different GST rates in the world'.[12]

Tax Rate(s)

The tax rate also varies from country to country. 'India has the highest tax rate out of all the countries that have implemented GST'.[13] The standard GST rate in most of the countries ranges between 15 per cent and 20 per cent. There are two countries, New Zealand and Singapore, that have everything at a single rate of tax. Indonesia has five rates along with a zero rate. China applies GST on only goods and the provision of repairs, replacement and processing services. The tax rate of Canada varies from 12 per cent to 15 per cent. The GST rate of European Countries is around 19 per cent. They 'have one rate of GST as they do not have poor families, unlike in India, where families cannot be burdened with the same tax as the rich'.[14] The average national GST rate in Brazil is 20 per cent. The average GST of OECD countries is around 19.2 per cent (see Table 15.2). The world-wide tax rate for GST, VAT and sales tax may be seen in the Annexure 15.1.

OECD Consumption Tax Trends 2016

The consumption tax trends give information on VAT/GST and excise duty rates in OECD member countries. The OECD publishes consumption tax trends on regular basis with a lag of 2–3 years. It reviews the latest developments in consumption taxes in OECD

---

[12] World Bank, *India Development Update*, 110.

[13] India Today Web Desk, 'India's GST Rates Highest in the World'.

[14] Ibid.

countries. It gives the information of tax rates and reviews current issues of consumption taxes. The consumption tax trends of member countries may be seen in Table 15.2. The table depicts standard GST/VAT rate of member countries as well as VAT revenue ratio (VRR) for 2014. The average VAT/GST standard rate in the OECD was

Table 15.2 *Consumption Tax Trends*

S. No.	Country	Standard VAT Rates 2016 (%)	VRR 2014
1.	Australia	10.0	0.49
2.	Austria	20.0	0.59
3.	Belgium	21.0	0.47
4.	Canada	05.0	0.49
5.	Chile	19.0	0.63
6.	Czech Republic	21.0	0.58
7.	Denmark	25.0	0.59
8.	Estonia	20.0	0.70
9.	Finland	24.0	0.54
10.	France	20.0	0.48
11.	Germany	19.0	0.55
12.	Greece	23.0	0.37
13.	Hungary	27.0	0.57
14.	Iceland	24.0	0.46
15.	Ireland	23.0	0.49
16.	Israel	17.0	0.63
17.	Italy	22.0	0.37
18.	Japan	08.0	0.70
19.	Korea	10.0	0.69
20.	Latvia	21.0	0.51
21.	Luxembourg	17.0	1.23

(continued)

(*continued*)

S. No.	Country	Standard VAT Rates 2016 (%)	VRR 2014
22.	Mexico	16.0	0.32
23.	Netherlands	21.0	0.48
24.	New Zealand	15.0	0.97
25.	Norway	25.0	0.56
26.	Poland	23.0	0.44
27.	Portugal	23.0	0.48
28.	Slovak Republic	20.0	0.48
29.	Slovenia	22.0	0.60
30.	Spain	21.0	0.41
31.	Sweden	25.0	0.57
32.	Switzerland	08.0	0.71
33.	Turkey	18.0	0.42
34.	United Kingdom	20.0	0.44
	OECD	19.2	0.56

Source: OECD, 'Consumption Tax Trends 2016', http://www.oecd.org/tax/consumption/consumption-tax-trends-country-notes.htm

17.7 per cent on 1 January 2009. It increased to 19.2 per cent as of 1 January 2016. The standard rate of VAT/GST in most of the countries ranges between 16 per cent and 20 per cent. There are 22 out of 34 OECD countries that have revised their standard rate of GST/VAT at least once since 2009.

The VRR is a measure of revenue raising performance of VAT system. The ratio of one reflects a VAT system that applies a single VAT/GST rate to a comprehensive base of total expenditures on goods and services consumed in an economy, with a perfect performance of tax. The average VRR of OECD for 2014 was 0.56.

I

Model of GST/VAT

The model of GST framework varies from country to country. The different countries of the world have adopted different models of VAT/GST to levy tax (Table 15.3). There are three models to implement GST/VAT; these are as follows:

1. *Dual GST*: The tax is levied by both the centre and states on a pre-decided rate under dual GST model. The GoI introduced dual GST model in the country. In India, both the central and state governments levied tax equally on the supply of goods and services.
2. *National GST*: This is another option to implement GST/VAT. Under national GST, 'the two levels of government would combine their levies in the form of a single national GST, with appropriate revenue sharing arrangements among them. The tax could be controlled and administered by the Centre, States, or a separate agency reporting to them'.[15] Australia too has implemented national GST. The centre levied and collected the tax and the proceeds are allocated entirely to the states.
3. *State GSTs*: The third option to implement GST/VAT is SGST/VAT. Under this model, the indirect taxes would be levied by the states. The centre would continue to levy direct taxes—income taxes, customs duties and excise duties. The revenue loss of centre due to withdrawn of indirect tax 'could be offset by a suitable compensating reduction in fiscal transfers to the states. This would significantly enhance the revenue capacity of the states and reduce their dependence on the centre. The USA is the most notable example of these arrangements, where the general sales taxes are relegated to the states'.[16]

---

[15] Ahmad and Poddar, 'GST Reforms and Intergovernmental', 16.
[16] Ibid., 18.

Table 15.3 *Model of GST/VAT*

S. No.	Country	Model	Who	Proceeds
1.	India	Dual GST	Levied and collected by both centre and states	Revenues are shared among centre and states
2.	Australia	National GST	Levied and collected by the centre	Proceeds are allocated to entire states
3.	China	National VAT	The law and administration are centralized	The revenues are being shared with provinces.
4.	Canada	National GST	Levied at a combined federal and provincial rate of 13 per cent Tax design and collection are controlled by the centre	Revenues are shared among the participating provinces
5.	Austria	National	Tax design is controlled by the centre; states collect taxes	
6.	Germany	National	Tax design is controlled by the centre; states collect taxes	

Source: Authors.

II

Table 15.4 gives a comparative picture of taxation system of five countries that has opted GST for their indirect tax. These countries are India, Brazil, Canada, UK and Singapore.

Brazil, Canada and India have adopted a federal GST where the tax is levied by both the central and the provincial governments.[17]

---

[17] Brazil's tax is known as VAT.

Table 15.4 Comparative Picture of GST/VAT of Five Countries

S. No.	Particulars	India	Brazil	Canada	UK	Singapore
1.	Name	GST	Value Added Tax	Federal GST + HST	Value Added Tax	Goods and Services Tax
2.	Year of Introduction	1 April 2017	ICMS 1989 IPI 1964 ISS 1978	1 January 1991	1 April 1973	1 April 1994
3.	Tax Rate	0% (for food staples), 5%, 12%, 18% and 28% + cess for luxury items	ICMS: 17% standard rate 18% in Sao Paulo, Minas Gerais and Parana 19% in Rio de Janeiro IPI: 0–36.5% and average about 10% ISS: 2–5%	GST 5% and HST varies from 13% to 15%	Standard 20% Reduced 5%, exempt, zero rated	Standard rate 7% Reduced rates: zero rated, exempt
4.	Threshold Limit	₹20 Lakh and ₹10 lakh for NE states	Commencement of taxable activity	CAD30,000 (Approx. ₹16.46 lakh)	GBP85,000 (Approx. ₹79.62 lakh)	SGD1 million (Approx. ₹5.25 crore)
5.	Arising of Liability	Accrual Basis: Issue of invoice or receipt of payment — earlier	–	Accrual Basis: Date of issue of invoice or date of receipt of payment — earlier	Accrual Basis: Issue of invoice or receipt of payment or supply — earliest Cash Basis (t/o up to 1.35 mn): Payment	Accrual Basis: Issue of invoice or receipt of payment or supply — earliest Cash Basis (t/o up to SGD1 mn): Payment
6.	Returns	Monthly + 1 Annual	Monthly	Monthly, quarterly and annually	Quarterly, and small business has option of annual	Quarterly, monthly (optional)

Source: Authors.

Canada, Brazil, Singapore and France have successfully implemented GST/VAT in their countries. Malaysia is the only country that adopted GST but, within three years, they came back to their earlier tax system—Sales and Service Tax (SST). Let us study the international experience of GST/VAT country wise in the following sub-headings.

Canada

Canada introduced GST on 1 January 1991. The government levies a 5 per cent sales tax known as GST on supply of Canada-made goods and services except certain items that are exempt or zero rated (Table 15.5). 'The tax rate includes an additional provincial component of 8% or 10%, depending on the province. The combined 13% or 15% tax is known as the Harmonized Sales Tax (HST)'.[18] HST was introduced on 1 April 1997. There was a strong opposition to the introduction of GST from various political parties which was overcome, and GST was introduced. It has dual tax model.

HST is being levied at 13 per cent in three participating provinces. It is a combined federal rate of 5 per cent and provincial rate of 8 per cent. The design and collection of tax is being controlled by the centre. However, the provinces have flexibility to vary their tax rate. 'The revenues from the tax are shared among the participating provinces on the basis of consumer expenditure data for the participating provinces'.[19]

Registration

The registration under GST and HST is mandatory for those who are running their businesses in Canada or providing their sales and/or services and their last four quarters turnover exceeds C$30,000. The registered concerns for GST/HST get a business number (BN), which must be displayed on the invoices.[20]

---

[18] EY, *Worldwide VAT, GST and Sales.*

[19] Ahmad and Poddar, 'GST Reforms and Intergovernmental'.

[20] https://www.chargebee.com/docs/canadian-gst-hst.html

Table 15.5 *Sales Taxes are Levied in Canada, Based on Region*

S. No.	Provinces	Tax	Tax Rate (%)		
			Province	Federal	Total
1.	Alberta	GST	0.0	5	5
2.	British Columbia	GST + PST	07.0	5	12
3.	Manitoba	GST + PST	08.0	5	13
4.	New Brunswick	HST	10.0	5	15
5.	Newfoundland and Labrador	HST	10.0	5	15
6.	Northwest Territories	GST	0.0	5	5
7.	Nova Scotia	HST	10.0	5	15
8.	Nunavut	GST	0.0	5	5
9.	Ontario	HST	08.0	5	13
10.	Prince Edward Island	HST	10.0	5	15
11.	Québec	GST + QST	9.98	5	14.98
12.	Saskatchewan	GST + PST	06.0	5	11
13.	Yukon	GST	0.0	5	5

Source: http://www.calculconversion.com/sales-tax-calculator-hst-gst.html

Brazil

Brazil is an emerging market country and one of the leading economies of South America. The Brazilian indirect tax system was one of the most complex tax systems in the world. There were a number of duties and often it was difficult to differentiate one from another. 'A total of 90 taxes, duties and contributions were charged in Brazil. Some were almost unknown, like the Fee for Metrological Services, for example'.[21] The country was collecting a high 32 per cent of GDP in tax revenue.

Brazil is a federal country. It has three levels of tax authorities—federal, state and municipal. The country has introduced VAT and it has two types—federal VAT (IPI) and state VAT (ICMS). IPI was introduced in 1964, ICMS was in 1989, ISS in 1968, PIS-PASEP in

---

[21] Utsumi, 'Brazilian Tax System'.

Table 15.6 *Taxes in Brazil*

S. No.	Tax	Federal Tax	State Tax	Municipal Tax
1.	IPI	✓		
2.	ICMS		✓	
3.	ISS			✓
4.	COFINS	✓		
5.	PIS	✓		
6.	Import Duties	✓		

Source: Authors.

1970s, and COFINS in 1991. Some of them may apply concurrently. Taxes that are in force in Brazil can be divided into three categories on the basis of governmental sphere (Table 15.6).

Federal Tax VAT (IPI): The Impostos sobre Produtos Industrializados (IPI) is a federal excise tax that is regulated and collected by the federal government. It is a non-cumulative tax. Under IPI, the amount paid at one stage can be deducted at further stages. It is applied for both national and foreign 'finished goods'. It attracts tax when it leaves the factory or when it is imported. The Federal VAT (IPI) rate varies from 0 per cent to 300 per cent and averages around 15 per cent. 'At the federal level there are four indirect taxes (COFINS, Customs Duties, IPI and PIS), representing more than 35 per cent of federal tax collections and 25 per cent of total tax collections'.[22]

State VAT (ICMS): The Imposto sobre Circulação de Mercadorias e Serviços (ICMS) is a state VAT that is regulated and collected by each state government. It is levied by individual states on the supply of any goods, sales, services, communication services and transportation. The tax pertains to the transfer of merchandise from one party to another. The tax collects up to 82 per cent of all the taxes collected. The Brazilian states have defined their own ICMS rate, but

[22] Pinto, 'Tax Burden in Brazil'.

Table 15.7 *State Tax Rate in Brazil*

S. No.	States	ICMS Tax Rate (%)
1.	São Paulo	18
2.	Paraná	18
3.	Minas Gerais	18
4.	Rio de Janeiro	19
5.	Remaining states	17

Source: Authors.

the federal government may set the minimum rate. The total number of states in Brazil is 26. All the states and federal districts set their own indirect tax rates. The tax rates range from 17 per cent and 19 per cent.[23] The ICMS standard rate is 17 per cent. The state tax may be seen in Table 15.7.

Municipal Service Tax (ISS): The Imposto sobre Serviços de Qualquer Natureza is regulated and collected by each municipal government. It is a form of sales tax and also known as ISS or ISSQN. It attracts tax on the supply of any services that are not taxable under the state authorities (ICMS). It is a tax paid by companies and the civil society. The federal government has fixed the tax rate at minimum of 2 per cent and maximum of 5 per cent for municipal service tax. There is a specific services list for each municipal law. The general list of all taxable services is defined in federal (complementary) law.

Registration

It is mandatory for business entities to register themselves before the tax authorities of federal and states to sell their products on a commercial basis. A municipal registration also required for rendering services.

---

[23] https://www.avalara.com/vatlive/en/country-guides/south-america/brazil/brazil-indirect-tax-compliance-and-rates.html

Malaysia

The government started work to implement GST in 1983. The government sent a research team to South Korea to study the potential of GST. Tun Daim Zainuddin, the then minister of finance, announced on 21 October 1988 that the government is considering implementation of GST. Dato' Seri Anwar, the then minister of finance, announced on 30 October 1992 that government is going to implement GST from the 1993 Malaysian budget. But, later, it was deferred. Dato' Seri Abdullah Bin, the then prime minister, announced in the budget of 2005 dated 10 September 2004 that GST would come into effect by 1 January 2007. Later, it was also deferred. In 2005, government sent a team to Australia, New Zealand and Indonesia to study the mechanism of GST. In 2009, GST Bill was tabled at Dewan Rakyat. Datuk Seri Nazib Razak, the then prime minister, announced on 25 October 2013 that GST would become operational from 1 April 2015.

Finally, Malaysia implemented GST on 1 April 2015 after a long debate of 32 years. GST was a 'federal consumption tax based on the valued-added concept with a broad base, payable by intermediaries on all stages of the supply chain, with the tax burden ultimately borne by the consumer'.[24] The new GST led to a sharp rise in inflation that took one year to subside. 'After initial hiccups, things have settled down with 70% respondents reporting that business grew in last 12 months'.[25]

Earlier, the country had a single-stage federal sales tax and a single-stage federal service tax. Sales tax was imposed on goods and was governed by the Sales Tax Act, 1972. Service tax was levied on taxable services. It was governed by the Service Tax Act, 1975. Both the taxes were abolished on 1 April 2015.

There was opposition to the introduction of GST in the initial stages and even later. There was a huge anti-GST protest in the capital, Kuala Lumpur. Because of that, government decided on 31 July 2018 to abolish GST and return to the SST regime. Subsequently, the Ministry of Finance tabled five Bills to the Dewan Rakyat in August 2018. The

---

[24] Max, 'Malaysia's New GST: A Brief Comparison'.

[25] Singh, 'A Look at How GST'.

first was the Goods and Services Tax (Repeal) Bill 2018. The other bills were Service Tax Bill 2018, Sales Tax Bill 2018, Free Zones (Amendment) Bill 2018 and Customs (Amendment) Bill 2018. The bills were passed and became the law of the land.

The SST Bill was mostly similar to the earlier tax legislation, Sales Tax Act, 1972 and Service Tax Act, 1975. SST replaced GST from 1 September 2018 in Malaysia.

Now, Malaysian indirect tax is known as SST.

[It is] a single-stage tax, where the sales ad valorem tax is charged upon taxable goods manufactured and sold by a taxable person in Malaysia and taxable goods imported into Malaysia. Service tax is charged on taxable services provided in Malaysia and not on imported or exported services.... Sales tax will be imposed at the rate of 5%, 10% or a specific rate for petroleum products and the service tax will be at the rate of 6%.[26]

Singapore

The indirect tax of Singapore is known as GST. Singapore introduced GST on 1 April 1994. GST is a 'multi-stage tax that is collected at every stage of the production and distribution chain'.[27] 'The introduction of GST was part of a government reform intended to shift taxes from an income-based to a consumption-based system in order to boost Singapore's international competitiveness'.[28] GST is the second largest source of government revenue after corporate IT. 'The government has said that the GST will be raised to 9% sometime between 2021 and 2025.'[29] It is because 'government's spending on healthcare, infrastructure and security has gone up and is expected to increase further'.[30] The 'increase will provide the Government

---

[26] GuideMeSingapore, 'Malaysia SST'.

[27] The Goods and Services Tax Act, 1993, 1–2.

[28] The Goods and Services Tax Act, 1993, 6–9.

[29] *The Business Times*, July 3, 2018.

[30] *The Straits Times*, Feb 19, 2018.

Table 15.8 *Taxable and Non-Taxable Goods and Services*

	Taxable Supplies		Non-Taxable Supplies	
Items	*Standard Rated Supplies at 7%*	*Zero Rated Supplies at 0%*	*Exempted Supply No GST*	*Out of Scope Supplies GST not Applicable*
Goods	Major local sales falls in this category. Sale of TV set in a retail shop of Singapore is an example of this category.	Export of goods. Sale of Notebook (Laptop) to overseas customer address is an example of this category.	Importation, sale and rental of unfurnished residential property, local supply of investment, precious metals	Sale of goods where goods delivered from overseas to another place of overseas, private transactions
Services	Major local provisions of services fall under this rate. Provision of spa to a customer in Singapore is an example of this category.	International services. Air ticket from Singapore to Thailand is an example of this category.	Financial services. Issue of debt security is an example of this category.	

Source: IRAS website (www.iras.gov.sg).

with revenue of almost 0.7% of Singapore's gross domestic product per year'.[31]

The initial tax rate was 3 per cent that later increased to 7 per cent on 1 July 2007 (see Table 15.8). 'Singapore's GST rate still remains among the lowest in the Asia-Pacific, and well below the current Asia-Pacific average of 10.8%'.[32] 'Taxes in Singapore are relatively low, because competitiveness is a key consideration undergirding its tax policy'.[33]

[31] Ibid.

[32] *Singapore Business Review*, March 30, 2010.

[33] *The Business Times*, July 3, 2018

'All goods and services are taxable and known as taxable supplies. However, some items are specifically exempt from GST by law. Exempted items include financial services and the sale or lease of residential properties'.[34]

> If you are a bona fide traveller (excluding holders of a work permit, employment pass, student pass, dependent pass or long-term pass issued by the Singapore Government, and crew members), you will be given GST relief on new articles, souvenirs, gifts and food preparations that you bring into Singapore which are for your personal use and not meant for sale'.[35]

The sales and leases of residential properties and most financial services are exempted. The tax rate is zero rated for the export of goods and international services. 'There is no GST relief for liquor, tobacco products, petroleum and goods imported for commercial purposes'.[36]

Registration Threshold

GST is levied on consumption and not on income. Hence, business concern whose taxable turnover exceeds $1 million must register for GST. If taxable turnover of business concern does not exceed $1 million, they may still choose to voluntarily register for GST after careful consideration.

Returns Filing

All the business concerns registered under GST have to file return and account to Internal Revenue and Tax Authority of Singapore (IRAS). The main features of return file are as follows:

1. The return should be filed on monthly or quarterly basis
2. It should be filed electronically

---

[34] Rikvin, Singapore Company Registration Specialists.

[35] https://www.customs.gov.sg/individuals/going-through-customs/arrival/duty-free-concession-and-gst-relief

[36] www.gov.sg/factually/content/is-it-true-that-i-have-to-pay-gst-on-items-purchased-overseas

3. The return and payment of GST are due one month from the end of the accounting period
4. Business concerns must file a nil return if there are no GST transactions during an accounting period

France

The indirect tax of France is known as *taxe sur la valeur ajoutee* or TVA. It is a VAT and was introduced by a French economist in 1954 to replace the tax on production. France is the first country that introduced VAT. The objective of the introduction of new tax was to remove tax evasion. Its original coverage was limited. It was extended over time. 'It was then extended across the whole economy in 1968'.[37] 'The value added tax system has been a great success in France since the very beginning.... At present, the value added tax contributes substantial share of the state finance in France'.[38] It accounts for more than 50 per cent of state revenues.[39]

Tax Rate

The standard VAT rate in France is 20 per cent and reduced rate being 10 per cent, 5.5 per cent or 2.1 per cent. VAT rates applicable in mainland France are given in Table 15.9.[40]

Registration Threshold

The businesses that are 'based outside France are required to register for French VAT purpose when they are carrying out transactions for which they are responsible for the payment of French VAT, if any, even if they only carry out zero rated supplies. Alternatively, they are not entitled to register for VAT if they only carry out supplies for which

---

[37] French VAT, https://www.avalara.com/vatlive/en/country-guides/europe/france.html

[38] Economic Watch, 'Value Added Tax (VAT) in France'.

[39] TRA: https://tra.org/wp-content/uploads/2016/02/France-VAT-Guidebook.pdf

[40] Ibid.

Table 15.9 *VAT Rate in France*

S. No.	VAT Rate (%)	Items
1.	2.1	Applies to the sale of pharmaceuticals if it is reimbursed by social security and sale of newspapers and certain magazines
2.	5.5	Food, beverages without alcohol, books, services to old people and handicapped persons, supply of works of art by their authors
3.	10	Home services like childcare, cleaning, home courses, etc., works and repairs on residential buildings built from more than two years, bio-fertilizers, passengers' transport, sale of immediate consumptions such as restaurant, beverages without alcohol, pharmaceuticals which are not reimbursed by social security and sights
4.	20	Others (It applies in overseas territories and Corsica)

Source: https://tra.org/wp-content/uploads/2016/02/France-VAT-Guidebook.pdf (accessed 26 November 2019).

the French VAT is due on a reverse charge basis by their client registered for VAT purpose in France'.[41]

III

The indirect tax system is known as GST or VAT in more than 165 countries of the world. VAT is a more common, noticeable and acceptable tax format. GST is the same concept as VAT all over the world. In other words, GST is a substitute of VAT. VAT, an indirect tax is the main source of tax revenue for most of the countries. It is accepted by major countries of the world because of its effectiveness. It removes cascading effect of taxes and gives a common nation-wide market for goods and services. Hence, every country has introduced GST/VAT. The indirect tax must be effectively implemented and reformed from time to time to finance majority of the public expenditures for social welfare. The rate of tax, number of returns, registration thresholds, name of tax and introduction year of GST/VAT of 122 countries may be seen in Appendix E.

[41] Ibid.

Policy Review and the Way Forward

The erstwhile taxes—CENVAT, State VAT, CST, Service Tax and Sales Tax—have now become passé and GST is the buzzword. The new tax regime, GST, came into existence on 1 July 2017, and it has been in existence for over two-and-a-half years now.

The assembly elections of Uttar Pradesh and Gujarat were scheduled in 2017, and the assembly elections of Telangana, Madhya Pradesh, Rajasthan, Chhattisgarh and Mizoram were scheduled in 2018. The government wanted to take credit of implementation of GST in the above said assembly elections. Hence, the NDA II government was in hurry to implement GST.

The government prepared CAB 2014 with four grammatical mistakes (see the following figure). To remove the mistakes, they further issued corrigenda on 19 December 2014. The bill was referred to the Select Committee of Rajya Sabha on 14 May 2015. The Select Committee submitted its report to Rajya Sabha on 22 July 2015. The committee took only two months to examine the bill. It also shows in how much hurry the government was.

The opposition is still criticizing the complicated GST It is still drawing complaints from the industry regarding filing of returns, ITC and refund of credit. There are a number of issues that have to be solved within a required time frame. Haseeb Drabu, the former finance

---

LOK SABHA
———
CORRIGENDA
to
THE CONSTITUTION (ONE HUNDRED AND TWENTY-SECOND AMENDMENT)
BILL, 2014
[To be/As introduced in Lok Sabha]

1. Page 2, line 32, -

    for "Contitution,–"

    read "Constitution,–"

2. Page 4, line 16, -

    for "of its recommendation."."

    read "of its recommendations."."

3. Page 5, in the marginal citation against clause 18, -

    for "by the Council."

    read "by Council."

4. Page 8, *omit* line 11.

---

minister of Jammu and Kashmir has opined, 'There is still a long way to go before "one nation–one tax" is achieved in letter and spirit. But there is no denying that one tax, one commodity is already a reality'.[1] Rahul Renavikar, MD of Acuris Advisors says, 'The time is opportune to refresh and introduce sweeping changes in the existing structure, procedures and processes to make it more flawless and simple'.[2]

The GST Act is still a work in progress. The government has made a number of changes in GST so far. Experts on the subject were asking the government prior to the introduction of GST to take time and make

---

[1] Ibid.

[2] Renavikar, 'GST 2.0: Why Two-Rate'.

it a flawless law. But government was in a hurry to introduce it. No wonder, therefore, that it is issuing notifications regarding amendments in rules, changes in slabs and waiver of penalty on regular basis. Similar notifications are also issued by all the states under the respective SGST Act.

The first notification was issued on 22 June 2017 which notified certain sections under CGST. Since its inception, 607 notifications have been issued so far.[3] These notifications relate to notifying sections, notifying rules and amendments to the rules and wavier of penalty, etc. Besides, these notifications, 132 circulars and 18 orders have been also issued by CBIC with regard to offices, ease of exports and extension of last date for filling up forms, etc.

The government is trying to solve the glitches and improve the effectiveness of GST. There is still a lot of work which needs to be done to ensure that GST creates a world-class environment for businesses to flourish. But there is a long way to go.

GST is a good concept, but badly implemented. The present GST is not tax payer friendly. The Bombay High Court has also rapped the government for poor execution of GST. The court said that the present system is affecting the 'image, prestige and reputation of the country'.[4]

CAG on GST Implementation

The Comptroller and Auditor General (CAG) examined GST and submitted a detailed report[5] to the President of India under Article 151 of the Constitution of India on 30 July 2019. CAG has raised many concerns. Talking about rates, it observed that goods and services of same nature have been subjected to multiple tax rates. Different rates have been levied on hotels and lodges for the same room rent.

---

[3] 329 ,126 137 and 15 notifications have also been issued under CGST, IGST, UTGST and GST (Compensation to States) Act respectively.

[4] Seth, 'GST Regime is Not Tax Friendly'.

[5] CAG, Report No. 11 of 2019 (Indirect Taxes—Goods and Services Tax).

It observed that even after two years of its rollout, system validated Input Tax Credit (ITC) through 'invoice matching' is not in place and a non-intrusive e-tax system still remains elusive.

It pointed out that complexity of return mechanism and the technical glitches resulted in roll back of invoice matching, rendering the system prone to ITC frauds. Thus, on the whole, the envisaged GST tax compliance system is non-functional.

The system of payment and settlement of tax that was envisaged for GST was based on invoice matching and availment of ITC, as well as settlement of IGST on the basis of invoice matching. Neither is possible as of now, as an invoice-matching system has not kicked in.

With reference to return filing, CAG said while it was expected that compliance would improve as the indirect tax regime stabilizes, there was yet no improvement in the number of GSTR 3B returns filed. While 87 per cent taxpayers filed GSTR 3B in April 2018, this declined to 79 per cent by December 2018. It indicates that compliance declined.

The growth in indirect taxes of the union government slowed down to 5.80 per cent in 2017–2018 as compared to 21.33 per cent during 2016–2017.

The CAG said post-implementation, the centre's revenue from GST (excluding central excise on petroleum and tobacco) registered a decline of 10 per cent in 2017–2018 compared to revenue of subsumed taxes in 2016–2017.

The deficiencies in the GST system also point to a serious lack of coordination between the executive and the developers.

Way Forward

The indirect tax regime of GST has completed two-and-a-half years on 31 December 2019. Increasing tax evasion, and slow refund process remain major challenges for the government, as it gears up for a reformation of the tax system.[6] However, the government has announced a few measures like the introduction of the new return system—Sahaj and Sugam—for small taxpayers on a trial basis from 1 July 2019 and on a mandatory basis from 1 October 2019.[7] The government is also going to introduce single cash ledger for tax, interest, penalty, fee and others. The previous 20 heads are merged into five major heads.

Keeping all the problems in mind, government should rewrite the GST legislation after taking advice from experts specially Vijay Kelkar. The following points should be kept in mind while redesigning the present GST.

GST Network

GST was implemented without adequate preparation by the agency. The GSTN server also often failed. Therefore, taxpayers were struggling to file their returns. Taxpayers complained that 'the system is prone to slowing down to a crawl, generating error messages and crashing'.[8] The Parliamentary Standing Committee on Finance also emphasized that 'for flawless implementation of GST, the basic prerequisites are seamless IT infrastructure, uniform administrative paradigms, unified tax credit clearing mechanism, etc.' The Committee urged the central government 'to provide assistance and capacity building at State level, which would help in developing robust IT practices, ranging from overall procedure of e-filing of tax return to audit of tax and result in enhanced GST collections at the State level'. It further said that 'without a well-designed IT infrastructure across the country, the benefits of GST may remain elusive'. The government should work on IT infrastructure and make a system which would be acceptable to trade and commerce.

---

[6] *The Morning Standard*, July 1, 2019, 13.

[7] 'Government to Introduce Further Reforms in GST on Monday to Mark 2 Years of Rollout', *The Economic Times*, July 1, 2019.

[8] *The Economic Times*, November 2, 2017.

One Indirect Tax

GST was introduced with the objective of subsuming all indirect taxes. It has replaced 17 central and state indirect taxes. But a number of products such as alcohol and petroleum, electricity, fuel, land and real estate, excluding construction contracts, are still outside the ambit of GST. It will increase the tax base for the government and help in realizing higher revenues if these items are also brought within the ambit of GST.

Alcohol and Petroleum Product

The UPA government did not keep alcohol and petroleum products under GST. The NDA II government went a step forward and made a provision that alcohol and petroleum products would be included within the ambit of GST from the date which the GST Council would recommend. GST accounts for 60 per cent of the indirect tax revenue of the government. The balance 40 per cent is realized from the excise tax on alcohol and petroleum products. The Union Minister for Petroleum Dharmendra Pradhan has also pleaded for the inclusion of these products under GST. 'Petroleum products should be included under the goods and services tax (GST)', he has said.[9] The Thirteenth Finance Commission had also recommended that petroleum products should be under the purview of GST. We are also of the firm view that alcohol and petroleum products should come under the ambit of GST.

Simplicity of Tax Rates

There are five slabs of tax rates for goods and services. Moreover, we have two additional nominal rates—3 per cent and 0.25 per cent—and a compensation cess. The highest slab is 28 per cent. The government says that GST has brought down the tax rate for 97.5 per cent commodities to 18 per cent or less. Then, what is the relevance of 28 per cent slab.

---

[9] Jethmalani and Pengonda, 'Tank Full of Issues'.

Is it only for 2.5 per cent commodities? The multiple tax slabs brought back all the problems of multiplicity of rates.

The government says that it is not possible to make three slabs of tax rates. They should not forget that earlier we had three rates of CENVAT and a single service tax rate of 15 per cent with two cesses. Earlier, NDA I had already brought down multiple excise rates to three rates (a mean rate, a merit rate and a demerit rate) with additional rates of few luxury goods in 1999 with a philosophy: 'one excise' or, in today's context, 'one GST rate'. Further, in the budget speech for 2000–2001, the government converged three ad valorem rates into a single rate of 16 per cent.

The one rate service tax is also split into various rates. It is a step backwards and will lead to more problems. That is why it is flawed. The government also says that they have opted multiple rates to maintain equity between the goods meant for the poor and rich. However, it is for this purpose that we have direct taxes. The world over, direct taxes are used for equity and social justice. Indirect tax should not be used for that purpose. For various valid reasons it must be kept as simple as possible.

Stop Making Changes

The government has so far made changes in tax rate 213 times.[10] The government has issued 220 notifications regarding rates of GST.[11] The items have shifted from one slab to another slab on a regular basis. As yet, government has transferred 178 items from the 28 per cent tax rate slab to 18 per cent, 2 items from the 28 per cent tax rate to 12 per cent, 13 items from the 18 per cent tax rate to 12 per cent, 6 items from the 18 per cent tax rate to 5 per cent, 8 items from the 12 per cent tax rate to 5 per cent and 6 items from the 12 per cent tax rate to 0 per cent. It is necessary to stop making changes in rates

[10] ET Bureau, 'One Year of GST'.

[11] 69, 73, 69 and 9 rate related notifications each have been issued under the CGST Act, IGST Act, UTGST Act and GST (Compensation to States) Act, respectively.

and procedure so frequently. They have only increased the confusion among businesses.

Administrative Control

The administrative control is divided on the basis of turnover of the assesse. This has also led to serious difficulties. Instead of dividing the assesses between the centre and the states in the proportion of 1:9 or 5:5, it is better that states should be given exclusive authority to deal with assesses up to a turnover of ₹10–20 crore and the centre can deal with assesses with higher revenue.

One Nation, One Tax

GST has been hailed as 'one nation, one tax' since its inception. It was introduced in the hope that it would convert all indirect taxes into one tax. But instead, we have (a) the CGST Act, 2017; (b) the IGST Act; (c) the UTGST Act; (d) the Goods and Services Tax (Compensation to States) Act; and (e) 30 SGST Act.

Single Registration

In the present regime of GST, a number of registrations are required. It creates problem for business concerns. The government should adopt a single registration process with IGST for the respective states being paid by such centralized registrants and doing away with GST on cross-charge for services.

Single Login and Password

The businesses which are operating in many states and UTs have to obtain separate GSTIN for each of the states and UTs. They have to also file their GSTR state-/UT-wise on GSTN portal. For this purpose, they have to use a number of user names and passwords as the number of states or UTs they operate in. It should be simplified by giving them a single login and password. It will save time, and they do not need to remember multiple login IDs and passwords.

Return Filing

GST had proposed GSTR 1, GSTR 2 and GSTR 3. The businesses have to file three returns per month. They need to file 36 monthly returns per year per state/UT. It proved to be unworkable and necessitated the GSTR 3B return, which is a monthly summary. The provisions of return filing are ill-advised and need to be reconsidered.

Reduce Tax Evasion

GST was introduced with the intention of reducing tax evasion. But tax evasion is still a matter of concern. As per the GST Council officials, so far, the government has detected GST evasion of about ₹20,000 crore during April–February, of which ₹10,000 crore has been recovered. Our attention should be on curbing evasion and speedy refund process.

Appendix A

Indirect Tax Reforms in India: A Chronology

1935 : Sales tax made by GoI Act as a provincial subject

1939 : Sales tax first time introduced in India in the State of Madras

1941 : Sales tax introduced in the State of Punjab

1953 : Government formed Taxation Enquiry Commission, led by John Mathai

1956 : Kaldor Committee (confined to only direct taxes)

1965 : Government constituted Fourth Finance Commission for the examination of indirect taxes

1968 : S. Bhoothalingam Committee

1970 : Wanchoo K. N. Committee (direct tax enquiry committee)

1971 : Central Excise (Self-Removal Procedure) Review Committee formed

1972 : Raj Committee on taxation of agriculture wealth and income

1976 : L. K. Jha ITEC suggests introduction of VAT in India

1986 : (February) Finance Minister V. P. Singh proposes a major overhaul of the excise taxation structure in budget 1986–1987
     : Government introduced MODVAT in select commodities

1991 : Government-constituted TRC, the committee led by Raja J. Chelliah, recommended the introduction of VAT

1992 : Government constituted K. L. Rekhi Committee

1994 : Government service tax

1999 : Government constituted a group of chief ministers to work on VAT; Basu asked states to adopt of uniform floor rates of sales tax on commodities from 2000

2000 : Yashwant Sinha constituted Standing Committee of Finance Ministers later the committee converted into EC of Finance Ministers headed by Asim Das Gupta, who became the Chairman of EC

2002 : Task Force on Indirect Taxes formed
: Government constituted a Task Force on the implementation of FRBMA 2003
: CENVAT introduced on all commodities at central level

2003 : Vajpayee government formed a task force under Vijay Kelkar to recommend tax reforms
: VAT introduced in first Indian State of Haryana

2004 : Adviser to Finance Ministry Vijay Kelkar asked government to replace the existing tax with GST

2005 : VAT introduced in 24 states/UTs, including Himachal Pradesh, Jammu and Kashmir, Delhi, Punjab and Chandigarh

2006 : VAT introduced in five more states, including Rajasthan
: (28 February) Chidambaram set 1 April 2010 to introduce GST
: The union finance minister said the EC of Finance Ministers will prepare a road map for GST.

2007 : VAT implemented in Tamil Nadu and Puducherry
: Finance minister announces introduction of GST in India from 1 April 2010
: Thirteenth Finance Commission was constituted to work on GST

2008 : (1 January) VAT came into existence in Uttar Pradesh; it was the last state

: CST reduced to 2 per cent

: (30 April) EC of finance ministers submitted 'A Model and Roadmap Goods and Services Tax in India'

2009 : (10 November) EC head by Asim Dasgupta released its 'First Discussion Paper on GST'

: (15 December) Task Force of the Thirteenth Finance Commission submitted its report

: (29 December) Thirteenth Finance Commission submitted its report

: Finance Minister Pranab Mukherjee announced the basic structure for GST, retains 1 April 2010, deadline.

2010 : Finance Minister Pranab Mukherjee deferred GST to 1 April 2011

2011 : (22 March) UPA II government tabled CAB 2011 in Lok Sabha to bring GST

: (29 March) GST Bill referred to the Parliamentary Standing Committee on Finance

: Asim Dasgupta resigned from EC and was replaced by Sushil Modi

2012 : The Parliamentary Standing Committee on Finance started discussion

: Finance Minister Chidambaram in the meeting with finance ministers of states decided to resolve all the issues by December 2012 to rollout GST

2013 : The Parliamentary Standing Committee on Finance submitted its report

: UPA II revised the bill and sent to EC for consideration

: Gujarat Chief Minister Narendra Modi opposed the bill and said that state would incur loss of ₹14,000 crore every year due to GST

2014 : CAB 2011 lapsed due to dissolution of the fifteenth Lok Sabha

: BJP-led NDA II government came back to power

: NDA II government approved CAB 2014
: Finance Minister Arun Jaitley tabled CAB 2014 in Lok Sabha (19 December); opposition demanded that the bill be sent to Standing Committee

2015 : (1 April) Finance Minister Jaitley announced that the government is keen in implementing GST
: (6 May) Lok Sabha passed CAB 2014
: (12 May) CAB 2014 tabled in Rajya Sabha
: (14 May) Congress-led opposition demanded to refer the bill to Select Committee of Rajya Sabha. They also asked to cap GST rate at 18 per cent.
: (13 August) Government failed to win the support of Upper House to pass the Bill
: Rajya Sabha referred the Bill to its Select Committee
: (22 July) Select Committee presented its report on CAB 2014 Bill to Rajya Sabha

2016 : (July) Centre and states agreed against capping the GST rate of 18 per cent in the Constitution Amendment Bill
: (3 August) Rajya Sabha approved the Bill as congress and BJP both were agreed on the bill
: GST Council to begin work
: (8 August) Lok Sabha passed GST, CAB 2014
: CAB was passed by more than 15 states
: (8 September) President Pranab Mukherjee gave assent to the Constitution (101st Amendment) Act, 2016
: (10 September) The notification for bringing into force Article 279A (Constitution of GST Council) with effect from 12 September 2016
: (22 September) GST Council met for the first time
: (3 November) GST Council made five slabs tax structure 0, 5, 12, 18, and 18 per cent along with an additional cess on luxury and sin goods.

2017 : The government set 1 July 2017 for the rollout of GST
: (18 February) GST Council finalized the draft of Compensation Bill
: (4 March) GST Council approved CGST and IGST Bill

- : (20 March) Cabinet approved CGST, IGST, UPGST and GST Compensation Bills
- : (27 March) Finance minister tabled CGST, IGST, UPGST and GST Compensation Bills in the Parliament; both the Houses passed the bills
- : GST Council fitted over 1,200 goods into five tax slabs. Over 80 per cent goods of mass consumption were either exempted or taxed under the 5 per cent slab
- : GST Council fixed cess on luxury and sin goods to create kitty for compensation for states
- : (21 June) All states except Jammu and Kashmir passed SGST legislation
- : (28 June) Mamata Banerjee-led TMC decided to skip midnight launch of GST
- : (29 June) Congress also decided to skip launch of GST
- : (Midnight of 30 June) GST rollout

Appendix B

The Constitution (Amendment) Bill of UPA Government and NDA Government

CAB 2011 was introduced in Lok Sabha by the then Finance Minister Pranab Mukherjee on 22 March 2011. CAB 2014 was introduced by the then Finance Minister Arun Jaitley on 19 December 2014. The aim of both the Bills was to introduce a new tax structure with the amendment in the Constitution of India. Where CAB 2011 contained 19 sections, CAB 2014 contained 21 sections. A comparative picture of both the bills may be seen in the following table:

Citation	Clause	CAB 2011	CAB 2014
Short title and commencement	1	*1. This Act may be called the Constitution (115th Amendment) Act, 2011.*	*1. This Act may be called the Constitution (122nd Amendment) Act, 2014.*
		2. It shall come into force on such date as the central government may, by notification in the Official Gazette, appoint, and different dates may be appointed for different provisions of this Act and any reference in any such provision to the commencement of this Act shall be construed as a reference to the commencement of that provision.	2. It shall come into force on such date as the Central Government may, by notification in the Official Gazette, appoint, and different dates may be appointed for different provisions of this Act and any reference in any such provision to the commencement of this Act shall be construed as a reference to the commencement of that provision.
Insertion of new Article 246A	2	*After Article 246 of the Constitution, the following article shall be inserted:*	
Special provision with respect to GST		'246A. Notwithstanding anything contained in articles 246 and 254, Parliament and the Legislature of every State, have power to make laws with respect to goods and services tax imposed by the Union or by that State respectively.	'246A. (1) Notwithstanding anything contained in articles 246 and 254, Parliament, and, subject to clause (2), the Legislature of every state, have power to make laws with respect to goods and services tax imposed by the Union or by such State.
		Provided that Parliament has exclusive power to make laws with respect to goods and services tax where the supply of goods, or of services, or both takes place in the course of inter-State trade or commerce. Explanation. For the purpose of this article, "State" includes a Union territory with Legislature'.	(2) Parliament has exclusive power to make laws with respect to goods and services tax where the supply of goods, or of services, or both takes place in the course of inter-state trade or commerce. Explanation. The provisions of this article, shall, in respect of goods and services tax referred to in clause (5), of Article 279A, take effect from the date recommended by the Goods and Services Tax Council'.

(continued)

(continued)

Citation	Clause	CAB 2011	CAB 2014
Amendment of Article 248	3	In Article 248 of the Constitution, in Clause (1), for the word 'Parliament', the words, figures and letter 'Subject to Article 246A, Parliament' shall be substituted.	In Article 248 of the Constitution, in Clause (1), for the word 'Parliament', the words, figures and letter 'Subject to Article 246A, Parliament' shall be substituted.
Amendment of Article 249	4	In Article 249 of the Constitution, in Clause (1), after the words 'with respect to', the words 'goods and services tax or' shall be inserted.	In Article 249 of the Constitution, in Clause (1), after the words 'with respect to', the words, figures and letter 'goods and services tax provided under Article 246A or' shall be inserted.
Amendment of Article 250	5	In Article 250 of the Constitution, in Clause (1), after the words 'with respect to', the words 'goods and services tax or' shall be inserted.	In Article 250 of the Constitution, in Clause (1), after the words 'with respect to', the words, figures and letter 'goods and services tax provided under Article 246A or' shall be inserted.
Amendment of Article 268	6	In Article 268 of the Constitution, in Clause (1), the words 'and such duties of excise on medicinal and toilet preparations' shall be omitted.	In Article 268 of the Constitution, in Clause (1), the words 'and such duties of excise on medicinal and toilet preparations' shall be omitted.
Omission of Article 268A	7	Article 268A of the Constitution [as inserted by Section 2 of the Constitution (88th Amendment) Act, 2003] shall be omitted.	Article 268A of the Constitution, as inserted by Section 2 of the Constitution (88th Amendment) Act, 2003 shall be omitted.
Amendment of Article 269	8	In Article 269 of the Constitution, in Clause (1), after the words 'consignment of goods', the words, figures and letter 'except as provided in Article 269A' shall be inserted.	In Article 269 of the Constitution, in Clause (1), after the words 'consignment of goods', the words, figures and letter 'except as provided in Article 269A' shall be inserted.

		After Article 269 of the Constitution, the following article shall be inserted:	
Insertion of new Article 269A	9		
Levy and collection of GST in course of inter-state trade or commerce		'269A. (1) Goods and services tax on supplies in the course of inter-State trade or commerce shall be levied and collected by the Government of India and such tax shall be apportioned between the Union and the States in the manner as may be prescribed by Parliament by law. Explanation I. For the purposes of this clause, supply of goods or of services or both in the course of import into the 'territory of India shall be deemed to be supply of goods, or of services, or both in the course of inter-state trade or commerce. Explanation II. For the purpose of this article, "State" includes a Union territory with Legislature.	'269A. (1) Goods and services tax on supplies in the course of inter-State trade or commerce shall be levied and collected by the Government of India and such tax shall be apportioned between the Union and the States in the manner as may be provided by Parliament by law on the recommendations of the Goods and Services Tax Council. Explanation. For the purposes of this clause, supply of goods, or of services, or both in the course of import into the territory of India shall be deemed to be supply of goods, or of services, or both in the course of inter-State trade or commerce. Explanation II removed from CAB 2014
		(2) Parliament may, by law, formulate the principles for determining when a supply of goods, or of services, or both takes place in the course of inter-State trade or commerce'.	(2) Parliament may, by law, formulate the principles for determining the place of supply, and when a supply of goods, or of services, or both takes place in the course of inter-State trade or commerce'.
Amendment of Article 270	10	In Article 270 of the Constitution	
		1. In Clause (1), for the words, figures and letter 'Articles 268, 268A and 269', the words, figures and letter 'Articles 268, 269 and 269A' shall be substituted;	1. In Clause (1), for the words, figures and letter 'Articles 268, 268A and 269', the words, figures and letter 'Articles 268, 269 and Article 269A' shall be substituted;

(continued)

(continued)

Citation	Clause	CAB 2011	CAB 2014
		2. After Clause (1), the following clause shall be inserted, namely: '(1A) Goods and services tax levied and collected by the Government of India shall also be distributed between the Union and the States in the manner provided in Clause (2)'.	2. After Clause (1), the following clause shall be inserted, namely: '(1A) The goods and services tax levied and collected by the Government of India, except the tax apportioned with the States under Clause (1) of Article 269A, shall also be distributed between the Union and the States in the manner provided in Clause (2)'.
Amendment of Article 271	11	In Article 271 of the Constitution, after the words 'in those articles', the words 'except the goods and services tax' shall be inserted.	In Article 271 of the Constitution, after the words 'in those articles', the words, figures and letter 'except the goods and services tax under article 246A' shall be inserted.
Insertion of new Article 279A. Goods and Services Tax Council	12	'279A. (1) The President shall, within sixty days from the date of commencement of the Constitution (One Hundred and Fifteenth Amendment) Act, 2011, by order, constitute a Council to be called the Goods and Services Tax Council.	After Article 279 of the Constitution, the following articles shall be inserted: '279A. (1) The President shall, within sixty days from the date of commencement of the Constitution (One Hundred and Twenty-second Amendment) Act, 2014, by order, constitute a Council to be called the Goods and Services Tax Council.

The Goods and Services Tax Council shall consist of the following members:

(a) the Union Finance Minister ...... Chairperson;
(b) the Union Minister of State in charge of Revenue ...... Member;
(c) the Minister in charge of Finance or Taxation or any other Minister nominated by each State Government ...... Members.

(3) The Members of the Goods and Services Tax Council referred to in sub clause (c) of clause (2) shall, as soon as may be, choose one amongst themselves to be the Vice-Chairperson of the Council for such period as they may decide.

(4) The Goods and Services Tax Council shall make recommendations to the Union and the States on
(a) the taxes, cesses and surcharges levied by the Centre, the States and the local bodies which may be subsumed in the goods and services tax;
(b) the goods and services that may be subjected to or exempted from the goods and services tax;
(c) the threshold limit of turnover below which goods and services tax may be exempted;
(d) the rates of goods and services tax; and
(e) Any other matter relating to the goods and services tax, as the Council may decide.

(a) the Union Finance Minister ...... Chairperson;
(b) the Union Minister of State in charge of Revenue or Finance ...... Member;
(c) the Minister in charge of Finance or Taxation or any other Minister nominated by each State Government ...... Members.

(3) The Members of the Goods and Services Tax Council referred to in sub-clause (c) of clause (2) shall, as soon as may be, choose one amongst themselves to be the Vice-Chairperson of the Council for such period as they may decide.

(4) The Goods and Services Tax Council shall make recommendations to the Union and the States on
(a) the taxes, cesses and surcharges levied by the Union, the States and the local bodies which may be subsumed in the goods and services tax;
(b) the goods and services that may be subjected to, or exempted from the goods and services tax;
(c) model Goods and Services Tax Laws, principles of levy, apportionment of Integrated Goods and Services Tax and the principles that govern the place of supply;

(continued)

(continued)

Citation	Clause	CAB 2011	CAB 2014
			(d) the threshold limit of turnover below which goods and services may be exempted from goods and services tax; (This was as Part 12c in CAB 2011) (e) the rates including floor rates with bands of goods and services tax; (This was as Part D in CAB 2011) (f) any special rate or rates for a specified period, to raise additional resources during any natural calamity or disaster; (g) special provision with respect to the States of Arunachal Pradesh, Assam, Jammu and Kashmir, Manipur, Meghalaya, Mizoram, Nagaland, Sikkim, Tripura, Himachal Pradesh and Uttarakhand; and (h) Any other matter relating to the goods and services tax, as the Council may decide. (This was as Part 12e in CAB 2011)
		(5) While discharging the functions conferred by this article, the Goods and Services Tax Council shall be guided by the need for a harmonized structure of goods and services tax and for the development of a harmonized national market for goods and services.	(5) The Goods and Services Tax Council shall recommend the date on which the goods and services tax be levied on petroleum crude, high-speed diesel, motor spirit (commonly known as petrol), natural gas and aviation turbine fuel. (This clause is an addition in CAB 2014)

(6) One-third of the total number of members of the Goods and Services Tax Council shall constitute the quorum at its meetings.	(6) While discharging the functions conferred by this article, the Goods and Services Tax Council shall be guided by the need for a harmonized structure of goods and services tax and for the development of a harmonized national market for goods and services. (This was as Part 5 in CAB 2011)
(7) The Goods and Services Tax Council shall determine the procedure in the performance of its functions.	(7) One-half of the total number of Members of the Goods and Services Tax Council shall constitute the quorum at its meetings. (This was as Part 6 in CAB 2011)
(8) Every decision of the Goods and Services Tax Council taken at a meeting shall be with the consensus of all the members present at the meeting.	(8) The Goods and Services Tax Council shall determine the procedure in the performance of its functions. (This was as Part 7 in CAB 2011)
(9) No act or proceedings of the Goods and Services Tax Council shall be invalid merely by reason of (a) any vacancy in, or any defect in, the constitution of the Council; or (b) any defect in the appointment of a person as a Member of the Council; or (c) Any irregularity in the procedure of the Council not affecting the merits of the case. Explanation. For the purposes of this article, "State" includes a Union territory with Legislature'.	(9) Every decision of the Goods and Services Tax Council shall be taken at a meeting, by a majority of not less than three-fourths of the weighted votes of the members present and voting, in accordance with the following principles, namely: (a) the vote of the Central Government shall have a weightage of one third of the total votes cast, and (b) The votes of all the State Governments taken together shall have a weightage of two-thirds of the total votes cast, in that meeting. (This was as Part 8 in CAB 2011)

(continued)

(continued)

Citation	Clause	CAB 2011	CAB 2014
			(10) No act or proceedings of the Goods and Services Tax Council shall be invalid merely by reason of (a) any vacancy in, or any defect in, the constitution of the Council; or (b) any defect in the appointment of a person as a member of the Council; or (c) Any procedural irregularity of the Council not affecting the merits of the case. (This was as Part 9 in CAB 2011)
			(11) The Goods and Services Tax Council may decide about the modalities to resolve disputes arising out of its recommendations'. (This clause is an addition in CAB 2014)
Insertion of new Article 279B. Goods and Services Tax Dispute Settlement Authority		'279B. (1) Parliament may, by law, provide for the establishment of a Goods and Services Tax Dispute Settlement Authority to adjudicate any dispute or complaint referred to it by a state government or the Government of India arising out of a deviation from any of the recommendations of the Goods and Services Tax Council constituted under article 279A that results in a loss of revenue to a state government or the Government of India or affects the harmonized structure of the goods and services tax.	No provision

(2) The Goods and Services Tax Dispute Settlement Authority shall consist of a Chairperson and two other members.

(3) The Chairperson of the Goods and Services Tax Dispute Settlement Authority shall be a person who has been a Judge of the Supreme Court or Chief Justice of a High Court to be appointed by the President on the recommendation of the Chief Justice of India.

(4) The two other members of the Goods and Services Tax Dispute Settlement Authority shall be persons of proven capacity and expertise in the field of law, economics or public affairs to be appointed by the President on the recommendation of the Goods and Services Tax Council.

(5) The Goods and Services Tax Dispute Settlement Authority shall pass suitable orders including interim orders.

(6) A law made under Clause (1) may specify the powers which may be exercised by the Goods and Services Tax Dispute Settlement Authority and provide for the procedure to be followed by it.

(continued)

(continued)

Citation	Clause	CAB 2011	CAB 2014
		(7) Notwithstanding anything in this Constitution, Parliament may by law provide that no court other than the Supreme Court shall exercise jurisdiction in respect of any such adjudication or dispute or complaint as is referred to in Clause (1). Explanation. For the purpose of this article, "State" includes a Union territory with Legislature'.	
Amendment of Article 286	13	*In Article 286 of the Constitution*	
		1. In Clause (1) (A) for the words 'the sale or purchase of goods where such sale or purchase takes place', the words 'the supply of goods or of services or both, where such supply takes place' shall be substituted; (B) in Sub-clause (b), for the word 'goods', at both the places where it occurs, the words 'goods or services or both' shall be substituted;	1. In clause (1) (A) for the words 'the sale or purchase of goods where such sale or purchase takes place', the words 'the supply of goods or of services or both, where such supply takes place' shall be substituted; (B) in Sub-clause (b), for the word 'goods', at both the places where it occurs the words 'goods or services or both' shall be substituted;
		2. In Clause (2), for the words 'sale or purchase of goods takes place', the words 'supply of goods or of services or both' shall be substituted;	2. In Clause (2), for the words 'sale or purchase of goods takes place', the words 'supply of goods or of services or both' shall be substituted;

	3. For Clause (3), the following clauses shall be substituted, namely: '(3) Any law of a State shall, in so far as it imposes, or authorises the imposition of a tax on the sale or purchase of goods declared by Parliament by law to be of special importance in inter-State trade or commerce be subject to such restrictions and conditions in regard to the system of levy, rates and other incidents of tax as Parliament may by law specify. (4) Nothing in clause (3) shall apply to a law of a State insofar as it imposes or authorises the imposition of goods and services tax'.	3. Clause (3) shall be omitted.
Amendment of Article 366	14	*In article 366 of the Constitution*
	1. After Clause (12), the following clause shall be inserted, namely: '(12A) "goods and services tax" means any tax on supply of goods or services or both except taxes on the supply of the following goods, namely: (i) petroleum crude; (ii) high-speed diesel; (iii) motor spirit (commonly known as petrol); (iv) natural gas; (v) aviation turbine fuel; and (vi) alcoholic liquor for human consumption'. 2. Clause (29A) shall be omitted.	1. After Clause (12), the following clause shall be inserted, namely: '(12A) "goods and services tax" means any tax on supply of goods, or services or both except taxes on the supply of the alcoholic liquor for human consumption; 2. After Clause (26), the following clauses shall be inserted, namely: '(26A) "Services" means anything other than goods; (26B) "State" with reference to articles 246A, 268, 269, 269A and article 279A includes a Union territory with Legislature'.

(continued)

Citation	Clause	CAB 2011	CAB 2014
Amendment of Article 368	15	In Article 368 of the Constitution, in Clause (2), in the proviso, in Clause (a), for the words and figures 'article 162 or article 241', the words, figures and letters 'article 162, article 241, article 279A or article 279B' shall be substituted.	In Article 368 of the Constitution, in Clause (2), in the proviso, in Clause (a), for the words and figures 'article 162 or article 241', the words, figures and letter 'article 162, article 241 or article 279A' shall be substituted.
Amendment of Sixth Schedule	16	In the Sixth Schedule to the Constitution, in Paragraph 8, in Sub-paragraph 3, (i) in Clause (c), the word 'and' occurring at the end shall be omitted; (ii) in Clause (d), the word 'and' shall be inserted at the end; (iii) after Clause (d), the following clause shall be inserted, namely: '(e) Taxes on entertainment and amusements'.	In the Sixth Schedule to the Constitution, in Paragraph 8, in Sub-paragraph 3, (i) in Clause (c), the word 'and' occurring at the end shall be omitted; (ii) in Clause (d), the word 'and' shall be inserted at the end; (iii) after Clause (d), the following clause shall be inserted, namely: '(e) Taxes on entertainment and amusements'.
Amendment of Seventh Schedule	17	*In the Seventh Schedule to the Constitution*	
		(a) in List I (Union List)	
		1. For Entry 84, the following entry shall be substituted, namely: '84. Duties of excise on the following goods manufactured or produced in India, namely: (a) petroleum crude; (b) high-speed diesel; (c) motor spirit (commonly known as petrol); (d) natural gas; (e) aviation turbine fuel; and (f) tobacco and tobacco products'.	1. For Entry 84, the following entry shall be substituted, namely: '84. Duties of excise on the following goods manufactured or produced in India, namely: (a) petroleum crude; (b) high-speed diesel; (c) motor spirit (commonly known as petrol); (d) natural gas; (e) aviation turbine fuel; and (f) tobacco and tobacco products'.

2. Entries 92 and 92C shall be omitted; (b) in List II (State List) 1. For Entry 52, the following entry shall be substituted, namely: '52. Taxes on the entry of goods into a local area for consumption, use or sale therein to the extent levied and collected by a Panchayat or a Municipality'. 2. For Entry 54, the following entry shall be substituted, namely: '54. Taxes on the sale, other than sale in the course of inter-state trade or commerce or sale in the course of international trace and commerce of, petroleum crude, high-speed diesel, natural gas, motor spirit (commonly known as petrol), aviation turbine fuel and alcoholic liquor for human consumption'. 3. Entry 55 shall be omitted; 4. For Entry 62, the following entry shall be substituted, namely: '62. Taxes on entertainments and amusements to the extent levied and collected by a Panchayat or a Municipality or a Regional Council or a District Council'.	2. Entries 92 and 92C shall be omitted; 1. Entry 52 shall be omitted; 2. For Entry 54, the following entry shall be substituted, namely: '54. Taxes on the sale of petroleum crude, high-speed diesel, motor spirit (commonly known as petrol), natural gas, aviation turbine fuel and alcoholic liquor for human consumption, but not including sale in the course of inter-state trade or commerce or sale in the course of international trade or commerce of such goods'. 3. Entry 55 shall be omitted; 4. For Entry 62, the following entry shall be substituted, namely: '62. Taxes on entertainments and amusements to the extent levied and collected by a Panchayat or a Municipality or a Regional Council or a District Council'.

(continued)

(continued)

Citation	Clause	CAB 2011	CAB 2014
Arrangement for assignment of additional tax on supply of goods to states for two years or such other period recommended by the Council	18 for CAB 2014	There was no provision in CAB 2011. It is an addition in CAB 2014.	1. An additional tax on supply of goods, not exceeding 1 per cent. in the course of inter-state trade or commerce shall, notwithstanding anything contained in Clause (1) of article 269A, be levied and collected by the Government of India for a period of two years or such other period as the Goods and Services Tax Council may recommend, and such tax shall be assigned to the states in the manner provided in Clause (2). 2. The net proceeds of additional tax on supply of goods in any FY, except the proceeds attributable to the union territories, shall not form part of the Consolidated Fund of India and be deemed to have been assigned to the states from where the supply originates. 3. The Government of India may, where it considers necessary in the public interest, exempt such goods from the levy of tax under Clause (1). 4. Parliament may, by law, formulate the principles for determining the place of origin from where supply of goods take place in the course of inter-state trade or commerce. (This clause is an addition in CAB 2014)

Compensation to States for loss of revenue on account of introduction of goods and services tax	19 for CAB 2014	There was no provision in CAB 2011. It is an addition in CAB 2014.	Parliament may, by law, on the recommendation of the Goods and Services Tax Council, provide for compensation to the states for loss of revenue arising on account of implementation of the goods and services tax for such period which may extend to five years. (This clause is an addition in CAB 2014)
Transitional provision	18 for CAB 2011/20 for CAB 2014	Notwithstanding anything in this Act, any provision of any law relating to tax on goods or services or on both in force in any state immediately before the commencement of this Act, which is inconsistent with the provisions of the Constitution as amended by this Act shall continue to be in force until amended or repealed by a competent Legislature or other competent authority or until expiration of one year from such commencement, whichever is earlier.	The same provision in CAB 2014, but in Clause 20.
Power of the President to remove difficulties	19 for CAB 2011/21 for CAB 2014	1. If any difficulty arises in giving effect to the provisions of the Constitution as amended by this Act (including any difficulty in relation to the transition from the provisions of the Constitution as they stood immediately before the date of assent of the President to this Act to the provisions of the	The same provision in CAB 2014, but in clause 21.

(continued)

(continued)

Citation	Clause	CAB 2011	CAB 2014
		Constitution as amended by this Act), the President may, by order, make such provisions, including any adaptation or modification of any provision of the Constitution or law, as appear to the President to be necessary or expedient for the purpose of removing the difficulty: Provided that no such order shall be made after the expiry of three years from the date of such assent. 2. Every order made under Sub-section (1) shall, as soon as may be after it is made, be laid before each House of Parliament.	

Source: Computed by the authors from CAB 2011 and CAB 2014.

Appendix C
Parliamentary Standing Committee Report on GST

The Constitution (115th Amendment) Bill, 2011 was tabled in Lok Sabha on 22 March 2011. The bill was referred by the Speaker of Lok Sabha to the Parliamentary Standing Committee on Finance, headed by Yashwant Sinha on 29 March 2011 for examination and report thereon.[1] The Parliamentary Standing Committee on Finance submitted 73rd Report on CAB 2011 (GST), on 7 August 2013. The committee has given significant recommendations on a host of issues related to the GST design, including the rate structure, fiscal autonomy of the states, compensation mechanism and exemptions from GST. The Bill envisages the harmonization of the indirect tax regime by subsuming a number of taxes currently levied by the centre and state by introducing a dual levy on the supply of goods and services, one by the centre and one by the state. The Composition of Standing Committee on Finance for 2012–2013 was as below:

---

[1] Under rule 331E of the Rules of Procedure and Conduct of Business in Lok Sabha.

	Shri Yashwant Sinha—Chairman
	Members
	Lok Sabha
1.	Shri Suvendu Adhikari
2.	Dr Baliram
3.	Shri Sudip Bandyoypadhyay[a]
4.	Shri Udayanraje Bhonsle
5.	Shri Nishikant Dubey
6.	Shri Gurudas Dasgupta
7.	Shri Rahul Gandhi
8.	Shri Deepender Singh Hooda
9.	Shri Chandrakant Khaire
10.	Shri Bhartruhari Mahtab
11.	Dr Chinta Mohan
12.	Shri Sanjay Brijkishorlal Nirupam
13.	Shri Prem Das Rai
14.	Shri S. S. Ramasubbu
15.	Vacant[b]
16.	Shri Adv. A. Sampath
17.	Shri Thakur Anurag Singh
18.	Dr M. Thambidurai
19.	Shri Shivkumar Udasi
20.	Shri Dharmendra Yadav
	Rajya Sabha
21.	Shri Naresh Agrawal
22.	Shri Rajeev Chandrasekhar
23.	Smt. Renuka Chowdhury
24.	Shri Piyush Goyal
25.	Shri Satish Chandra Misra
26.	Dr Mahendra Prasad
27.	Shri Ravi Shankar Prasad
28.	Shri P. Rajeeve
29.	Shri Praveen Rashtrapal
30.	Dr Yogendra P. Trivedi

Notes: [a] Nominated as Member of the Standing Committee on Finance w.e.f. 13 December 2012.

[b] Dr Kavuru Sambasiva Rao, MP ceased to be the Member of the Committee w.e.f. 17 June 2013 consequent upon his induction to the Union Council of Ministers.

The Bill proposes the establishment of a GST Council which will recommend harmonized tax rates, and a GST Dispute Settlement Authority which will look into disputes regarding these rates. Parliament will have exclusive power to levy GST on imports and inter-state trade. The committee made the following observations:[2]

Design of the GST

The committee noted that the GST Bill envisaged harmonization of the indirect tax regime by subsuming a variety of taxes levied by the centre and the states. The implementation of GST would allow the centre and state governments to avoid multiple layers of taxation that currently exists in India, leading to the creation of a single market.

The most important aspect of the Bill is the consensus required with all the states in the design of the GST structure and all the other contours. The committee noted that there has been divergence in views among states, who have serious apprehensions on erosion of state autonomy. A fine balance is therefore required to be maintained between the imperatives of a common market with unified tax structure vis-à-vis the fiscal requirements of states. The centre needs to play a pro-active role in this regard.

The committee is of the view that any tax reform should have an objective of improving economic efficiency, encouraging economic activity and benefiting the common man and should be put in place giving due regard to the constitutional scheme of distribution of powers and fiscal autonomy of the states. In a federal set up, implementation of a comprehensive tax reform like GST hinges on mutual trust and cooperation between centre and state governments. The committee is of the opinion that before proceeding to enact the Constitution (115th Amendment) Bill, 2011, broad consensus on key issues concerning the implementation of GST should be arrived at between the centre and the state governments.

---

[2] The observations are extracted from 73rd Report of the Parliamentary Standing Committee on Finance.

While designing the desired tax reforms, the government should also learn from the experiences of other countries, while taking into account the political, social and economic variations obtaining in our country. Adequate groundwork would thus be essential before setting upon to operationalize the proposed GST regime. Keeping in view the apprehensions expressed by states, a credible study would also be required to evaluate the impact of the GST regime on the revenues of states. If the success of VAT in states has to be replicated, it may be necessary to leave enough flexibility and fiscal space for the states. It may also be made optional for states as was done in the case of VAT. In the succeeding paras, the committee has commented upon specific issues arising out of some of the clauses in CAB and has suggested changes, wherever required.

Compensation Mechanism

The committee notes that differences had emerged between the centre and states on account of CST compensation to the states arising out of phasing out of CST. Further, during their interactions with state governments, the committee observed that one of the major concerns over the implementation of GST is RNR. Some states generating high tax revenue have expressed apprehensions on the possibility of suffering revenue losses after the implementation of GST.

The committee notes with concern that no structured mechanism has been formulated so far to attend to this problem. The committee would, therefore, recommend that a well-defined automatic compensation mechanism may thus be built in, which would ensure that trajectories of revenues being contemplated are maintained at least in the short turn. Suitable amendments may accordingly be made in the Bill providing for a built-in permanent compensation mechanism with a view to addressing the legitimate revenue concerns of states. For this purpose, a GST Compensation Fund may be created under the administrative control of the GST Council.

Administration and IT Mechanism

The committee concurs with the view that for flawless implementation of GST, the basic prerequisites are seamless IT infrastructure, uniform administrative paradigms, unified tax credit clearing mechanism, etc. The committee notes that in this regard an Empowered Group on IT Infrastructure headed by Nandan Nilekani has been constituted to put in place a strong IT infrastructure on GST in a time-bound manner. For smooth and effective implementation of GST, the committee would urge the central government to provide technical assistance and capacity building at state level, which would help in developing robust IT practices, ranging from overall procedure of e-filing of tax return to audit of tax and result in enhanced GST collections at the state level. Without a well-designed IT infrastructure across the country, the benefits of GST may remain elusive. It is also imperative that although a dual GST regime has been proposed, a situation of trade/business dealing with a dual administration and multiplicity of authorities should be avoided, as it may create more hassles rather than ease them. Although not part of CAB, this issue needs clarity, so that dual GST regime becomes acceptable to trade and commerce at large and fosters tax compliance.

Integrated Goods and Services Tax

IGST model envisages that the centre will levy tax at a rate approximately equal to (CGST + SGST) rate on inter-state supply of goods and services. It will be collected by the centre and transferred to states depending upon whether the state is net exporter or net importer for the given period of settlement. The committee notes that the settlement of accounts will be done by the centre that would function as a clearing house for this purpose. The proceeds of the IGST arising out of inter-state trade or commerce shall thus be used for the settlement of accounts among the states for the flow of ITC in the course of inter-state transactions based on 'destination principle' thereby providing a continuous credit chain across states. The committee further notes that to the extent goods or services are supplied from one state to another for further distribution, IGST transactions would be revenue neutral. However, in practice, there may be a possibility of a positive balance in the proceeds of IGST at the end of an FY. The committee, therefore, desires that a suitable proviso in the Article 269A in both Clause 9 and Clause 10 of Amendment Bill may be made for the distribution of remaining proceeds of IGST when the accounts of the FY have been settled. It has also been submitted to the committee by some experts that the IGST model could be onerous in terms of compliance and administrative burden and that since it is meant for effectively tax interstate trade on destination principle, the central government need not get involved in this process. A simpler model (Modified Bank Model) as recommended by the Task Force on GST set up by the Thirteenth Finance Commission has been suggested for the settlement of proceeds arising out of inter-state trade. The committee notes that the central government will only act as a clearing agent with regard to IGST, which remains in effect a clearing mechanism between states for inter-state transactions. The committee would thus suggest that the alternate model, suggested by the Task Force on GST constituted by the Thirteenth Finance Commission, could be considered with a view to simplifying and easing compliance and administrative burden and ensuring a smooth clearing house mechanism between states for facilitating the process of IGST after consideration by the GST Council.

Further, as the destination-based IGST model favours predominantly consumer states more than producer states, the revenue concerns of these states also need to be factored in and duly addressed. The proposed model should not thus act as a dampener or disincentive for states with a strong manufacturing base.

GST Dispute Settlement Authority

In concurrence with the views expressed by state governments and the Chairman, EC, the committee believes that the proposed provision of GST Dispute Settlement Authority would affect the fiscal powers of the Parliament and the state legislatures. The committee, therefore, desires that the proposed Article 279B providing for GST Dispute Settlement Authority should be omitted, as this body would have the effect of overriding the supremacy of the Parliament and the state legislatures. However, since any dispensation involving several entities/ interests requires a mechanism to resolve disputes/differences, it may be expedient to make a provision in Article 279A itself empowering the GST Council to decide about the modalities to resolve disputes arising out of its recommendations.

Harmonized Tax Structure

The committee notes that Clause 5 of the proposed Article 279A requires the GST Council to be guided by the need for a harmonized structure of GST and for the development of a harmonized market for goods and services. However, since the words have not been defined in the proposed Bill, the committee is of the view that such ambiguity should not remain in the Bill. They would therefore recommend that the word 'harmonized structure' may be clearly amplified or defined. It should also be clarified that the provisions contained in Clause 5 are in the nature of guiding principles for the council and not mandatory or obligatory in nature.

Consensus

The committee notes that the decisions in the GST Council would be taken based on consensus which implies that all the members present would have to agree to a proposal; even if one state differs, the decision cannot be passed. The committee feels that keeping in view the diversity in socio-economic interests of the states, achieving such a consensus is likely to be very difficult. As it would be critical in ensuring that all the valid interests are properly reflected in the recommendations of the GST Council, the committee would therefore recommend amendments to Clause (8) of Article 279A so as to provide for voting instead of consensus for decisions of the GST Council. Accordingly, as agreed upon by the EC, one-third weightage for central representatives and two-thirds weightage for state represent-atives may be given with the decision taken by the council being passed with more than three-fourths votes of the representatives present in the meeting. Similarly, amendment to Clause (6) of Article 279A may also be made for increasing the quorum to half from the proposed one-third. In this context, the committee would recommend that in tune with the spirit of cooperative federalism, it would be in order if the proposed GST Council functions like the present EC, which has a good track record of not only reforming the tax system but also resolving differences amicably in an institutional mode.

Declared Goods

In order to ensure that there is no unilateral decision by the centre regarding taxation of 'declared goods' kept outside the purview of GST (Clauses 3 and 4 of amendment proposed in Article 286) and also to uphold the spirit of cooperative federalism, which is crucial for the structure of dual GST, the committee recommends that Clause 3 should be amended so that in place of 'subject to such restrictions and conditions in regard to the system of levy, rates and other incidents of tax as Parliament may by law specify', the phrase 'subject to such restrictions and conditions of tax as Parliament may by law specify on the recommendations of the GST Council constituted under 279A' may be substituted. This change is expected to allay the fears of states to some extent on loss of fiscal autonomy. In this context, it would also be expedient to insert a new sub-clause in Clause (4) of Article 279A to provide both states and centre the requisite flexibility to raise additional resources during period of natural calamities and disasters. The proposed Clause 4 of Article 279A may also be suitably amended to provide for special schemes for north-eastern states, Jammu and Kashmir and other special category states. Similarly, the central government should also have the flexibility to levy surcharge or cess whenever required or during extra-ordinary circumstances.

Entry Tax

The committee notes that Entry 52 of the Seventh Schedule is worded in the Bill as 'taxes on the entry of goods into a local area for consumption use or sale therein to the extent levied and collected by a Panchayat or Municipality'. As most of the states seem to be opposed to this proposed amendment, the committee does not agree with this formulation. It will not be desirable to go back to the earlier system of levy and collection of octroi by local bodies, and this will be a retrograde step, which would hinder free flow of trade and increase compliance burden. The committee therefore desires that entry tax in general should be subsumed in GST. The relevant clause/sub-clause in the Bill may be modified accordingly so as to empower the states to collect entry tax for distribution among local bodies instead of leaving it to be collected by different local bodies.

Floor Rate

Tax on sale of goods is the biggest and most buoyant source of revenue for states. The committee is of the opinion that the states should have some limited leverage to vary the rate of tax depending on exigencies. The committee, therefore, desires that a system of band with floor rate should be adopted while introducing GST, so that states have some elbow-room within stipulated limit to calibrate the rate of tax depending on needs of the situation and the dynamics of circumstances. The committee is of the view that based on the European model, there could be a floor rate and a ceiling rate within which the states will have the freedom to have a high or a low rate. Taking into account the need for state autonomy, the states may thus be allowed to increase their GST rate within a narrow band. There could however be a provision to levy higher rates on demerit goods, whenever necessary. The proposed Article 279(A) may accordingly be modified providing for such a flexibility in rate.

Threshold of limits of turnover, etc., for exempting certain class of taxpayers like small traders/manufacturers/service providers may also be left to the wisdom of the GST Council. Although it is ideally desirable that the GST regime is made comprehensive and all-encompassing for the present, the existing exemption for small business may continue in line with the government policy to encourage and promote small enterprises including self-employed sector.

Exclusions

Article 366 of the Constitution is proposed to be amended vide Clause 14 in the Bill, wherein taxes on the supply of specified goods is proposed to be excluded from the purview of GST. The committee believes that such specific exclusions need not be provided in a CAB, as this will needlessly make the GST regime very rigid. Since the ultimate goal is to have an integrated, comprehensive and seamless

GST regime subsuming various central and state indirect taxes and levies, the committee recommend that the above-mentioned exclusion provision may be omitted from CAB. In any case, the proposed provision inserting Article 279A in the Constitution empowers the GST Council vide Clause 4(a) and (b) to make recommendations on subsuming or exempting or excluding certain goods/services from the purview of GST. The committee thus believes that the constitutional mandate being provided to the GST Council is resilient enough to address emerging situations.

GST Monitoring

Considering the fluidity and uncertainties involved in ushering in radical changes in the tax system, the committee believes that there is a need to set up a GST monitoring/evaluation cell, which should closely follow on a continuous basis the immediate impact of GST on key aspects such as growth in GDP, inflation, hoarding, compliance costs for taxpayers, administrative bottlenecks and, last but not least, the retail prices paid by the ultimate consumer. The efficacy of the proposed GST model in lieu of the existing CST dispensation with regard to inter-state trade/transactions and the requirement for a robust, error-free IT platform also needs to be monitored with a view to assessing and ensuring that India becomes a truly common market. Certain pro-consumer measures should be initiated as well, such as, passing on tax credit benefit to retail consumers for cushioning them against possible increase in prices post GST and ensuring that cascading effect on consumer prices is well and truly avoided as envisaged. The GST Monitoring/Evaluation Cell may function under the aegis of the proposed GST Council. This may be incorporated as a clause/sub-clause in the proposed Article 279A of the Bill so as to put monitoring of GST on a firmer footing.

Conclusion

In conclusion, the committee is of the view that fears expressed in some quarters about the proposed GST Council being made a constitutional body and infringing upon or even overriding the supremacy of the Parliament or state legislature is not correct as it is envisaged as a recommendatory body. The fruitful experience with the EC of State Finance Ministers so far does not seem to give any credence to such apprehensions. This body has provided a useful platform for consensus-building between centre and states and has evolved democratic practices over time to discuss and resolve issues. The committee would thus expect the proposed GST Council to follow the principles of cooperative federalism and democratic governance. As this will be a political and a recommendatory body, it would be in a position to play a constructive and enabling role vis-à-vis the legislature, which needless to emphasize would remain supreme in matters of legislation including taxation. In the committee's view, the mandate entrusted to the GST Council under the proposed Article 279A of CAB does not in any way alter the existing constitutional scheme in so far as the legislature, both union and state, is concerned. On the whole, the committee is of the view that CAB should not ideally include specific aspects relating to rates, exemptions, exclusions, thresholds, administrative arrangements, etc. What should be included in the laws and rules should not form part of the Constitution of India. The present Bill relating to GST, in the committee's view, has not been well-drafted from this perspective and, therefore, requires amendments as suggested above.

Appendix D
Select Committee Report on GST

CAB 2014 was passed by Lok Sabha on 6 May 2015. After that, the Bill was sent to Rajya Sabha. However, due to disagreements over a few provisions of the Bill, it was referred to the Select Committee of Rajya Sabha for examination. The committee was asked to submit its report by the last day of the first week of the next session (Monsoon Session). The Bill contained 21 clauses on which the committee had been asked to submit a report and these clauses proposed to, inter alia, amend the Constitution of India by inserting new Articles 246A, 269A and 279A with respect to special provision to GST, levy and collection of GST in course of inter-state trade or commerce and GST Council, respectively. Apart from that, the bill also purports to amend Articles 248, 249, 250, 268, 269, 270, 271, 286, 366 and 368 of the Constitution of India and amendment of the Sixth and the Seventh Schedule of the Constitution as well. The Bill also seeks to repeal Article 268A of the Constitution.

The Select Committee was constituted on 12 May 2015. The Select Committee comprised of 21 members and was headed by Bhupender Yadav, a member of the Parliament. The composition of Select Committee was as below:

1. Shri Bhupender Yadav (Chairman)
2. Dr Chandan Mitra
3. Shri Ajay Sancheti
4. Shri Madhusudan Mistry

5. Shri Mani Shankar Aiyar
6. Dr Bhalchandra Mungekar
7. Shri Naresh Agrawal
8. Shri K. C. Tyagi
9. Shri Derek O'Brien
10. Shri A. Navaneethakrishanan
11. Shri Satish Chandra Misra
12. Shri K. N. Balagopal
13. Shri Dilip Kumar Tirkey
14. Shri C. M. Ramesh
15. Shri Praful Patel
16. Shrimati Kanimozhi
17. Shri Anil Desai
18. Shri Naresh Gujral
19. Mir Mohammad Fayaz
20. Shri D. Raja
21. Shri Rajeev Chandrasekhar

Recommendations/Observations[1]

The Select Committee held discussions on various dates and heard the views of various stakeholders including ministries, states, trade bodies, associations, financial institutions and experts, besides conducting field visits. The committee viewed the Bill and submitted its report on 22 July 2015. The report endorsed most of the provisions of the GST Bill and also made certain recommendations. However, there were a few dissent notes submitted by the Congress, AIADMK and Left parties to the committee. Let us discuss the major recommendations/observations of the committee in the following sub-headings:

Finances of Local Bodies

The committee strongly felt that the revenues of local bodies need to be sustained and protected for ensuring that standards of local

---

[1] The observations are extracted from the report of Select Committee of Rajya Sabha.

governance are maintained. The committee, thus, strongly recommends that the state governments take adequate measures to ensure that adequate revenues flow to the local bodies, and their resources are not adversely affected. The committee noted that Articles 243H and 243X contain provisions for state legislatures to authorize panchayats and municipalities to collect and appropriate taxes in the State List.

Band Rates

The committee further noted that Articles 243I and 243Y provide for setting up of State Finance Commissions to make recommendations regarding devolution of funds to local bodies. The committee noted that the above provisions notwithstanding, local bodies find managing their resource requirements quite challenging. In light of the above, with respect to Article 279A Clause 4(e), the committee strongly recommends that the word 'band' used in the proposed Article may be defined in GST laws, as 'Band': Range of GST rates over the floor rate within which CGST or SGST may be levied on any specified goods or services or any specified class of goods or services by the central or a particular state government as the case may be.

Additional Tax up to 1 per cent

The Bill empowers the centre to levy an additional tax, up to 1 per cent, on the supply of goods in inter-state trade. This tax will be given to the state from where the supply of the good originates. The committee felt that the provision of 1 per cent additional tax in its present form is likely to lead to cascading of taxes. Therefore, the committee strongly recommends that the term 'supply' be explained to mean 'all forms of supply made for a consideration'.

Dispute Resolution

The modality to resolve any differences internally lies with the council. If any Dispute Settlement Authority is created separately, it will certainly hamper the functioning of the GST Council in general and legislatures in particular. Thus, it would be judicious not to have a separate and distinct authority having far reaching powers and which could pre-empt and supersede the powers of Parliament and state legislatures in the long run.

Shareholding of GSTN

The committee felt GSTN shall play a crucial role in implementation of GST as it shall provide the IT infrastructure for implementation of GST. The committee noted that the non-government shareholding in GSTN is dominated by private banks, and this is not desirable. The committee strongly recommended that the government may take immediate steps to ensure non-government financial institution shareholding be limited to public sector banks or public sector financial institutions.

The committee also recommended that for having no discernible blemishes in the implementation of GST, it is imperative that not only IT preparedness is at very high level but also prerequisites such as IT infrastructure, unified tax credit clearing mechanism, etc., may be put in place.

GST Rates of Banking Services

The committee considered that if the GST rate is more than the service tax rate of 14 per cent, the increase in the tax rate will further increase the cost of banking services. This results into cost of doing business being much higher in India as compared to other competing countries. Therefore, the committee recommended that to be internationally competitive, the GST rate for banking industry should be minimum.

Rate Determination

The committee felt that although the GST Council has been entrusted with the task of fixing the rate including floor rates with bands in mutual consent with other state governments that are part and parcel of the Council. But implementation of GST in other countries has shown GST rate is a very important factor in earning the trust of the consumers. If the GST rate is kept high, it will surely erode the confidence of the consumers badly and may lead to high inflation. Therefore, the committee is of the considered view that while fixing the rate, the GST Council may opt for a broad base and moderate rate as it is an essential feature of a good tax system and as far as possible multiplicity of tax rates may be avoided.

Compensation to States for Loss in Revenue

The committee had recommended that revenue loss to the states should be compensated for a period of five years by the centre.

Appendix E

VAT, GST and Sales Tax Rates in the World

S. No.	Jurisdiction	Introduction Year	Name of Tax/ Local Name	Return Period	Registration Thresholds	Standard Rate	Other Rates
1.	Albania	1995	VAT/ TVSH	Monthly	Annual turnover of ALL 2 million	20%	6%, 0%
2.	Argentina Armenia	1975 1977	VAT IIBB	Monthly	VAT: If sale is higher of: ARS 1,050,000 for goods and ARS 70,000,000 for services IIB: Commencement of sales activity	VAT: 21% IIB: Industrial 1%–4%, Commercial and services: 3.5%–5%, and Commission and intermediation: 4.9%–8%	VAT: 27%, 10.5%, 0%
3.	Armenia	2018	VAT/ Avelacvets arzheqi hark	Monthly	AMD 115 million for the preceding or current calendar year	20%	0%

(continued)

(continued)

S. No.	Jurisdiction	Introduction Year	Name of Tax/ Local Name	Return Period	Registration Thresholds	Standard Rate	Other Rates
4.	Aruba	2007 2014	Revenue Tax Health Tax	Monthly	None	RT: 1.5% HT: 1%–2%	N/A
5.	Australia	2000	GST	Monthly Quarterly Annual	AUD 75,000 (AUD 150,000 for non-profit bodies)	10%	0%
6.	Austria	1973	VAT/ Umsatzsteuer	Monthly Quarterly Annual	EUR 30,000 (entities established in Austria)	19%, 20%	13%, 10%
7.	Azerbaijan	1992	VAT/DV	Monthly	Taxable turnover exceeding AZN 200,000 for a period of 12 consecutive months	18%	0%
8.	Bahamas	2015	VAT	Monthly Quarterly Semi-annually	BSD 100,000 in annual turnover	7.5%	0%
9.	Bahrain	2019	VAT			5%	0%
10.	Barbados	1997	VAT	Bimonthly Monthly	BBD 200,000	17.5%	22%, 7.5%, 0%

11.	Belarus	1991	VAT/NDS	Quarterly/ Monthly (as per choice of taxpayer)	None	20%	25%, 10%, 0%
12.	Belgium	1971	VAT/BTW	Monthly Quarterly	None	21%	0%, 6%, 12%
13.	Bolivia	1986	VAT/IVA	Monthly	Commencement of sales activity	Nominal: 13% Effective: 14.94%	0%
14.	Bonaire, Sint Eustatius and Saba (BES Islands)	2011	General Expenditure Tax	Quarterly	None	Goods: 6%–8% Services: 4%–6%	30%, 25%, 22%, 18%, 10%, 7%, 5%, 0%
15.	Botswana	2002	VAT	Bimonthly Monthly	BWP 1 million	12%	0%
16.	Brazil	1989 1964 1968 1970s 1991	VAT ICMS IPI ISS PIS-PASEP COFINS	Monthly	Commencement of Taxable activity for ICMS, IPI and ISS, sales activity for PIS-PASEP /COFINS	IPI 0%–365% ICMS 0%–35% ISS 0%–5% PIS-PASEP 0.65% 1.65% COFINS 3%, 7.6%	NA
17.	Bulgaria	1994	VAT	Monthly	BGN 50,000	20%	9%, 0%

(continued)

(continued)

S. No.	Jurisdiction	Introduction Year	Name of Tax/ Local Name	Return Period	Registration Thresholds	Standard Rate	Other Rates
18.	Canada	1991 1997	GST HST	Monthly Quarterly Annual	CAD 30,000	GST: 5% HST: 13%–15% QST: 9.975%	0%
19.	Chile	1974	VAT	Monthly	None	19%	15%–50%
20.	China	1994	VAT	One day to one quarter	See footnote	6%, 11%, 17%	17%, 11%, 6%, 5%, 3%
21.	Colombia	1983	VAT	Bimonthly/ quarterly	Gross income in the previous year less than USD 37,100	19%	5%, 0%
22.	Costa Rica	1982	VAT	Monthly	None	13%	10%, 5%, 0%
23.	Croatia	1998	VAT/PDV	Monthly or quarterly	HRK 300,000	25%	13%, 5%
24.	Curaçao	1999	Turnover Tax	Monthly (or annually on request)	None	6%	9%, 7%
25.	Cyprus	1992	VAT	Quarterly	EUR 15,600 (in a 12-month period)	19%	9%, 5%, 0%

26.	Czech Republic	1993	VAT	Monthly Quarterly (optional)	CZK 1 million (for a total period of 12 consecutive calendar months)	21%	15%, 10%, 0%
27.	Denmark	1967	VAT	Monthly Quarterly Half-yearly	DKK 50,000 a year	25%	0%
28.	Dominican Republic	1992	Tax on the Transfer of Industrialized Goods and Services/ITBIS	Monthly	None	18%, 16%, 0%	–
29.	Ecuador	1981	VAT	Monthly	None	12%	0%
30.	Egypt	2016	VAT	Monthly	EGP 500,000 annual turnover	14%	5%, 0%
31.	El Salvador	1992	VAT	Monthly	Annual turnover of USD 5,714.29	13%	0%
32.	Estonia	1991	VAT	Monthly	EUR 40,000	20%	9%, 0%
33.	European Union	1993	VAT	Monthly	–	–	–

(continued)

(continued)

S. No.	Jurisdiction	Introduction Year	Name of Tax/ Local Name	Return Period	Registration Thresholds	Standard Rate	Other Rates
34.	Finland	1994	VAT	Monthly (in certain cases quarterly or annually)	EUR 10,000	24%	14%, 10%, 0%
35.	France	1954	VAT/TVA	Monthly	None	20%	10%, 5.5%, 2.1%
36.	GCC	2018	VAT	Quarterly	USD 100,000	5%	0%
37.	Georgia	1993	VAT	Monthly	GEL 100,000 in the preceding 12 months	18%	0.54%
38.	Germany	1968	VAT	Monthly or quarterly and/ or annual returns	None	19%	7%
39.	Ghana	1998	VAT	Monthly	Turnover exceeding GHS 200,000 in 12 months	15%	17.5%, 3%, 2.5%, 0%
40.	Greece	1987	VAT	Monthly Quarterly	None	24%	13%, 6%
41.	Guatemala	1992	VAT	Monthly	None	12%	5%, 0%
42.	Honduras	1964	VAT/ISV	Monthly	None	15%	18%

No.	Country	Year	Type	Filing Frequency	Registration Threshold	Standard Rate	Reduced Rates
43.	Hungary	1988	VAT	Monthly Quarterly Annual	Every taxable person	27%	18%, 5%
44.	Iceland	1990s	VAT	Bimonthly Annual	ISK 2 million	24%	11%, 0%
45.	India	2017	GST	Monthly Quarterly	INR 1 million for special category states INR 2 million in all other states	0%, 5%, 12%, 18%, 28%	3%, 0.25%
46.	Indonesia	1984	VAT/PPN	Monthly	IDR 4.8 billion of supplies of goods or services	10%	0%
47.	Ireland	1972	VAT	Bimonthly, triennially, biannually and annually	EUR 37,500– services EUR 75,000– goods	23%	13.5%, 9%, 0%
48.	Isle of Man	1973	VAT	Monthly Quarterly	GBP 85,000	20%	5%, 0%
49.	Israel	1976	VAT	Bimonthly Monthly	ILS 98,707	17%	0%
50.	Italy	1973	VAT	Annual	None	22%	10%, 5%, 4%

(continued)

(continued)

S. No.	Jurisdiction	Introduction Year	Name of Tax/ Local Name	Return Period	Registration Thresholds	Standard Rate	Other Rates
51.	Japan	1989	Consumption Tax	Monthly, quarterly, biannually and annually	None	8%	N/A
52.	Jersey	2008	GST	Quarterly Monthly	JEP 300,000	5%	0%
53.	Jordan	1994	GST	Two Month – GT Monthly – ST	Goods: JOD 75,000 Services: JOD 30,000	16%	10%, 5%, 4%, 0%
54.	Kazakhstan	1991	VAT	Quarterly Monthly	USD 218,630 for 2018	12%	0%
55.	Kenya	1990s	VAT	Monthly	KES 5 million	16%	0%
56.	Korea rep	1977	VAT	Quarterly	None	10%	0%
57.	Kosovo	2001	VAT	Monthly	Annual turnover of EUR 30,000	18%	8%
58.	Kuwait	2019	VAT	Monthly		5%	0%
59.	Latvia	1995	VAT	Monthly Quarterly	EUR 40,000	21%	12%, 0%

60.	Lebanon	2002	VAT	Quarterly	LBP 100 million in any period varying from one to four prior consecutive quarters	11%	0%
61.	Lithuania	1994	VAT	Monthly Semi-annually Quarterly	EUR 45,000	21%	9%, 5%, 0%
62.	Luxembourg	1969	VAT	Monthly Quarterly Annual	None	17%	14%, 8%, 3%
63.	Macedonia	2000	VAT	Monthly Quarterly	MKD 1 million	18%	5%, 0%
64.	Madagascar	1962	VAT	Monthly	MGA 100 million	20%	0%
65.	Malaysia	2018	SST	Bimonthly	MYR 500,000	Sales tax 5% or 10%, Service tax 6%	0%
66.	Maldives	2011	GST	Monthly Quarterly	MVR 1 million (USD 64,851)	GST: 6% TGST: 12%	0%
67.	Malta	1999	VAT	Quarterly	None	18%	7%, 5%
68.	Mauritius	1998	VAT	Monthly Quarterly	MUR 6 million	15%	0%

(continued)

S. No.	Jurisdiction	Introduction Year	Name of Tax/ Local Name	Return Period	Registration Thresholds	Standard Rate	Other Rates
69.	Mexico	1980s	VAT/IVA	Monthly	None	16%	0%
70.	Moldova	1998	VAT/TVA	Monthly	MDL 1.2 million	20%	8%
71.	Mongolia	1998	VAT	Monthly	MNT 50 million	10%	0%
72.	Morocco	1986	VAT/TVA	Monthly or quarterly	NIL	20%	14%, 10%, 7%
73.	Myanmar	1990s	Commercial Tax	Quarterly and yearly	MMK 50 million	Goods and services: 5%	3%, 1%
74.	Namibia	2000	VAT	Bimonthly	NAD 500,000	15%	0%
75.	Netherlands	1969	VAT/BTW	Monthly Quarterly Annually	None	21%	6%, 0%
76.	New Zealand	1986	GST	One, two, three, and six month	NZD 60,000	15%	0%
77.	Nicaragua	1984 2003 revised	VAT/IVA	Monthly	None	15%	0%
78.	Nigeria	1993	VAT	Monthly	None	5%	0%
79.	Norway	1970s	VAT	Bimonthly Annual	NOK 50,000	25%	15%, 12%, 0%
80.	Oman	2019	VAT	Monthly		5%	0%

81.	Pakistan	1990s	Sales Tax	Monthly, quarterly and annual	PKR10 million or annual utility bills exceed PKR 800,000	Goods: 17% Services: 13%–16%	19.5%, 10%, 8%, 6%, 5%, 4%, 3%, 2%, 1%, and 0%
82.	Panama	1976	VAT	Monthly/quarterly	Gross annual income of USD 36,000 or monthly average above USD 3,000	7%	15%, 10%
83.	Papua New Guinea	2004	GST	Monthly	PGK 250,000	10%	0%
84.	Paraguay	1992	VAT	Monthly Quarterly Biannual	None	10%	5%
85.	Peru	1991	VAT	Monthly	None	18%	0%
86.	Philippines	1988	VAT	Monthly Quarterly	Gross sales or receipts in excess of PHP 3 million in a 12-month period	12%	0%
87.	Poland	1993	VAT	Monthly	PLN 200,000	23%	8%, 5%, 0%

(continued)

(continued)

S. No.	Jurisdiction	Introduction Year	Name of Tax/ Local Name	Return Period	Registration Thresholds	Standard Rate	Other Rates
88.	Portugal	1986	VAT	Monthly Quarterly	None	Mainland 23% Madeira 22% Azores 18%	Mainland 13%, 6% Madeira 12%, 5% Azores 9%, 4%
89.	Puerto Rico	2006	Sales and Use Tax	Monthly	None	10.50%	4%, 1%
90.	Qatar			Monthly		5%	0%
91.	Romania	1993	VAT	Monthly	EUR 65,000	19%	9%, 5%
92.	Russian Federation	1991	VAT	Quarterly	None	18%	10%, 0%
93.	Rwanda	2001	VAT	Monthly or quarterly	RWF 20 million (in 12 months) RWF 5 million (in a quarter)	18%	0%
94.	Saint Lucia	2012	VAT	Monthly	XCD 400,000	12.50%	10%, 0%
95.	Saudi Arabia	2018	VAT	Quarterly Monthly	SAR 375,000	5%	0%
96.	Serbia	2005	VAT	Monthly or quarterly	Annual turnover of RSD 8 million	20%	10%, 0%

97.	Seychelles	2013	VAT	Monthly Quarterly	SCR 2 million of taxable supplies for any 12-month period	15%	0%
98.	Singapore	1994	GST	Quarterly Monthly	SGD 1 million	7%	0%
99.	Sint Maarten	1997	Revenue Tax	Monthly	None	5%	N/A
100.	Slovak Republic	1993	VAT/DPH	Monthly	EUR 49,790 in a maximum period of 12	20%	10%, 0%
101.	Slovenia	1999	VAT/DDV	Monthly or Quarterly	EUR 50,000 in the preceding 12 months	22%	9.5%, 0%
102.	South Africa	1991	VAT	Monthly, bimonthly, half yearly or annually	Annual taxable supplies of more than ZAR 1 million	15%	0%
103.	Spain	1986	VAT/IVA	Monthly Quarterly	None	21%	10%, 4%
104.	Suriname	1997	Turnover Tax	Monthly	None	Goods: 10% Services: 8%	25%, 0%
105.	Sweden	1969	VAT	Monthly Quarterly Annually	SEK 30,000	25%	12%, 6%

(continued)

(continued)

S. No.	Jurisdiction	Introduction Year	Name of Tax/ Local Name	Return Period	Registration Thresholds	Standard Rate	Other Rates
106.	Switzerland	1995	VAT	Quarterly Half yearly Monthly	CHF 100,000, global turnover	7.70%	3.7%, 2.5%, 0%
107.	Taiwan	1931 2015 revised	VAT and GBTR	Bimonthly	None	VAT: 5% GBRT: 0.1%–25%	0%
108.	Tanzania	2015	VAT	Monthly	TZS 100 million in a year	18%	0%
109.	Thailand	1992	VAT	Monthly	Annual revenue of THB 1.8 million	7%	0%
110.	Trinidad and Tobago	1990s	VAT	Two monthly	TTD 500,000	12.50%	0%
111.	Tunisia	1988	VAT	Monthly	TND 100,000	19%	13%, 7%
112.	Turkey	1984	VAT	Monthly	None	18%	8%, 1%
113.	Uganda	1996	VAT	Monthly	Annual amount of UGX 150 million	18%	0%
114.	Ukraine	1992	VAT/PDV	Monthly	Taxable supplies in excess of UAH 1 million during preceding 12 calendar months	20%	7%, 0%

No.	Country	Year	Tax type	Frequency	Threshold	Rate	Reduced rates
115.	United Arab Emirates	2018	VAT	Quarterly Monthly	AED 375,000	5%	0%
116.	United Kingdom	1973	VAT	Quarterly Monthly	GBP 85,000	20%	5%, 0%
117.	United States		Sales Taxes	–	–	0%–7.25%	N/A
118.	Uruguay	1972	VAT/IVA	Monthly	None	22%	10%, 0%
119.	Venezuela	1993	VAT	Monthly	None	12%	8%–20%, 0%
120.	Vietnam	1999	VAT	Monthly or quarterly	None	10%	5%, 0%
121.	Zambia	1995	VAT	Monthly	ZMW 800,000 in any 12 consecutive months	16%	0%
122.	Zimbabwe	2004	VAT	Monthly	Compulsory registration: USD 60,000	15%	0%

Source: Computed by the authors from EY, 'Worldwide VAT, GST, Sales Tax Guide 2018', https://www.ey.com/gl/en/services/tax/worldwide-vat--gst-and-sales-tax-guide---rates

Bibliography

Reports

Buydens, Stéphane. *Consumption Tax Trends 2008*. Paris, France: OECD Publishing, 2009.

CBIC. *Goods and Service Tax (GST): Concept & Status*. New Delhi: GoI, 2018.

———. 'Goods and Service Tax (GST) Concept and Status', August 1, 2019, 51–55.

EC of Finance Ministers. *Annual Report (2005–06)*. New Delhi: Government of India.

———. *Annual Report (2006–07)*. New Delhi: GoI.

———. *Annual Report (2007–08)*. New Delhi: GoI.

———. *Annual Report (2008–09)*. New Delhi: GoI.

———. *Annual Report (2009–10)*. New Delhi: GoI.

———. *Annual Report (2010–11)*. New Delhi: GoI.

———. *Annual Report (2011–12)*. New Delhi: GoI.

———. *Annual Report (2015–16)*. New Delhi: GoI.

———. *A White Paper on State-Level Value Added Tax*. New Delhi: GoI, 2005.

———. *A White Paper on State-Level Value Added Tax*. New Delhi: GoI, 1999.

———. *Annual Report for 2005–06*. New Delhi: GoI.

EY. *Worldwide VAT, GST and Sales Tax Guide 2018*. EYGM Limited, 2018. https://www.ey.com/Publication/vwLUAssets/ey-2019-Worldwide-VAT-GST-and-Sales-Tax-Guide/$FILE/ey-2019-Worldwide-VAT-GST-and-Sales-Tax-Guide.PDF

GoI. *13th Finance Commission Report 2009*. https://fincomindia.nic.in/ShowContent.aspx?uid1=3&uid2=0&uid3=0&uid4=0&uid5=0&uid6=0&uid7=0 (accessed on 18 January 2019)

———. *4th Finance Commission Report 1965*.

———. *73rd Report of Parliamentary Standing Committee on Finance 2012–13*.

———. *Budget for the Year 1953–54*, 14.

———. *Budget Speech, 1987–88*, Para 103.

GoI. *Budget Speech, 1993–94.*

———. *Budget Speech, 1994–95.*

———. *Budget Speech, 1995–96.*

———. *Budget Speech 1996–97.*

———. *Budget Speech 1997–98.*

———. *Budget Speech, 1998–99.*

———. *Budget Speech, 1999–2000*, Para 61.

———. *Budget Speech, 2000–01*, Para 89–90.

———. *Budget Speech, 2001–02.*

———. *Budget Speech, 2003–04.*

———. *Budget Speech, 2004–05.*

———. *Budget Speech, 2005–06.*

———. *Budget Speech, 2006–07.*

———. *Budget Speech, 2007–08.*

———. *Budget Speech, 2008–09.*

———. *Budget Speech, 2009–10.*

———. *Budget Speech, 2010–11.*

———. *Budget Speech, 2011–12.*

———. *Budget Speech, 2012–13.*

———. *Budget Speech 2013–14.*

———. *Budget Speech, 2014–15.*

———. *Budget Speech, 2015–16.*

———. *Budget Speech, 2016–17.*

———. *Budget Speech, 2017–18.*

———. *Budget Speech, 2018–19.*

———. *Budget Speech, 2019–20.*

———. *Central Excise (Self Removal Procedure) Review Committee Report 1971.*

———. *Economic Survey, Various Issues.*

———. *Finance Minister Budget Speech, 1978–79,* 18.

———. *Indian Public Finance Statistics 2015–16.*

———. *Indirect Tax Enquiry Committee Report 1971.*

———. *Rekhi Committee on Indirect Taxes Report 1992.*

———. *Report of the Fourth Finance Commission,1965,* 1.

———. *Report of the Indirect Taxation Enquiry Committee, Part I.* New Delhi: Ministry of Finance, 1977.

———. *Report of the Indirect Taxation Enquiry Committee, Part II.* New Delhi: Ministry of Finance, 1978.

———. *Report of the Select Committee.* July 22, 2015.

———. *Report of the Taxation Enquiry Commission, 1953–54.* New Delhi: Ministry of Finance, 1955.

———. *Task Force on implementation of FRBM Act 2003 Report 2004.*

———. *Task Force on Indirect Taxes Report 2002.*

———. *Tax Reform Committee Report 1992.*

———. *Union Budget 2000–01,* Para 87.

GoI. *Union Budget, 2012–13.*

———. *Union Budget, Various Issues.*

John, Norregaard, and Tehmina S. Khan. *Tax Policy: Recent Trends and Coming Challenges*, Working Paper No. WP/07/274, IMF 2007.

NCEAR. *Impact of Goods and Services Tax on India's International Trade*. New Delhi: 13th Finance Commission, 2009.

NIPFP. *Reform of Domestic Trade Taxes in India*. New Delhi, 1994.

OECD. *International VAT/GST Guidelines*. 2017.

———. *Revenue Statistics 2017: Tax Revenue Trends in the OECD.*

Press Information Bureau. *GST Compensation to States*. August 10, 2018. http://pib.nic.in/newsite/PrintRelease.aspx?relid=181826

———. *GST Revenue Collection for April 2018.* 2018.

———. *GST Revenue Collection for August 2018.* 2018.

———. *GST Revenue Collection for July 2018.* 2018.

———. *GST Revenue Collection for May 2018.* 2018.

———. *GST Revenue Collection for September 2018.* 2018.

———. *GST Revenue Collection for the Month of December 2018.* 2019.

———. *GST Revenue Collection for the Month of January 2019.* 2019.

———. *GST Revenue Collection for the Month of November 2018.* 2018.

———. *GST Revenue Collection for the Month of October 2018.* 2018.

———. *GST Revenue Collections for the Financial Year 2017–18.* 2018.

———. *GST Revenue Figures: As on 25th September 2017.* 2017.

———. *Total Collection under GST for the Month of December 2017.* 2017.

World Bank. *India Development Update: India's Growth Story*. Washington, DC: World Bank, 2018.

Articles

Aanchal Magazine and Sunny Verma. 'Goods and Services Tax: Businesses Struggle with Multiple Tax Rates, Returns'

Acharya, Shankar. 'India's Tax Reforms'. *Business Standard*, April 26, 2005.

Aggarwal, Pawan K. *Modified Value Added Tax (MODVAT): Structure and Resource Mobilization*. New Delhi: NIPFP, 1996.

Ahmad, Ehtisham, and Satya Poddar. 'GST Reforms and Intergovernmental Considerations in India'. Working Paper No. 1, Department of Economic Affairs, Ministry of Finance, Government of India, New Delhi, 2009, 16.

Anand, Geeta. 'After Killing Currency, Modi Takes a Leap with India's Biggest-Ever Tax Overhaul'. *The New York Times*, 2017, June 30.

Anand. 'NDDB Urges Finance Minister to Rationalize Taxes on Dairy Items'. *Business Standard*, June 10, 2019.

Bhutani, Mukesh, and Tarun Jain. 'GST: A Year of Learning and Attainment'. *Business Standard*, July 2, 2018.

Bird, Richard M. 'Tax Reforms in India'. *EPW*, December 11, 1993.

Bloomberg. 'Good, Bad and Ugly of India's New National Sales Tax Journey'. *The Economic Times*, July 25, 2017.

Burgess, Robin, Stephen Howes, and Nicholas Stern. 'Value-Added Tax Options for India'. *International Tax and Public Finance* 2, no. 1 (1995): 109–141.

Business Line Bureau. 'Budget 2019: CAIT for Lowering GST Rates for Various Products'. *Business Line*, June 13, 2019.

———. 'GST Bills Passed in Rajya Sabha without Amendments'. *Business Line*, April 6, 2017.

Chakravarty, Praveen, and Vivek Dehejia. 'India Is an Outlier in Its Tax Policy'. *Live Mint*, April 27, 2018.

Chakrborty, S. 'Exporters Face a Long Wait for Refunds'. *Business Standard*, July 2, 2018.

Chawla, Prakash. 'GST: A Game-Changer for India'. *Press Information Bureau*, August 4, 2016.

Chidambaram, P. 'The GST Bill Is History in the Making: P. Chidambaram'. *Financial Express*, June 14, 2015.

Dash, Dipak. 'A Year of GST: Riding A Truck to Get E-Way Bill Experience'. *Times of India*, June 30, 2018.

Datar, Arvind P., and K. Vaitheeswaran. 'A GST Good and Simple'. *The Indian Express*, September 28, 2017.

Deccan Herald. 'CAIT Urges India Inc. to Push for GST Passage'. May 25, 2016.

domain-b.com. 'Sushil Modi, Empowered Committee has no GST Role to Play Now: Sushil Modi'. December 9, 2017.

Dutta, Prabhash K. '98 Days of GST: How Council Has Changed Business Rules Since July 1 Rollout'. *India Today*, October 6, 2017.

Economic Watch. 'Value Added Tax (VAT) in France'. June 29, 2010.

Edwin, Tina. 'Dual GST Rate Regime Could Fast-Track Political Consensus'. *The Quint*, December 6, 2015.

ET Bureau. 'One Year of GST: The Successes, Failures and What's Next on the Agenda'. *The Economic Times*, June 29, 2018.

ET Contributors. 'One Year of GST: Reality Check of Government Initiatives'. *The Economic Times*, June 30, 2018.

ET Online. 'GST Collections Cross 1 Lakh in January: Finance Ministry'. *The Economic Times*, February 2, 2019.

———. 'GST Revenue Collection Exceeds 1 Lakh Crore in April, FM Hopes It to Rise Further'. *The Economic Times*, May 2, 2018.

Expert Web Desk, 'India Ushers in GST: How Global Media Covered Country's New Tax Regime'. *The Indian Express*. July 1, 2017.

Express Editorial. 'One Year of GST: A Look at the Journey so Far'. *The Indian Express*, July 1, 2018.

Express News Service. 'GST has Become Bad Word, No Positive Impact on Growth, Says Chidambaram'. *The Indian Express*, July 2, 2018.

Governance Now. 'Recalling a Time when BJP Opposed GST'. June 29, 2017.

GuideMeSingapore. 'Malaysia SST: What Are the Changes?' August 20, 2018. https://www.guidemesingapore.com/in-the-news/2018/malaysia-sst-what-are-the-changes

IANS. 'Sushil Modi Urges Amit Mitra to Postpone Empowered Committee's Meeting'. *Financial Express*, December 8, 2017.

India Today Web Desk. 'India's GST Rates Highest in the World: All about GST in India and Other Countries'. *India Today*, July 3, 2017.

Jethmalani, Harsha, and Pallavi Pengonda. 'Tank Full of Issues in Bringing Petrol and Diesel under GST'. *Live Mint*, April 10, 2018.

Kelkar, Nachiket. 'GST Gave Big Boost to India's GDP Growth: Adi Godrej'. *The Week*, June 29, 2018.

Kelkar, Vijay. 'GST: Make Haste Slowly'. *Live Mint*, October 19, 2016.

Krishnan, V. S. 'Milestones in Central Excise'. *Business Line*, April 1, 2000.

Kumar, Manoj. 'GST Effect: Hundreds of Thousands Laid Off Despite Growth'. *The Indian Express*, September 6, 2018.

———. 'India's Tax Effect: Hundreds of Thousands Laid off Despite Growth'. *Reuters*, September 6, 2018.

Mahanta, Vinod, and Sachin Dave. 'EU Countries Looking at India's GST Closely to Implement in Their Countries: PwC's Bello'. *The Economic Times*, May 23, 2018.

Mail Today Bureau. 'India's GST Highest in the World: Here's What Some Other Countries Charge'. *Business Today*, July 1, 2017.

Mani, Sriram. 'GST Impact on Household Finances, One Year Later'. *Live Mint*, July 11, 2018. https://www.livemint.com/Money/O1qMH5zxrtmQWVVo PYoOvJ/GST-impact-on-household-finances-one-year-later.html

Marlow, Iain, Archana Chaudhary, P. R. Sanjai, and Kartik Goyal. 'Businesses Brace for Chaos as India Rolls Out Tax Milestone'. *Washington Post/Bloomberg*, June 30, 2017.

Mehra, Puja, 'The Birth of Service Tax (1994–95)', *The Hindu*, July 7, 2014.

Menon, Sachin. 'Indirect Taxes: Rationalise CENVAT Credit as a Step to Align with the Proposed GST'. *Business Today*, February 17, 2016.

Mohan, Archis. 'How GST Changed Indian Politics'. *Rediff.com*, 2018, July 01.

Padmanabhan, Anil. 'One Year of GST: It is Politics versus Economics'. *Live Mint*, July 2, 2018.

Parthasarathy, Jayashree, and P. C. Anand. 'The New Set of CENVAT Rules'. *Business Line*, July 03, 2000.

Pinto, Lidia. 'Tax Burden in Brazil: Indirect Taxes'. *The Brazil Law Blog*, October 16, 2012.

Prabhu, Suresh. 'E-Wallet will Address GST Refund Issue of Exporters'. *Business Line*, March 18, 2018.

PTI. '8.2% GDP Growth an Outcome of Modi Govt's Reforms in FDI, GST: CII'. *Business Standard*, September 4, 2018.

PTI. 'BJP Slams Govt. on Plan to Introduce GST Bill in Parliament'. *Hindustan Times*, February 20, 2011.

————. 'GDP May Grow to 7% in FY19 as GST Impact Wanes: HSBC'. *The Economic Times*, January 24, 2018.

————. 'Govt Spent ₹1.32 bn on GST Advertisements; Print Media Got Biggest Share'. Business Standard, September 3, 2018.

————. 'GST to be 5% on Footwear below ₹500, 18% on Rest'. *The Economic Times*, June 3, 2017.

————. 'New Monthly GST Return Filing System to be Rolled Out from October: FinMin'. *Business Standard*, June 11, 2019.

————. '"Milestone" GST Reforms Should Be Further Simplified, Says IMF'. *NDTV Profit*, 2018, August 8.

————. 'Now, Only 35 Goods in Highest Tax Bracket of GST'. *The Economic Times*, July 22, 2018.

————. 'President Pranab Mukherjee Gives Assent to Four Supporting Legislations on GST'. *The Economic Times*. April 13, 2017.

————. 'Rahul Gandhi's idea of single rate for GST 'flawed', says Arun Jaitley'. *Business Standard*. July 1, 2018.

————. 'VAT Implemented in 20 States Today'. *The Times of India*, April 1, 2005.

Purohit, M. C. *Problems of Introducing Value Added Tax in India: Direction for Reforms*. New Delhi: NIPFP, 1992.

Rajagopalan, T. N. C. 'Unsung Heroes Who Made GST a Reality'. *Business Standard*, July 2, 2018.

————. 'It Took Three Decades and Many Hands'. *Business Standard*, July 3, 2017.

Rajaraman, Indira. 'GST Features Contributing to GDP Growth Slowdown'. *Live Mint*, October 6, 2017.

Rao, S. L. 'Father of Tax Reforms'. *The Hindu*, June 22, 2010.

Renavikar, Rahul. 'GST 2.0: Why Two-Rate Structure Is Needed'. *Financial Express*, June 11, 2018.

Reuters. 'Foreign Media on GST: Ready or Not, Indian Businesses Brace for Biggest-Ever Tax Reform'. *India Today*, June 28, 2017.

————. 'GST Effect: Hundreds of Thousands Laid off Despite Growth'. *The Indian New Express*, September 6, 2018.

Sahoo, Sahadev. 'Rationale Behind Congress' Opposition to GST Bill'. *The Pioneer*, March 29, 2016.

Schofield, Max. 'Malaysia's New GST: A Brief Comparison with Its Former Sales Tax and Service Tax Regime'. *International Tax Blog*, April 24, 2015.

Seth, Dilasha. 'GST Council to Consider E-Invoicing for Firms with over ₹500-cr Turnover'. *Business Standard*, June 10, 2019.

————. 'GST Regime Is Not Tax Friendly, Fix Glitches on GSTN, Bombay HC Raps Govt'. *The Business Standard*, February 10, 2018.

Seth, Dilasha. Compliance Still a Challenge for Small Business, *Business Standard*, July 2, 2018.

Shaikh, Mohammed Uzair. 'GST Roll-Out a Historic Moment, Culmination of 14-Year-Long Journey: President'. *India News*, July 1, 2017.

Sharma, Vinod, and Gaurav Choudhury. 'Social Peace, Political Consensus Important for Economic Reforms: Manmohan Singh'. *Hindustan Times*, July 24, 2016.

Sidhartha. 'State, Union Territories Have up to 43% GST Revenue Gap'. *The Economic Times*, July 23, 2018.

Singh, Shelley. 'A Look at How GST Was Rolled Out in Other Countries'. *The Economic Times*, June 29, 2017.

Srivastava, Shruti. 'GST Slugfest: Coming a Full Circle'. *The Indian Express*, November 22, 2018.

Subramanya, Rupa. 'A Missed Opportunity'. *India Today* 2018, August 20: 66.

Suneja, Kirtika. 'Refund Mechanism Still a Pain Point for Exporters'. *The Economic Times*, July 2, 2018.

The Asian Age. 'India Will Set Example for World with GST: Modi'. June 20, 2017.

The Economic Times. 'Paves Way for Rolling Out of GST from July 1'. April 13, 2017.

TNN. 'Gujarat Opposes GST Regime'. *The Times of India*, October 23, 2013.

———. 'Milk and Mercedes Can't Be Taxed at Same Rate, Says PM'. *The Times of India*, July 2, 2018.

———. 'It Should Be Called 'RSS tax', Says Chidambaram'. *The Times of India*, July 2, 2018, 9.

Utsumi, Igor. 'Brazilian Tax System'. *The Brazil Business*. April 29, 2014.

Owens, Jeffrey. 'Improving Performance of VAT System is a Priority in the Context of the Economic Crisis'. *World Commerce Review* 5, no. 3 (2011): 8.

Owens, Jeffrey, and Piet Battiau. 'VAT's Next Half Century: Towards a Single-Rate System? *OECD Observer* 284, no. Q1 (2011): 20.

Books

Banerje, Abhijit, and Esther Duflo. *Good Economics for Hard Times: Better Answers to Our Biggest Problems*. New Delhi: Juggernaut, 2019.

Banerjee, Abhijit, Gita Gopinath, Raghuram Rajan, and Mihir S. Sharma, eds. *What the Economy Needs Now*. New Delhi: Juggernaut, 2019.

Kumar, Virendra. *Committees and Commissions in India: 1971–73, Vol. 2*. New Delhi: Concept Publishing Company, 1988.

Lekhi, R. K. *Public Finance*. New Delhi: Kalyani Publishers, 2007.

Murty, S. *Structural Transformation of Indian Economy*. New Delhi: Atlantic Publishers and Distributors, 1996.

Rao, R. Kavita, and Sacchidananda Mukherjee. *Evolution of Goods and Services Tax in India*. New Delhi: Cambridge University Press, 2019.

Sinha, Yashwant. *Confessions of a Swadeshi Reformer: My Years as Finance Minister*. New Delhi: Penguin Books India, 2007.

———. *Relentless: An Autobiography*. New Delhi: Bloomsbury, 2019.

Sinha, Yashwant, and Aditya Sinha. *India Unmade: How the Modi Government Broke the Economy*. New Delhi: Juggernaut, 2019.

Sinha, Yashwant, and Vinay K. Srivastava. *The Future of India Economy: Past Reforms and Challenges Ahead*. New Delhi: Rupa India, 2017.

Sury, M. M. *Taxation in India, 1925 to 2007: History, Policies, Trends & Outlook*. New Delhi: New Century Publication, 2006.

Newspapers

ASEANBUSINESS STAFF. 'At a Glance: Taxes in Singapore'. *The Business Times*. July 4, 2018.

Borpuzari, Pranbihanga. 'GST: Composition Scheme for Small Taxpayers Extended to ₹1.5 Crore'. *The Economic Times*. August 5, 2019.

Chua, Tony. 'Singapore's Indirect Tax Rate Still among Region's Lowest'. *Singapore Business Review*. March 30, 2010.

Financial Express. 'GST 2.0: Why Two-Rates Structure Is Needed'. *Financial Express*. June 11, 2018.

———. 'Kelkar Heads the Task Force on Indirect Tax'. September 4, 2002.

IANS. 'Sushil Modi Urges Amit Mitra to Postpone Empowered Committee's Meeting'. *Financial Express*, December 8, 2017.

Lam, Lydia. 'Singapore Budget 2018: GST to Be Raised from 7% to 9% Some Time between 2021 and 2025'. *The Straits Times*. February 19, 2018.

Mail Today Bureau. 'India's GST Highest in the World: Here's What Some Other Countries Charge'. *Business Today*. July 1, 2017.

Nair, Remya. 'GST Led to Greater Formalization of Economy by Increasing Taxpayer Base: Sushil Kumar Modi'. *Live Mint*. July 1, 2018.

Poddar, Satya, and Amaresh Bagchi. 'Revenue-Neutral Rate for GST'. *The Economic Times*, November 15, 2017.

Sikarwar, Deepshikha. 'Infosys Is to Blame for GST Network Glitches, Say Government Officials'. *The Economic Times*. November 2, 2017.

Vikraman, Shaji. 'VAT, GST and the Long, Bumpy Road to Tax Reform'. *The Indian Express*, April 5, 2017.

Websites

French VAT. https://www.avalara.com/vatlive/en/country-guides/europe/france.html

GST Revenue. http://pib.nic.in/PressReleseDetail.aspx?PRID=1541584

http://www.cbic.gov.in/

http://www.gstcouncil.gov.in/

https://gstawareness.cbec.gov.in/

https://www.customs.gov.sg/individuals/going-through-customs/arrival/duty-free-concession-and-gst-relief

https://www.gst.gov.in/

https://www.gstn.org/

Lawbaba, 'Concept and History of Indirect Taxation in India'. October 13, 2017. http://lawbaba.in/history-indirect-taxation-india/

Ministry of Finance, Singapore. https://www.mof.gov.sg/Policies/Tax-Policies/Goods-and-Services-Tax

Sudheer, C. S. 'History of Tax'. https://indianmoney.com/articles/history-of-tax

www.gov.sg/factually/content/is-it-true-that-i-have-to-pay-gst-on-items-purchased-overseas

Index

About the Authors

Yashwant Sinha is a veteran politician of the country and a very senior leader. He has worked as the Finance Minister and Minister of External Affairs of the Government of India. He was also the Chairman of the Parliamentary Standing Committee on Finance, New Delhi, between 2009 and 2014. He has played an integral role in the story of economic reforms of India. It was he who was at the helm when the economy was in the worst crisis, keeping the vigil before the dawn of reforms. Mr Sinha is widely credited for pushing through several major reforms that put the Indian economy on a firm growth trajectory. Among them are lowering of real interest rates, introducing tax deduction for mortgage interest, freeing up the telecommunications sector, helping fund the national highway authority and deregulating the petroleum industry. Mr Sinha is also known for being the first finance minister to break the 53-year-old tradition of presenting the Indian budget at 5:00 PM local time, a practice held over from British Rule days that sought to present the Indian budget at a time convenient to the British Parliament (11:30 AM GMT) rather than Indian Parliament. He has written a comprehensive account of his years as the finance minister in a book titled *Confessions of a Swadeshi Reformer: My Years as Finance Minister* (2007). He is the co-editor of *Future of Indian Economy: Past Reforms and Challenges Ahead* (2017) and co-author of *India Unmade: How the Modi Government Broke the Economy* (2018). Recently, he has authored *Relentless: An Autobiography* (2019).

Vinay K. Srivastava is presently working as an Associate Professor at the Institute of Technology and Science, Ghaziabad. Earlier, he was the Dean in the School of Management at Raffles University, Neemrana, and Dean Academics (Management) at Raj Kumar Goel Institute of Technology (RKGIT), Ghaziabad. He is the Founder Honorary Secretary of Indian Society for Management Development and Research (ISMDR) and Managing Editor of *ARASH*. He is also the founder Editor of *Saaransh* and *Raffles Business Review*. He is the author of *Privatisation of Public Enterprises in India* (2007) and co-editor of *Public Enterprises and Changing Scenario* (2014) and *The Future of Indian Economy: Past Reforms and Challenges Ahead* (2017). He has published over 70 articles in various journals, magazines and newspapers.